the food lover's guide to seattle

Katy Calcott

photographs by Nicholas Calcott

SASQUATCH BOOKS
SEATTLE

*To my sister, Dora Nathaniel, who was in my heart
through every step of this book.
1955–1999*

Printed in the United States of America
Distributed in Canada by Raincoast Books, Ltd.
07 06 05 04 03 02 01   5 4 3 2 1

Cover design: Karen Schober
Cover photograph: ©Owen Franken/CORBIS
Interior photographs: Nicholas Calcott
Interior design: Elizabeth Boyce
Interior composition: Jenny Semet

Library of Congress Cataloging in Publication Data
Calcott, Katy.
        The food lover's guide to Seattle / Katy Calcott.
                p.   cm.
        ISBN 1-57061-247-1
        1. Food—Guidebooks. 2. Grocery trade—Washington (State)—Seattle—
Guidebooks. 3. Cookery, American—Pacific Northwest style. I. Title.

TX354.5 .C35 2001
381'.45641'025797772—dc21

Sasquatch Books
615 Second Avenue
Seattle, Washington 98104
(206) 467-4300
www.SasquatchBooks.com
books@SasquatchBooks.com

the food lover's guide to seattle

contents

recipe list

acknowledgments

The real forces behind this eighteen-month-long odyssey through Seattle and environs are the shopkeepers, bakers, chocolate makers, fishmongers, greengrocers, cheesemongers, coffee roasters, importers, manufacturers and sundry producers I talked to. They cheerfully took time from busy schedules, patiently answered my repeated queries, steered me in new directions, gave me samples, and bent over backwards to make sure I had what I needed to write about them. I thank them from the bottom of my heart.

Without my husband, Peter, this book would never have gotten off the ground. His unflagging support and helpful suggestions, hand-holding through innumerable computer crises, and taste buds par excellence were the reason this book ever saw the light of day. The book additionally comes to life with images created by Nicholas Calcott, first-class photographer/taster/eldest son. And without second son Julian's considerable appetite, I dread to think what size I would have become. Thank you, boys.

My friends and relations continually provided the use of their taste buds, and their critical advice, and I learned something from each. My neighbor, Claire Hodgson Meeker, initially encouraged me to approach Sasquatch and provided countless hours of advice and encouragement. My friends Ken and Tien White and Brendan and Anita Gannon read and critiqued sections, and tasted more barbecue than they care to remember. My friend Monica Devens, although not a foodie, was still able to steer me when I floundered. My cousin Charles Chitayat and brother-in-law Lance Choo encouraged and provided recipes. My brother and sister-in-law, Roby and Angie Nathaniel, and my mom, Clara Nathaniel, listened patiently to my complaining and/or accompanied me on my explorations. Thank you also to Ron Chew of the Wing Luke Asian Museum; Paul Williams, marine biologist for the Suquamish Indian Tribe; Bruce Aidells; Jon Rowley; and all of the contacts I made within the area's ethnic communities.

Finally, the helpful advice and suggestions of my editor at Sasquatch, Gary Luke, played a major role in keeping this mammoth project on track. Thanks, all.

introduction

I am obsessed with good food—shopping for it and cooking it. I spend more hours than you can imagine dreaming of food, chasing down elusive ingredients, and imagining the taste of a perfectly cooked dish. And I am not alone. It is my obsession and delight that has prompted me to write this book. But it is the many adventurous people who consider food shopping not only a necessity but a relaxing activity, to whom I dedicate my efforts. I have explored the Seattle area with one goal in mind: to find the best specialty food and ethnic markets and give you the tools to do your own exploring.

This book will tell you all about the best food markets in the Seattle area, as well as the people who run them. Where do you go if you're planning a Mexican meal and *have* to have fresh masa for your tamales? Ever wonder where to get the best kimchi in town? Looking for a market boasting live tanks with fish still flopping and writhing, where the proprietor dismembers your catch with a few strokes of his cleaver so swiftly that the heart is still beating? (That may not appeal to everyone, but it is a guarantee of freshness—and should you overcome your squeamishness, you'll find the result is unparalleled sweet tenderness.) Want to try a kind of bread you've never tasted before, created by one of the area's many artisan bakers? This book will deliciously guide you through these and many other such culinary adventures.

The Seattle area abounds with an incredible selection of foodstuffs. Specialty food markets are located in all our neighborhoods. Some offer a limited selection—maybe only a few items that are made on the premises or are a point of pride for the owner. Some cater predominantly to their ethnic community or neighborhood. Food shopping is a great excuse to travel to new or unfamiliar neighborhoods for a different perspective. And you don't need to use any frequent flyer miles.

When people talk about food, I listen. In this book, I have tried to convey the passion and curiosity of these market proprietors, the often roundabout journeys they make, and the accrued insights and experiences that result. These are people who feel strongly that food is nourishment for the soul as well as the body. They are businesses that choose to stay small so that their owners can retain control and a sense of integrity.

I was touched and changed by the many people I met while doing my research, and each foray into a new neighborhood brought the thrill of new discoveries and fabulous eating. I hope you'll have a similar experience as you join me on this voyage of discovery through the best, most enticing food terrain in the Seattle area.

Bon appétit!

how to use this book

The Food Lover's Guide to Seattle is divided into three sections: specialty food markets, superstores, and ethnic food markets. Within each section, the information is arranged by food category, store, or ethnic community, respectively. Within categories and communities, markets are grouped by broad geographic boundaries, as follows:

Central Seattle:
> South of the Montlake Cut and Ship Canal
> North of Interstate 90

North:
> North of the Montlake Cut and Ship Canal
> Includes Bothell and Woodinville

South:
> South of Interstate 90
> Includes Renton, Kent, Burien, and Sea-Tac

East:
> South of Bothell
> East of Lake Washington

West:
> West Seattle

Small businesses, especially food-related businesses, are notoriously precarious. I have tried to limit the entries in this book to businesses with at least some longevity (more than two years in operation), but of course there are no guarantees. In addition, hours may change. To be safe, call before you go.

In summarizing my conversations with hundreds of diverse individuals about the intricacies of their businesses and their communities, I have tried to be as accurate and as true to people's visions as possible. Naturally, any mistakes are my own, and I offer my apologies for any errors herein.

New food shops are opening in Seattle all the time. If you'd like to help me keep up to date on the latest developments, or want to send me other feedback on this book, e-mail me at seattlefoodlover@aol.com.

bread

cakes, pastries, pies, and other baked goods

cheese

chocolates, candies, nuts, and ice cream

coffee, tea, and spices

fish

meat and poultry

prepared food and deli items

produce and farmers markets

wine and beer

bread

bread When I was a kid, I was taught that if you dropped a piece of bread on the floor, you immediately picked it up and kissed it in apology. Bread is too fundamental, too central to human survival to ever be less than a revered symbol. In those days, though, I rebelled: I lusted after squishy white bread. My favorite snack was a slice of Wonder bread, smooshed flat in the center and then toasted. Instead, I got a crusty, flat "slipper" of a loaf—naan-e-barbari—that my Persian mother went to great lengths to find. Today, when I could easily make a whole meal out of the exceptional bread available in the Seattle area, along with some perfectly ripe cheese and a glass of wine, it's hard to recall those childish desires.

There is no excuse for not eating superior bread in Seattle. Lucky Seattleites benefit from the obsessions of scores of gifted bakers who have opened shops in recent years. Serious bakers are gripped with questions of yeast and flour characteristics and proofing time and oven temperature. They will experiment endlessly till they are absolutely satisfied with their product. Equally serious bread mavens will have their own obsessions about the best baguette or sourdough or rustic bread, and will think nothing of traveling far, like my mother, to get what they consider to be the best bread in town. Happily, today most of the artisan bakers in town sell their breads at area supermarkets. Their bakeries, though, are their "front parlors," where the public has the chance to meet them, taste the results of their experimentation, and buy a far larger selection of their products than will ever be seen in a supermarket.

The two godmothers of the local movement away from the tasteless, anemic, industrial bread that too many of us grew up eating are
Grand Central Bakery founder Gwenyth Bassetti and her original
baker, Leslie Mackie (who went on to open Macrina Bakery). Both
women began their bread-baking careers with an idea, fueled by
travel and interest, of what genuine artisan breads should taste like.
In the early '80s, there were few American role models for what they
envisioned. The breads they read about in Carol Field's seminal book
The Italian Baker triggered in both of them a profound desire to
restore a real taste to bread, and to recreate a tradition that has given
so many people so much pleasure for centuries. Their experiments,
along with those of George DePasquali at Essential Baking Co. and
Ciro Pascuitto at La Panzanella, among others, have effected no less
than a genuine bread revolution here in Seattle.

Even at its most expensive, you'd be hard pressed to spend more
than $4 or $5 for a loaf of good bread. If that seems like an uncon-
scionable price to pay for such a basic commodity, consider that
bread is the easiest and least expensive way to turn a meal into a treat.
A $3 loaf of classic, crusty Italian bread—rubbed first with garlic and
then with split tomatoes till both meat and juice have permeated the
entire surface of the bread, and lastly drizzled with first-quality olive
oil—makes a heavenly meal on its own. As Gwenyth asked me in
genuine puzzlement, how could any meal be considered complete
without a loaf of good bread alongside?

Wide World of Bread

As proof that Seattle has become a multicultural city, and that
bread is so central to meal-taking that virtually no immigrants
will be satisfied until the bread of their homeland can be repli-
cated here, I offer a list of some of my favorite international
breads available in the area.

American: hominy bread at Tall Grass Bakery; sticky buns at
Crusty Loaf

French: baguettes at Le Fournil or Le Panier

German: pretzels from Hess Bakery; Bohemian pumpernickel from
Morning Star Bakery (both available at the Continental Store)

Italian: any of the breads at La Panzanella; focaccia at Essential Baking Co.

Jewish: challah at Macrina Bakery; bagels at Bagel Oasis

Persian: *naan-e-barbari* at Old Country Bakery

Salvadoran: pupusas at Salvadorean Bakery

Scandinavian: *lefse* at Olsen's Scandinavian Foods; cardamom bread at Nielsen's Authentic Danish Pastries

"Parmesan" Bread Crumbs

Here's a great way to use all those stale ends and crumbs of bread that always lurk in the bread bin. It doesn't matter what sort of bread you have: focaccia, *pain au levain,* and baguettes all work nicely. Use this "Parmesan" just like the real thing: sprinkled on a dish just before serving for a delightful flavor and texture boost. The key is to add the crumbs at the very last minute so they will retain their crunch.

Stale bread, crumbed in a food processor, to make about 1 cup

3 tablespoons extra virgin olive oil

2 cloves garlic, minced

1 tablespoon finely chopped parsley

1 tablespoon finely chopped basil

1 dried chile pepper, seeded and crumbled; or 1 fresh jalapeño pepper, seeded and thinly sliced

Coarsely ground salt and pepper to taste

Preheat oven to 500 degrees F.

Toss bread crumbs with 1½ tablespoons of the olive oil.

Combine the remaining 1½ tablespoons olive oil, garlic, parsley, basil, chile or jalapeño pepper, salt, and pepper in bowl and set aside.

Place bread crumbs in ovenproof dish (a cast-iron skillet works well). Bake till toasted golden brown, about 5 minutes. Watch carefully or else it will burn.

Remove from oven and immediately pour herb mixture directly over crumbs. Stir to combine.

When sizzling stops, "Parmesan" is ready. It can be prepared several hours in advance, but try to use it the same day.

Note: I love these crumbs tossed on top of a salad, scattered on roasted tomatoes, sprinkled on sautéed shrimp, or even finishing off a pasta dish.

CENTRAL SEATTLE

The Crumpet Shop

1503 First Ave. (in Pike Place Market), Seattle
Phone: 206/682-1598
Hours: 8AM–4PM Monday–Saturday; closed Sunday

What's the best thing to put on a crumpet? Gary Lasater, owner of the Crumpet Shop, says it's "cream cheese with maple butter and toasted walnuts," but then admits that he has to pedal off the calories by bicycling home after eating one. Actually, you can slather a crumpet with anything your imagination and the contents of your fridge can dream up. But the best options take advantage of the nature of the little critter.

The Oxford Companion to Food defines a crumpet as a type of thick, perforated pancake made from a yeast-leavened batter containing milk. After cooking on a griddle, the bottom takes on a pale gold color and smooth surface, while the top stays pallid and studded with a mass of tiny holes, the better to absorb butter plus toppings.

Gary has owned this storefront bakery facing First Avenue since 1976. He learned his craft from a baker in Victoria, B.C., who was the supplier to that city's elegant Empress Hotel. He was in the middle of his morning bake the day I talked to him, and in between fussing over his charges, he chatted about proper crumpet-baking techniques and the frustrations of running a small business. Gary's crumpets are made fresh several times a day because they don't keep well. In fact, he says, it's "almost a disservice to have crumpets on a grocery shelf." He's right. His crumpets are scrumptious homey creations, with a mildly yeasty tang and an underlying sweetness, perfect with fruit preserves and butter.

The shop also sells teas from China, Ceylon, India, and Japan. They specialize in loose-leaf varieties, either single estate or blends of their own formulation. Gary's practice of buying carefully in small quantities ensures that everything is very fresh.

Crusty Loaf

2123 Queen Anne Ave. N, Seattle
Phone: 206/282-5623
Hours: 7AM–7PM Monday–Saturday; 8AM–6PM Sunday

You need only breathe deeply once when cruising the neighborhood around Crusty Loaf. The bakery's insidious yet delightful marketing scheme is to bake in midafternoon, so that passersby on their way home from work will find themselves inexplicably lured inside.

Walk into this charming little storefront on upper Queen Anne Avenue and two things will immediately hit you. First, there's the oven dominating the room. The show here takes place right in front of the customers. Naturally, everyone makes a beeline straight to the counter, where hunks of the daily bread selection are offered for sampling.

Crusty Loaf's breads are eye-catching because of their rustic simplicity. They're based on simple ingredients, organic flour, and traditional techniques. Take, for example, the sticky bun. Here it's not a dainty little pastry. Instead it's *bread*: intense and buttery with caramel and cinnamon, looking like a wildly splayed pinwheel.

The rosemary–sea salt bread is my absolute favorite. Perhaps it's because of my gender: women, I'm told, can't get enough of this bread. Why? No one seems to know. Customers also rave about the Irish soda bread, the Asiago cheese bread, and another of my favorites, the potato dill bread, which has recognizable chunks of potato embedded in a moist, herbaceous crust.

Grand Central Bakery

214 First Ave. S, Seattle
Phone: 206/622-3644
Hours: 7AM–6PM Monday–Friday; 9AM–5PM Saturday; closed Sunday

Every artisan baker in Seattle owes a debt to Grand Central Bakery. For one thing, dozens have used the bakery as a training ground. For another, Gwenyth Bassetti and her bakery have shown that the city is responsive to real food handmade by skilled craftspeople, and that a dedicated individual can thrive and make an honorable living from providing it.

Grand Central's story is well known, and it's possible to buy their bread in pretty much any supermarket around town. But Gwenyth has a soft spot for the original shop in Pioneer Square, from which the "revolution" originated. In addition, as she puts it, "This is where the bakers get to play and try out new things." Of course old favorites, such as the cinnamon roll made with seven grains, are always available too. (Gwenyth says that these were her own contribution and that she personally has made thousands of them.)

I myself am partial to Grand Central's breadsticks, available only at the retail store. Slightly salty, with a feisty kick of black pepper and Parmesan, they are simply irresistible. I have never been known to walk by the shop without stopping in for a fix.

Making good bread takes time. True artisan bread, as made at Grand Central, comes from long, slow fermentation (sometimes as long as two days) and hands-on efforts by the bakers. This bread doesn't go stale quickly. The flavors are strong. The crusts tend to be dark, almost caramelized, with crispness and satisfying chewiness. Each loaf is ample and unique, with variations in shape, color, and texture giving pleasure to the eye as well as the palate. That, I think, is what has fueled Grand Central's phenomenal growth.

Il Fornaio

600 Pine St., Seattle
Phone: 206/264-0994
Hours: 6:30AM–9PM every day

Some people might find the raisin bread at Il Fornaio too dark and bitter. Not me. I love this bread. A dark, almost charcoal-crusted loaf bursting with just the right number of golden and black raisins embedded in a creamy white interior, this rustic country loaf is an unmitigated wow. The ciabatta loaf is also exceptional. It's got a crust you can sink your teeth into, and a robust interior perfect for sopping up and encasing dripping-wet sandwich fillings.

Il Fornaio is a bakery that began in Italy with a mission to preserve regional bread traditions, and subsequently spread from the Bay Area to its first location in Seattle at Pacific Place, having built a formidable reputation for their breads. The bakery is hidden away in the ground level of the restaurant, which is a worthwhile stop on its own for a casual Italian meal. Be sure to pop in if you're in the neighborhood.

Le Panier

1902 Pike Pl. (in Pike Place Market), Seattle
Phone: 206/441-3669
Hours: 7AM–6PM Monday–Saturday; 8AM–5PM Sunday

Make it simple, keep it fresh, and the crowds will come: a winning formula for any food market, especially a bakery. Of course, it helps to be in the center of Pike Place Market with plenty of walk-through traffic.

Thierry Mougin and Kristi Drake know they've got a great location. They are also really focused on what they do best: traditional French breads and classic pastries. Thierry sees himself foremost as a bread baker, staying true to his French heritage. That translates into a marvelous assortment of breads of various sizes and shapes: perfectly crisp-crusted baguettes as close to what you'd get in Paris

The staff of life, ready for your daily meal.

as you're likely to see in Seattle, ring-shaped *couronnes*, *pain aux noix* (bread filled with walnuts) or *aux olives*, and a few others. The pastries run to the classic, with experimentation kept to a minimum.

Try to visit Le Panier on a winter morning, when the endless rain and clouds have worn down your spirit. The shop is warm and cozy and enveloped in delicious smells while the sleepy Market around it comes to life. This is when the croissants and the *pain au chocolat* are just coming out of the oven, and they are irresistible.

Macrina Bakery

2408 First Ave., Seattle
Phone: 206/448-4032
Hours: 7AM–6PM Monday–Saturday; 8AM–3PM Sunday

Leslie Mackie happened on her career as a baker almost by chance. She came to Seattle to work with restaurateur Tom Douglas as a pastry chef, but that project was delayed. As an interim solution, she knocked on the door of Grand Central Bakery, then just opening. Bakery founder Gwenyth Bassetti, who was also learning on the job, took her on, and Seattle has enjoyed the fruits of that collaboration ever since.

In 1993 Leslie branched out on her own and opened Macrina Bakery, and the café was added a year later. The bakery has been phenomenally successful, mostly because of the owner's personal stamp. As she puts it, "Creativity keeps us lively; we're a smaller operation, and we bend over backward to please our customers."

In turn, all of Seattle bends over backward for Macrina's breads. Hands down, this is the best all-around bakery in Seattle. Why? I say it is because Leslie has not compromised in any way, despite her breads' popularity, and has deliberately chosen to keep her operation small so that she can control every aspect of it.

The breads are all exceptional, and the full line isn't as readily available elsewhere as those of some other bakeries (another reason to visit). The basic white, the Guiseppe, is a first-rate crusty loaf; crumbs will litter your counter when you slice it, but no matter, you'll scoop them up to snack on. The rustic potato, made with unpeeled russet potatoes, and the rye (with or without caramelized onions) make great sandwich breads. The pear and cracked pepper bread, made seasonally, is absolutely fantastic slathered with some soft, ripe goat cheese.

Macrina makes wonderful rustic desserts too. I'm especially partial to the homey French apple tart. It's got everything I could ever want after dinner, the apples and butter making a magical combination.

The Mad Baker of Seattle

Ciro Pascuitto dragged me into his proofing room, a giant concrete shell empty but for a double line of plastic tubs and several bundles of grapevines hanging from the wall. "Here, smell the room. It's living, breathing, it's the foundation for everything that comes out of my bakery." Ciro and his wife Kim are the owners of La Panzanella, a jewel of a bakery on the southern edge of Capitol Hill. Ciro has some unorthodox ideas about baking, but more importantly, he is passionate about his bread—red-blooded, arm-waving, and voluble, with a sales pitch that had me completely captivated.

The key to La Panzanella's bread is the proofing, the period during which the dough is set to rise before shaping and baking. Proofing is done in the aforementioned room. The room *does* smell alive, vigorous and permeated with the aroma of wheaty fermentation, with an elusive tang of wood smoke mixed in. Periodically, a branch or two of grapevine is lit like incense to give a benediction and, more prosaically, to stabilize the humidity in the room. The entire process from proofing to shaping to final baking can take up to twenty-seven hours (as opposed to a typical state-of-the-art commercial bakery, which cuts that time to under two hours).

La Panzanella dough gets only one teaspoon of yeast for every fifty pounds of dough, an incredibly minuscule quantity. Ciro says that the space in the proofing room is the reason he can get by with using so little leavening. Bacteria and yeast have attached themselves to the walls and floors and the very ambient air, and they migrate to the fermenting dough from the outside in, like ants at a picnic. Amazingly enough, the whole process, from start to finish, is done entirely by hand: no machines to knead the dough, no cutters to divide the loaves, no industrial shapers to give the bread its final form. The result is a dense-textured bread with a full-bodied flavor of the grain.

To Ciro, bread is a metaphor for life. Indeed, watching the metamorphosis of flour to bread can be compared to the quest for the secret of a joyful life. "Bread is so fundamental to life—a neutral base to build from. Working with it puts value on change. It gives a sense of aging and mystery. My bread is like wine grapes. Soil is what gives wine its characteristic flavor, and here in this room my bread collects its flavors, slowly and sometimes unevenly. It's okay if it has flaws too."

He and Kim have gathered a community around themselves and the bakery. Friends drop in, bringing a basket of mushrooms or a liter of young, green olive oil from a trip to Italy, and are rewarded with bread and goodies in exchange. Every Wednesday at 1:45 in the afternoon (because anyone who can get away at that time must be interesting), they gather eight people, all strangers, around the large copper-clad table at the bakery for lunch, laughter, and wine. Customers put themselves in Ciro's hands and the menu is at his whim, always seasonal and featuring the best of the Northwest.

More important than anything else, of course, is the flavor of La Panzanella's bread. You taste one thing in a loaf of their bread and then, a split second later, you taste something else. What makes it unique? According to Ciro, it's very simple. "Start with good flour, give it time, and flour becomes flavor, not just bread."

La Panzanella

1314 E Union St., Seattle
Phone: 206/325-5217
Hours: 7:30AM–6:30PM Monday–Friday; 8:30AM–5:30PM Saturday; closed Sunday

NORTH

Bagel Oasis

2112 NE 65th St., Seattle
Phone: 206/526-0525
Hours: 8AM–5PM Monday–Friday; 7AM–4PM Saturday and Sunday

462 N 36th St., Seattle
Phone: 206/633-2676
Hours: 6:30AM–4PM Monday–Friday; 7AM–4PM Saturday and Sunday

I was having some work done in my house the day I got back from Bagel Oasis with a dozen assorted bagels. I figured that those guys looked like reliable bagel tasters, so I dropped the bag on the counter and offered them samples. They started taking bites out of each one, and pretty soon the work slowed down. They were in bagel heaven and didn't return to Earth till they were looking at the bottom of the bag.

Bagel Oasis is dedicated to making the perfect New York–style bagel, and they have come closer than anyone else in Seattle. The main branch, in Ravenna, is a plain, sparsely decorated shop, with bagels piled up inside old-fashioned wooden bins, a small refrigerated case selling lox and cream cheese, and not much else.

The bagels are worth a detour, especially for bagel purists who would prefer their favorite bread to not be the size of an inner tube, but instead to have suitable texture and crunch. These are water-

The bakers at Essential Baking Co. measure dough portions by hand.

boiled bagels, chewy but not too hard, flavorful but not too sweet, and light but not so airy that they collapse with a whoosh when you bite into them. The sesame and poppy seed varieties are excellent. The salt bagels have just enough salt, the garlic are suitably garlicky, and the rye-pumpernickel are a revelation. The latter, in fact, were my workmen's favorite.

Essential Baking Co.
1604 N 34th St., Seattle
Phone: 206/545-3804
Hours: 6AM–6PM Monday–Friday; 8AM–6PM Saturday; 8AM–3PM Sunday

According to Ptarmigan Teal, the general manager of Essential Baking Co., there has been a bakery on this site since 1925. When Buchan Bakery opened here in 1925, it was the first fully mechanized bakery in Seattle. The bakery was sold to Oroweat, and the operation grew into a behemoth of machine-run, conveyor-belted, never-touched-by-human-hands baking. It seems fitting that the old building now houses, in plain view of customers, the world's most spectacular bread oven: a 55,000-pound domed Llopis brick oven, with a volcanic ash hearth sixteen feet in diameter, that is completely nonautomated. The bakers rotate the giant, lazy Susan-like hearth by hand, and manually pour water for steam from a small pitcher.

Essential is the largest certified organic commercial bakery in Seattle. When the gorgeous new retail shop was opened in 1999, part of its mission was to showcase the personal and creative energy of the employees. Everything about the place bespeaks a labor of love.

George DePasquali is the head baker and creative director. The breads he likes to make are, for the most part, grounded in traditional ideas. That means you're not likely to find sun-dried tomato or pesto bread at Essential. What you will find are the four basic ingredients of bread baking—flour, salt, yeast, and water—endlessly manipulated to create a universe of possibilities.

That isn't to say that the bakers don't have baroque flights of fancy. A good example is the outstanding Sweet Perrin bread, available during the winter months, filled with big chunks of organic pears, figs, and roasted hazelnuts. The rosemary diamante bread, studded with fresh rosemary and sprinkled with kosher sea salt, is also a good bet. But the absolute star of the show, as far as I'm concerned, is the pizza bianco. Come about noon any day, and watch the baker carefully insert a four- or five-foot-long banner of dough into the brick oven. Ten or fifteen minutes later, out comes the most elementally satisfying, crunchily addictive flat bread you'll ever taste.

Note: Be sure to notice the wrought-iron shelving and decorative signboard hanging outside the bakery. One of the bakers moonlights as a talented sculptor.

Greatful Bread

7001 35th Ave. NE, Seattle
Phone: 206/525-3116
Hours: 7AM–7PM Monday–Friday; 8AM–5PM Saturday and Sunday

Honor Amourall is one of Seattle's more philosophical bakers. She believes that food gives off energy from the people making it. A baker full of pride and respect for her work will imbue her products with a palpable life force, she says, and you can taste it in her bread. It will be vastly different from the stuff produced by someone on a centralized assembly line churning out thousands of wretched plastic-wrapped industrial specimens.

Greatful Bread is an important gathering place for the community around its View Ridge location. From the elderly German gentleman who brings in flowers every day to the gaggle of middle-schoolers from nearby Eckstein to the evening poetry recitals and folk concerts, most locals find their way here at one time or another.

The bakery has a fine reputation for their thrice-a-day, steam-baked bagels and their incredibly oversized stromboli-brawny calzone cousins stuffed with cheese, mushrooms, olives, roasted peppers, broccoli, cauliflower, and zucchini. (Call them leftovers waiting to happen.) I was also particularly taken with the scones, which have an appealing, slightly funky homemade look to them, and sport a mass of blueberries wedged into the center of a crumbly, light biscuit dough. Only the counter help spoiled my visit, giving new meaning to the words "air" and "head."

Greenwood Bakery

7227 Greenwood Ave. N, Seattle
Phone: 206/783-7181
Hours: 6:30AM–7PM Monday–Saturday (in summer, 6:30AM–9PM);
7AM–6PM Sunday

This shop comes right out of your memories of small-town America. Stop in after school lets out, and watch moms and kids negotiate over the cookie trays. The Susan Shortbread with icing and sprinkles is a big hit. Throughout the day, the place is filled with a steady stream of regulars, neighborhood folks, and people driving in from outer burgs who grew up coming to this longtime family-run business. Greenwood devotees worried when the business was sold to John and Lara Baker in 1997, but their fears have since been allayed. John credits his store's success to keeping everything pretty much the same, maybe a little cleaned up.

This agreeable little bakery makes an impressive range of goodies in a very small back kitchen. Their breads are standouts, especially the basic *pain au levain*. It's made with a whole wheat starter and a pinch of yeast; it's sour, but not overly so, and it has a denser than average, chewy interior. The bagels here are hand rolled and boiled in water before baking, so they have the texture and crunch that bagels should. They are not quite to Bagel Oasis standards, but are a darn sight better than most of the pillowy, cottony, overinflated specimens around town.

Macaroon lovers will swoon over the versions here: chewy-dense with coconut and dipped in fresh-tasting chocolate, they won a recent Best of *Seattle Magazine* mention. All of the above, as well as pies, cheesecakes, quiches, scones, croissants, and a whole bunch of other stuff, are baked in an incredibly hardworking, geezerlike Rainier oven that's older than the store's owners.

Larry's Markets . . . . see Superstores

Le Fournil . . . see Cakes, Pastries, Pies, and Other Baked Goods

Tall Grass Bakery

5907 24th Ave. NW, Seattle
Phone: 206/706-0991
Hours: noon–8PM Monday–Friday; at Columbia City Farmers Market on
Wednesdays; at University District Farmers Market on Saturdays

"I'm not aspiring to be a French baker," says James Bowles. "I'm an American who gives credit to European traditions." James and his partner Russ Battaglia are the owners of Tall Grass Bakery, the innovative shop in Ballard that is breaking bread, so to speak, in a manner never before seen in Seattle.

In France, Italy, and Germany, many regional breads are made with various grains other than wheat, giving them a local distinction. For example, rye bread is made tangy with sourdough to bring out its natural flavor, and then is sold by the quarter, half, or whole log all over Europe. But Seattleites have not been willing to experiment with an all-rye bread containing no enrichments such as sweeteners, fats, eggs, or milk—not, that is, until they tasted Tall Grass's version (which James worked for over ten years to develop). This is a very rustic loaf, with a fissured surface studded with rough cracked rye meal, able to keep and develop its flavor for up to a week. Sliced thin and eaten with a sharp cheddar, it is unapologetically hearty and delicious.

Tall Grass makes other exceptional breads as well. Their hominy bread, half of which is cooked cornmeal, is served at Jimmy's Table and is the only bread that customers of the Madison Park restaurant have repeatedly raved over. The bakery's version of an all-spelt bread—something few bakeries will bother with—is wonderful.

In fact, a number of Tall Grass's recipes come from other shops' rejects. The bakery is small enough that they can bake what they want to, even if they produce only ten loaves at a time, so they try to develop what tastes good and then sell people on it. And boy, have people responded. At the University District Farmers Market, it's not unusual for them to sell 250 to 300 loaves in a three-hour period. The bakery stays open through dinner to take advantage of the evening rush. Laughing, James and Russ told me they felt that people were finally "getting it" when a little boy came in, sent by his mom to get a hot baguette just in time for dinner.

EASTSIDE

Old Country Bakery . . . . see Middle Eastern

WEST

Alki Bakery. . see Cakes, Pastries, Pies, and Other Baked Goods

cakes, pastries, pies, and other baked goods

Pity the poor baker in Seattle. Day after day, week in and week out, he or she must attend to the care and feeding of our formidable sweet tooth. Whether on a quick stop before boarding the ferry, in search of a toothsome nibble to accompany a latte, or seeking a carefully tied box of the day's luscious selections to carry home, Seattleites require a mountain of sticky, buttery, sweet, and utterly satisfying pastries every day. Luckily for us, there is a small, dedicated group of people who are willing to put in the long hours necessary to take care of that insatiable appetite.

In my explorations, one central fact hit home again and again: our pastry shops are neighborhood hangouts. I was told more than once how loyal a neighborhood is to their bakery, how likely folks are to sit, drink, and nibble for hours on end at this or that shop. Our pastry shops are run by friendly folk who are dedicated to their craft and toil long, often lonely hours to provide us with comfortable refuges where we can take a breather from our incessantly busy lives.

Seattle is a city where one can indulge a taste for a variety of ethnic bakeries. Choose from Scandinavian bakeries serving cardamom-scented yeasted buns; Chinese bakeries in the International District that seem to specialize in ultra-sweet, encased-in-frosting cakes; Italian pastry shops with ricotta cakes and panettones, crunchy cannolis, and gelati; Middle Eastern baklava shops; and more. Even if you choose to limit your sampling of ethnic foods to desserts, you could certainly circle the globe and still stay within our city limits.

All small food businesses face competitive pressures from sophisticated supermarkets and big-box retailers, which woo shoppers with gourmet baked goods, convenient hours, and free parking. Traditional bakers respond by emphasizing their high quality and service. The problem with high quality, of course, is that everyone has their own definition of it. For some it simply means the most expensive ingredients prepared in a labor-intensive, time-honored way.

But businesses have to survive. So they may start to cut corners— maybe use cheaper shortening or margarine rather than butter, maybe some dough enhancers and conditioners, maybe inexpensive fructose-enhanced fruit purees instead of whole fruit jams. They can and do still lay claim to baking from scratch and using all-natural ingredients. But it's a falsehood that ultimately dulls the meaning of the real terms. All too often, my experience has been that the fight for survival among small traditional bakers has not been kind to those still interested in making honest, top-quality food.

That's not to say they don't exist. It's just not a given that because a bakery has been in a community for umpteen years, it is still at the top of its game. And remember too that bakeries, like people, are not uniformly good at everything they do. Throughout this chapter, I have tried to indicate things that I particularly liked about each shop and warn you about those I didn't. My best advice: Go, taste for yourself, patronize these businesses, and help them to survive.

CENTRAL

Dilettante Chocolates . . . .
see Chocolates, Candies, Nuts, and Ice Cream

Gelatiamo . . . . . see Chocolates, Candies, Nuts, and Ice Cream

Grand Central Bakery . . . . see Bread

La Panzanella . . . . see Bread

Le Panier . . . . see Bread

Macrina Bakery . . . . see Bread

Madison Park Bakery

4214 E Madison St., Seattle
Phone: 206/322-3238
Hours: 6:30AM–6PM Tuesday–Friday; 6:30AM–5:30PM Saturday; closed
Sunday and Monday

Whenever my friends talk about old-style bakeries, this is the one they mean. Step into Madison Park Bakery and you'll feel that you've entered a warm, slightly faded time warp and you're holding your mom's hand while pressing your nose against the glass case. "You can choose anything, but just one," Mom would promise. Only now you can have as much as you want; the only limits are your wallet and your waistline.

The banana cake is the kind of old-fashioned Mom-pleaser that I know she would choose. Bursting with naturally sweet bananas and moist as can be, it's the kind of dessert that's been around forever and just can't be found at too many places anymore. I'd avoid some of the more gooey, frosting-heavy desserts, which tend to be simplistically sweet and one-dimensional.

Terry and Karen Hofman, owners since 1993, say that they have a bigger assortment of bakery items than anybody else in town. Breads, pies, cookies, cakes, holiday-themed items—they're all here, just as you would expect in a well-loved neighborhood bakery. But in my opinion, the best reason to come to Madison Park Bakery is the doughnuts. If you can, come at six in the morning, when they're just coming out of the fryer. They're puffy and light, crusted with sugar and absolutely scrumptious.

Nielsen's Authentic Danish Pastries . see Scandinavian

So You Wanna Open a Bakery . . .

Over the years, I have devised my own simple pleasure-meter for tasting desserts. If, after one or two bites, I can decorously put my fork down and be willing to share, I'm not impressed. If, on the other hand, it's "just one more bite" till all I'm left staring at are a few crumbs, then I know I've found a winner.

After visiting North Hill Bakery on Capitol Hill, I was left with a plate of crumbs. And the result of that experience is a lasting devotion to a phenomenal new addition to Seattle's bakery scene. Friends had told me about this recently opened bakery, run by two very experienced, very talented women. I had to see for myself. And foolishly enough, I even volunteered to show up at four in the morning, bakers' hours.

Tracey Peterson and Margaret Rumpeltes are both graduates of the culinary program at South Seattle Community College and, most recently, instructors in the Art Institute of Seattle's culinary program. Their combined experience has included cooking in an

Margaret Rumpeltes showing off her handiwork at North Hill Bakery.

Alaskan town north of the Arctic Circle and in Walla Walla, Washington, as well as stints at Julia's of Wallingford, the Columbia Edgewater Country Club in Portland, Rover's, and Macrina Bakery. Think of their desserts as "rustic contemporary" interpretations of sturdy American pastries: a little sleeker, a little prettier, and a lot sexier. A perfect example is their chocolate cream pie. Available either as a mini-tart or by the slice, it's a worldly, grown-up version of chocolate milk pudding set on a buttery pastry crust with generous quantities of whipped cream and even more chocolate flakes. There's no mistaking its origins . . . and the taste is utterly divine.

The space the bakery took over has been a bakery for sixty years. In its heyday during the '40s, '50s, and '60s it was known as Caroline's, then later as Hollyhock, a wholesale-only wedding cake bakery. Operating on a shoestring, Margaret and Tracey, along with their friends and family, repainted the all-pink room and scrubbed and cleaned every grubby nook and cranny before opening. They kept the Caroline's "C" molding and are happily using the original 1907 electric brick oven. Tracey's aunt used a toothbrush and a week's worth of elbow grease to restore an old 1940s Hobart mixer. Tracey and Margaret both note that the former owner and resident ghost, Felix, has signaled his approval.

A universal truth for bakers is that they start their day pretty darn early. From the moment I blearily stepped from the darkness outside into the bright lights of the bakery, I joined a practiced routine of controlled chaos. All the while working, Margaret chatted about the bakery, her work experience, her two young sons, her recipes, and North Hill's overriding commitment to success without cheating on quality.

At present, the bakery still needs some major (and expensive) pieces of equipment, especially a freezer and a sheeter (used for mechanically rolling and cutting dough). Sheeters are expensive, about $6,000 for a decent one, and must be carefully worked into the budget. In the meantime, everything is rolled and cut by hand. While the croissant dough warms to room temperature, Margaret pats out the oatmeal scones. She's forgotten to add the sultanas, but no matter; today's version will be raisinless.

Watching the effortless, rapid-fire movements of a craftsperson is a humbling experience. "I teach my students to use their hands. They're the best tools they have," says Tracey. To demonstrate, she hand-squeezes dead-on measures of pineapple, carrot, and raisin Morning Glory muffin batter into tins. Other bakeries might be able to learn something from this one: North Hill can sell its muffins (not oversized like many others) for less than a buck.

By the time the bakery opens at 6:30 in the morning and the first customers poke their heads in the door, the case is full of a tantalizing selection of muffins, scones, flaky croissants, and cookies, and the soft-crust breads are just coming out of the oven. Here's to a job well done by the bakers at North Hill.

North Hill Bakery

518 15th Ave. E, Seattle
Phone: 206/325-9007
Hours: 6:30AM–5:30PM Wednesday–Friday; 7AM–4PM Saturday and Sunday; closed Monday and Tuesday

Oatmeal Cranberry Cookies
North Hill Bakery

Makes approximately 24 2-ounce cookies

> *½ pound (2 sticks) butter, softened*
> *2½ cups packed brown sugar*
> *1 tablespoon vanilla*
> *2 eggs, at room temperature*
> *2¾ cups all-purpose flour*
> *1 tablespoon baking powder*
> *2 teaspoons baking soda*
> *1 teaspoon salt*
> *3 cups rolled oats*
> *2½ cups dried cranberries*

Preheat oven to 350 degrees F.

Cream butter with sugar until smooth.

Add vanilla to eggs, then add egg mixture to butter mixture in three batches, scraping well after each addition.

Sift flour with baking powder, baking soda, and salt, then mix with oats and add to butter-egg mixture.

Mix until blended, then add cranberries. Add a few drops of water if dough seems too stiff.

Let dough chill, then scoop or drop onto baking sheet lined with parchment and bake until golden brown, about 10 or 12 minutes. Note: Even if the dough feels stiff, the cookies will spread somewhat while baking. When they come out of the oven, they will probably collapse a bit and become chewy.

NORTH

Boulangerie
2200 N 45th St., Seattle
Phone: 206/634-2211
Hours: 7AM–7:30PM Sunday–Thursday; 7AM–8:30PM Friday and Saturday

For many years, Boulangerie was Seattle's lone purveyor of high-quality French baked goods. Now that there's competition, how does this little bakery hold up? Xon Luong, the baker here for over twenty years and the owner for about five, has struggled in recent times to find a successful formula for his operation. (Xon, who as you might guess is actually Vietnamese, not French, has been baking since he was a boy in Vietnam providing pastries and *pain Français* to the French military.)

As in any respectable French bakery, the breads and pastries are exceedingly fresh and moist. They are also significantly cheaper than those at, say Le Fournil. But be warned; eat those pastries quickly, before the grease has had a chance to soak through the bag. My son is exceedingly fond of the croissants here. They're flaky and messy, and (no small feat) they're big enough to satisfy a hungry teenage boy. The baguettes, by which any French bakery must be measured, are standard stuff—not bad, but, when measured against today's high standards, not terribly exciting.

Dessert Works
6116 Phinney Ave. N, Seattle
Phone: 206/789-5765
Hours: 8:30AM–2PM Tuesday–Saturday; closed Sunday–Monday

Tim Towner has been holed up in his end of Phinney Ridge for over ten years doing his best to satisfy Seattle's sweet tooth. Dessert Works is a mostly wholesale operation that takes special orders for retail, and it's an excellent source for special occasions. Tim says that about 20 percent of the business is retail and that everything is made to order. He specializes in chocolate, especially elaborate chocolate-wrapped cakes. What's special about his cakes is that they are incredibly light, since he doesn't use buttercream frostings. Instead, everything is layered with cream-based mousses. I tried the strawberry bagatelle, his signature item. Tim calls it "a decadent strawberry shortcake," and so it is, light with lovely strawberry juices streaked through. He likes to do about two or three wedding cakes a weekend—no more—so he can really concentrate and have them be as fresh as possible. Tim's creations are pricey, but that's because, he says, he's not willing to cut corners.

The Erotic Bakery

2323 N 45th St., Seattle
Phone: 206/545-6969
E–mail: eroticbakery@seanet.com
Hours: 10AM–7PM Monday–Saturday; noon–5PM Sunday

Wallingford's Erotic Bakery has been famous since 1986 for its sexy little cupcakes, cakes, adult novelties, and the best selection of risqué greeting cards in Seattle. Owner Robert Prado came here from Denver, which already had a shop purveying food erotica, and saw a niche that was open for him to exploit.

Now, you may not be crazy about marzipan, but a notable feature of the stuff is that it can be molded and colored into exceedingly realistic little shapes. The staff's artistry and talent is on full display in the bakery's cases, which showcase hand-painted tiny figures in various rude poses and play. Condoms encased in fortune cookies, chocolate lollipop male and female genitalia, and computerized picture cakes are some of the other "food"-related items for sale. Robert says that 80 percent of customers are female, and the store does a booming business providing cakes for bachelorette parties.

Greenwood Bakery . . . . see Bread

Honey Bear Bakery

101 S Main St. (in Elliott Bay Book Company), Seattle
Phone: 206/682-6664
Hours: 10AM–7:30PM Monday–Saturday; 11AM–7PM Sunday

17171 Bothell Way NE (in Third Place Books), Lake Forest Park
Phone: 206/366-3330
Hours: 8AM–10PM Sunday–Thursday; 8AM–11PM Friday and Saturday

Once upon a time, there was a little bakery in a place called Stehekin on the shores of Lake Chelan. It was owned by some counterculture throwbacks, Karl Gaskill and Rissa Warner, and folks came from miles around by boat or by air (for those were the only ways to get there) to load up on their cinnamon rolls and pumpkin muffins and scrumptious baked goodies.

When they packed it in in 1979 and moved to the city, they kept doing what they knew best, and the Honey Bear Bakery was born. Of course, their reputation preceded them, and they were mobbed from opening day forward. Just as in Stehekin, the bakery developed a cult following: customers thought nothing of driving from Bellevue, Edmonds, or parts even farther afield for the hearty whole-grain breads, extraordinary muffins and whole wheat sourdough cinnamon rolls, and good old-fashioned layer cakes. The potato-buttermilk bread was and still is the best of its kind in the city.

Cut to 1998: Karl and Rissa were tired and burnt out. After a lot of soul-searching, they made the decision to sell to developer Ron Sher, who added Honey Bear branches in his bookstores, Elliott Bay Book Company and Third Place Books. In 2001, bowing to market realities, the original Wallingford/Green Lake location was closed. Since then the bakery's menu has narrowed in scope, though many of the original bakery items are still available and I get the impression that, perhaps inevitably, the fanatical devotion to quality that was Honey Bear is cracking. Still, I can forgive a lot for a slice of the pear cassata cake, a frosted pound cake layered with ricotta, fresh pears, and candied ginger.

Honey Bear's pastries are not for small appetites. I haven't tasted the coconut cake, but it looks almost cartoonishly oversized, snow-white with frosting and shaved coconut. Likewise, the Danish, the muffins, and the scones all seem to be afflicted with a serious case of giganticus. What is the deal with this phenomenon? Does anyone seriously consume a scone the size of a football at one sitting?

Larsen's Original Danish Bakery

8000 24th Ave. NW, Seattle
Phone: 206/782-8285
Hours: 6AM–6:30PM Monday–Friday; 6AM–6PM Saturday; 7AM–5PM Sunday
Internet: www.larsensbakery.com

Poul Larsen didn't invent *kringles*, but just like McDonald's, he means to sell billions and billions of them. He's working on his second million, all made at his longtime "original" bakery in Ballard, and shipping them to loyal fans all over the country. Just what is a kringle? Think of a traditional Danish pastry made of layers of flaky crust enclosing almond paste and raisins, topped with sugar and almonds and twisted into a giant pretzel shape that literally melts over your tongue.

Larsen's stays true to its Danish heritage with a number of traditional Scandinavian breakfast pastries. They make a tasty cardamom-flavored braided bread, which is lovely first thing in the morning toasted and slathered with fresh butter. The bakery is also *the* source for *kransekage*, Danish-style wedding cakes (wrapped in marzipan rings). And while I'm not a cheesecake lover, the version here is a very creamy and classic New York style, sure to win the heart of any aficionado. (The French pastries, though, are eminently skippable.)

Go for the unwrapped *kringle* in the bakery case rather than the boxed version. Wrapping the cakes in cellophane predictably increases the sogginess quotient.

Note: There is no longer any relationship between this bakery and the Larsen's products sold at QFC. Poul sold his interest in that enterprise so that he could get back to the art of baking on a smaller scale. His employees say he's a lot happier.

Le Fournil

3230 Eastlake Ave. E, Seattle
Phone: 206/328-6523
Hours: 7AM–6PM Tuesday–Saturday; 7AM–2PM Sunday; closed Monday

French desserts are sexy. Just like the little black dress, they're appropriate anywhere, ooze good looks, and, unlike American-style desserts, are perfect in their diminutiveness. Le Fournil, a charming little patisserie/boulangerie on Eastlake, is filled with the minor masterpieces of its French owner, Nicolas Pare, and his pastry chef, Kevin Thompson. They are both talented, ambitious, and passionate about their work, and it shows. Nicolas is the boulanger and is responsible for the breads and croissants, whereas Kevin's domain is the jewel-like dessert case.

The product line is always changing, and it's all wonderful, sophisticated, and not overly sweet. The chocolate-pear tart is a perfect example of why customers are swooning over Le Fournil. It's a blend of pears marinated in a secret syrup, resting in a pool of chocolate batter and almond cream set on a shortbread crust. Each element works, and each ingredient has been coaxed and coddled to give maximum mouth-feel. In an inspired fit of frugality, Nicholas makes a bread pudding using leftover croissants, then goes overboard with the butter and sugar, making for a simply satisfying and utterly delicious dessert.

I'm going to go out on a limb and say that I think Le Fournil makes the best baguette in town. It's near-perfect: *bien cuite*, with a crackly, almost nutty crust and a light, airy, wheat-flecked *mie*, or interior. This is bread that calls to mind that great French triumvirate—bread, cheese, wine—and conjures up instant dinner solutions. There's also a nice variety of *pain de campagne*, as well as breads flavored with olives, walnuts, or rosemary.

Scandinavian Bakery................ see Scandinavian

Simply Desserts
3421 Fremont Ave. N, Seattle
Phone: 206/633-2671
Hours: noon–10PM Tuesday–Thursday; noon–11:30PM Friday and Saturday; noon–6PM Sunday; closed Monday

Most brownies taste like super-sweet and gooey fudge cakes to me. They're good, but you can quickly overload on the sugar and butter. The hazelnut chocolate brownies at Simply Desserts, on the other hand, taste like squashed chocolate soufflés studded with nuts—moist yet light enough that you can actually eat a whole one without feeling as if you've swallowed a lead weight.

Phil Tobin and Stacy Hagiya moved here from San Francisco to open Simply Desserts twenty years ago. Since they're largely self-taught (they were both art majors at the San Francisco Art Institute), they say they bake only things they like to eat. Desserts here are typically straightforward interpretations of American classics. Try the delectable berry pie and the recently introduced velvet torte, a bittersweet dark chocolate cake with a wallop of intensely chocolate richness.

In the old days, when this shop first opened, Fremont didn't exude the same urban pulse that it does today. As Phil says, "It was cheap before it was funky." Now, with the multistory Adobe Systems complex a block away and a surge of new upscale shops nearby, he worries that rising rents will push out some of the businesses responsible for the unique character of the neighborhood. That stamp of character and the "life, sweat, blood, and tears" that Phil and Stacy have put into the bakery are what makes it worth coming to.

Chocolate Fudge Torte
Simply Desserts

Crust
> 1 package Oreo cookies
> 1 to 2 ounces cold butter

Filling
> 5 ounces unsweetened chocolate
> 1/2 pound (2 sticks) butter
> 1/2 cup cream
> 2 cups sugar
> 4 eggs and 1 egg yolk
> 1 teaspoon vanilla

Preheat oven to 350 degrees F.

For crust, grind together Oreo cookies and cold butter. Spread evenly on bottom of 9-inch cheesecake pan.

Melt chocolate and butter in double boiler over medium heat. Add cream and sugar. Continue to cook over medium heat for at least 10 minutes or until sugar has dissolved. Let stand for 10 minutes.

In a medium bowl, mix eggs and vanilla. While beating, add warm chocolate mixture. Mix until smooth. Do not overbeat.

Pour into cheesecake pan and bake for 35 minutes, or until the outside puffs slightly and the middle begins to firm up. Do not overbake; the torte should firm up in the fridge and be very smooth when you cut it.

Refrigerate the torte until it is set, at least 3 to 4 hours, and serve with whipped cream.

60th Street Desserts

7401 Sand Point Way NE, Seattle
Phone: 206/527-8560
Hours: 7:30AM–5PM Monday–Thursday; 7:30AM–6PM Friday; 9AM–midnight Saturday; closed Sunday

Joan Williams used to sell her desserts at Costco. That was a nightmare. Given a tight labor market, the baking, packaging, delivering, and sometimes throwing out of unsold products left her with little time, excruciating wrist pains, and, most dishearteningly, meager profits to show for her efforts.

Things are a lot saner now. Two years ago, she moved her shop from its former View Ridge location to a new space with twice the square footage. Although it's primarily a wholesale business, a growing retail trade driven by neighborhood demand has added to the fun.

Joan's creations are first-rate innovations based on the down-home recipes she learned from her Iowa-raised grandmother. Try any of the tarts, for instance; they use an exemplary all-butter crust that's worked by hand so it's exceedingly flaky and doesn't look mass-produced. Toppings are made from fresh fruit, lemon curd, mousse, chocolate, or anything else the season or harvest offers. Triple chocolate chunk pecan tart is a sinful hybrid of chocolate, pecans, sugar, and butter, so good that I lay awake the other night planning my next dinner party around it.

The other nifty feature of this shop is the frozen case selling 60th Street's own pizza, cookie, and pie doughs. Heck, between the pizza dough and the pecan tart, I've got dinner covered. Joan plans to begin offering small savory mini-quiches that are perfect single-size servings. A few 60th Street desserts are sold at QFC and some Thriftways, and you can also find Joan at the University District Farmers Market.

SOUTH

International Biscuit Co.

5028 Wilson Ave. S, Seattle
Phone: 206/722-5595
Hours: 9AM–8PM Sunday; 7:30AM–8PM Monday–Thursday; 7:30AM till an hour and a half before sundown Friday; closed Saturday

Mottie Bendet came here from Brooklyn and in a New York minute took Seattle's Jewish community by storm. He bought International Biscuit a year and a half ago, converted it to a strictly kosher and largely lactose-free bakery (there are some products containing cheese), and then plans to move on to the Eastside to expand his empire. He calls his operation the "western frontier of Jewish food."

In typical rapid-fire speech, Mottie enthuses, "Think of us as a place where you can sit down and feel like you're in your mom's kitchen. Have a bite of chocolate rugelach. It'll feel like a slice of home." The old warhorses of Jewish cuisine are all here: cheese and potato blintzes, rugelach (made here in a huge puff pastry version as well as the more traditional dense twist), and *babkas* with either a chocolate or cinnamon-raisin filling.

Since my previous experiences with knishes all involved New York sidewalk carts, International Biscuit's version opened my eyes. I gotta admit, the dough is flaky, the fillings are deliciously oniony, and these knishes actually have some taste instead of resembling pasty mashed potatoes. Alas, I can't say the same about the ziti with mozzarella. If ever there was a more gluey, dry, shriveled mess, I can't think.

EASTSIDE

Amazing Cakes

14934 NE 31st Circle, Bldg D, Redmond
Phone: 425/869-2992
Hours: By appointment only

Neither words nor pictures could possibly do justice to this "amazing" bakery. Since 1993, Mike McCarey has been sculpting unnervingly lifelike one-, two-, or three-dimensional designs applied to a standard-shaped cake, or letting the cake itself be the sculpture. Need to com-memorate your daughter's membership in 4-H, pastime of raising chickens, and love of Renaissance fairy tales? No problem. Mike will take your idea and transform it into a life-size, fully gilted and bedecked prize rooster dressed in Renaissance splendor, all in your favorite cake flavor of white chocolate with orange and peach Schnapps.

Mike uses fondant, a sugary-sweet substance that can be rolled out and is extremely malleable, and hand-paints figurines using some-thing called sculptin (which I'm told is completely edible, although its contents remain a mystery). Although looks are everything with these cakes, they also tasted a lot better than I expected.

The biggest project Mike has ever worked on was a life-size grand-father clock with a fully functional clock face, created for a law firm that had the original in their main office. It took four guys to trans-port the four-hundred-pound cake to the party, and it cost the com-pany $13,000. Mike can also create a miniature cake and customize it with something special for your near and dear for as little as $17.

Hoffman's Fine Pastries

226 Parkplace Center, Kirkland
Phone: 425/828-0926
Hours: 7AM–8PM every day

When I asked him where and how he learned his craft, Ed Hoffman told me about working for one of the last old-style German bakers in Santa Cruz, California. "He didn't want to teach me, but he'd been an instructor, so he did it despite himself. It was a painful experience for both of us." Ed learned somehow, and moved on to open his well-regarded shop in downtown Kirkland. After fifteen years, he says that his biggest problem is that he doesn't have time to play anymore. He loves to create new products (he's been working on a bread recipe for five years and is still not satisfied). A baker to the core, Ed is opin-ionated about what makes really good pastry: rich cream but not oversweetness (after all, excess sugar can hide a lot of flaws), top-quality ingredients, and a natural balance between fruit and pastry.

Hoffman's signature item is the princess torte, covered marzipan with vanilla genoise, raspberry jam, and a filling of custard and whipped cream. (When his customers bemoan the calories, he replies, "Relax, it looks great on you.") But virtually everything in this shop is wonderful. I love the cookies—perfect oversized chocolate chip cookies with walnuts, and pinwheels and walnut icebox cookies, and many more, in a rotating selection.

WEST

Alki Bakery

2738 Alki Ave. SW, Seattle
Phone: 206/935-1352
Hours: 7AM–9PM Sunday–Thursday; 7AM–10PM Friday and Saturday; in summer, 7AM–10PM every day

5700 First Ave. S, Seattle
Phone: 206/762-5700
Hours: 6:30AM–4PM Monday–Friday; closed Saturday and Sunday

When you're out of lemons, sometimes you make lemonade. Misfortune rained down in the early morning hours of October 1998, when a car crashed through the windows of Alki Bakery following a high-speed police chase. Much to the dismay of its loyal customers, the bakery closed for almost a year of renovation.

It's back now, and even the old-timers love the spacious new quarters (especially on a sunny morning, with the sun sparkling on the water and the dazzling views of Bainbridge Island and the Olympics). The stroller brigade locks wheels on an otherwise quiet weekday morning, lured by the scent of the bakery's famous cinnamon rolls, cookies, scones, muffins, cakes, and pies. Lunch buzzes with devotees lining up for the house-roasted turkey, top round beef, ham sandwiches, and fresh soups.

And on the weekend . . . yikes, every sun-worshiping, roller-blading, volleyball playing, sand-frolicking West Seattleite must make an obligatory pit stop for a latte and a bite of the signature chocolate-banana flan. This outrageously decadent tart bursting with chocolate ganache, fresh bananas, pastry cream, and chocolate shavings should be nominated for some kind of award—say, "Most likely to earn you entrance through the Pearly Gates should you be buried with one." Only the baguette was disappointing, being insufficiently crusty for my tastes.

Frombach's Old Home Bakery

2332 California Ave. SW, Seattle
Phone: 206/932-5574
Hours: 6:30AM–2:30PM Monday–Friday; 6:30AM–noon Saturday; closed
Sunday

There's been a bakery at this end of California Avenue in West Seattle for as long as most people can remember. Joe McKeown says the best date he can come up with is 1956. That's long enough for a bakery to infuse its good, sweet smells into every crack and crevice of the neighborhood.

Joe was born into a family of bakers in Philadelphia. His grandfather, uncles, and cousins are scattered throughout Pennsylvania and New Jersey, and are all in the business. He laments that the business has changed drastically over the years. With the Admiral Thriftway around the corner, an old-fashioned from-scratch bakery faces an uphill struggle. Frombach's survives by doing about 75 percent of its business as wholesale.

If nothing else, it's worth coming directly to the bakery for its eight kinds of doughnuts, as well as maple bars and killer cookies. The fruit cobblers are an incredibly indulgent treat and are made with Deer Mountain jam from Granite Falls. If fruit cobblers like these grew on trees, moms all over Seattle would make sure they had them planted in their backyards. But they don't, so you'll have to come to Frombach's to taste for yourself.

The Original Bakery

9253 45th Ave. SW, Seattle
Phone: 206/938-5088
Hours: 7:30AM–6PM Tuesday–Friday; 7:30AM–5PM Saturday; 8:30AM–3PM
Sunday; closed Monday

I came into this shop appreciatively sniffing the air. The lovely aroma of baking mixed with a scent of burnt sugar was noticeable clear out the door. Bernie and Lorraine Alonzo have been keeping their West Seattle neighborhood well-fed and sweet smelling for at least twenty years.

Long ago, the competition between the neighborhood bakeries was fierce, and this one wanted to make sure the neighborhood knew which one had come first. The Original has been here since 1937, making it one of the oldest retail food businesses in Seattle. Bernie says that although the bakery looks the same, he's had to adapt to changing tastes. Years ago, customers would come in and buy ten or eleven loaves of bread at a time. Today he's introduced artisan-style breads and sells a lot more quick pastries such as muffins, Danish, and Bundt cakes. Those with long memories and a taste for the old Frederick & Nelson cinnamon pop-ups will be happy to learn that Bernie was taught the recipe by the original baker, and you can special-order them. The Danish are also made using Frederick & Nelson's recipe. Antiques and memorabilia of historic West Seattle line the faded walls of this shop, which adds to its nostalgic appeal. It's worth keeping in mind that the bakery is only a couple of blocks up from the Vashon Island ferry.

Pasteleria del Castillo .... see Latino

Salvadorean Bakery .... see Latino

cheese I would hate to live in a world without cheese.

I confess to eating the exact same breakfast almost every morning of my life: toast and cheese, sometimes grilled, sometimes with a tomato on top and sometimes with marmalade. I particularly enjoy artisan cheeses, those made by small producers using traditional methods, aged properly and sold at the perfect moment of ripeness.

Like me, more and more people in Seattle have gone cheese crazy. Witness the cheese plates offered in big-name restaurants around town, and the drop-dead gorgeous displays in some upscale markets. Although it's hard to imagine, not so many years ago few people in Seattle had tasted, let alone developed an appreciation for, fine cheese. Ten or fifteen years ago, the cheese you would most likely find in just about any Seattleite's refrigerator was good old Kraft American cheese, Velveeta, and of course that cardboard "Parmesan" shaken from a green can. As in so many other areas, we have turned 180 degrees, and are now discerning and demanding cheese consumers.

The basics of buying cheese are the same wherever you shop. Visit a good shop that stocks a respectable selection, take your time, linger over the signs and descriptions, and examine the possibilities before making your choice. Don't be afraid to ask for a taste before buying, and don't be too shy to reject it after sampling if it doesn't appeal to you. So many shops sell their cheese already cut and wrapped, but it is infinitely preferable to patronize a market that displays whole cheese wheels and will cut off a fresh piece for you. That way you can also examine the whole uncut wheel and its label, which tells you the cheese's maker and the town or region it comes from. When you get your cheese home, store it properly and eat it fast enough to prevent molds and off flavors from developing.

Cheeses can be made from the milk of any mammal. Today there is a bewildering profusion of tastes, from the youngest, mildest, squeaky-clean chèvres to the rankest, most pungent and earthy, soft-ripened rustic cheeses. Cheese should look fresh and appealing, with no obvious mold (unless it's a blue), cracks, or visible uncharacteristic discolorations. Keep in mind, though, that those wonderful artisan cheeses can look quite scruffy on the outside. Rest assured that this means more flavor.

The best, tastiest cheeses are made from fresh raw milk, just as it comes from the animal, living, breathing, and thriving with organisms. But the USDA at this time forbids the importation or sale of raw-milk cheeses unless they have been aged for more than sixty days. In addition, the agency is considering a ban on *all* raw-milk cheeses produced in this country. Many people feel that this would be the end for most small artisan cheese makers, because they just don't have the resources or the inclination to comply with the law. It comes down to a choice between a blander though safer product or a cheese that is marked by complexity and an authentic taste of its own *terroir*, or soil (to borrow a wine term).

The Pacific Northwest is home to a few wonderful independents marketing their own cheeses. Sally Jackson Cheeses, made in Oroville, Washington, are well known and widely available. The aged sheep's-milk cheese, in particular, will knock your socks off. Quillisascut Cheese Company is a favorite. Both LoraLea and Rick Misterly speak eloquently about their holistic approach to making farmhouse cheeses (see page 38). And since 1948, the Washington State University Creamery has been making full-bodied, aged Cougar Gold and milder, creamy Viking cheeses and packing them in fashionably retro green and gold cans, thereby avoiding the use of preservatives.

If you've lost your enthusiasm for cheese after tasting too many disappointing pasteurized-milk, factory-produced varieties, but you approach the cheese counters listed in this chapter with an open mind, then you will certainly come to understand what all the fuss is about.

Quillisasacut Cheese—A Washington Treasure

One of the more curious facts about cheese is that the process is essentially multiple stages of controlled spoilage. The cheese maker, whether a giant factory operation or a small-scale farmer, collects milk and, through careful manipulation of time, temperature, and microbes, controls the steps till the cheese arrives at its final flavor. Under the best circumstances, a seemingly magical alchemy occurs between nature and the cheese maker, and a gorgeous new cheese is created.

Rick and LoraLea Misterly bought a farm in northeast Washington in 1981 and began a meandering adventure that led them to their current status as one of Washington's premier cheese makers. "Sort of like planting a flower seed that we only knew was some sort of flower, but not whether it was a rose or a hollyhock. We didn't know what direction our farm would take when we first started. All we brought with us was our enthusiasm and the adventure that must have moved all of us in the West," says LoraLea. What started with one goat named Taffy evolved into an operation producing about 5,000 pounds of goat cheese annually, ranging from a firm, golden yellow manchego style (the *curado*) to others flavored with lavender and fennel, or peppercorn and dill, as well as a feta and a potted cheese. They named the cheese Quillisascut after a creek that runs through their valley. It is a Native American word meaning "place of scattered bushes."

LoraLea is the cheese maker and Rick is the spokesperson for the company. LoraLea grew up on a farm in Leavenworth, Washington, watching her mother make cheese with the summer milk surplus. She remembers the tastes of fresh curds, and real creamed cottage cheese and butter—tastes not duplicated by anything found in the local grocery stores.

When the couple gained their state license to sell cheese in 1987, the desire to carry on her family tradition seemed simple and fitting. They did a lot of experimentation in the beginning. Rick would taste the cheese and announce whether it was good: whether it resembled something he had tasted in Greece or some other exotic locale. When LoraLea finally started making cheese using a Spanish manchego recipe, something clicked—so much so that today they still follow the same recipe, with some modifications. They call it *curado* to reflect that early Spanish influence and separate it from the better-known industrial import. They describe the cheese as "real" with rustic nuances. Whether

A mountain of cheeses from around the world.

young and relatively mild, or aged and assertive, it always seems to have a slightly briny nuttiness and is full of flavor.

Sometimes they cut into a wheel of their cheese and say, "This is perfect." But as a cheese maker, LoraLea knows that fine cheese requires a communion between herself, the soil and weather, the animals, and even the facility where she makes the cheese as the seasons change. "Making the cheese every day requires observation at so many levels," she says. "It's a sensual thing. So I pay attention to the way things smell, they way things look, the way things feel to my hands, how they taste, and then I use my brain to control the information coming in."

All cheese, or at least all real farm-made cheese, is the result of a quest for perfection. The biggest stumbling block is government regulations requiring all cheese-milk to be pasteurized. While this might be a great thing for humankind, it is not nearly as good for cheese. Raw-milk cheese is a much truer reflection of the land it comes from, and banning it may quite possibly mean that, within our lifetime, every cheese will taste exactly the same.

CENTRAL

DeLaurenti . . . . see Mediterranean

James Cook Ltd.

2421 Second Ave., Seattle
Phone: 206/256-0510
Hours: 10AM–6PM Monday–Saturday; closed Sunday
Internet: www.jamescookcheese.com

James Cook's cheese is expensive; there's no way around it. When you charge anywhere from $14 to $27 a pound, you had better consistently deliver the goods. Though I've been known to let out a gasp of disbelief at the price, everything I have ever bought from him has been nothing short of sublime.

The specialty of this new shop in Belltown is unique farmstead treasures, made by hand by small-scale farmers from the milk of their own herds. Being Scottish, James is partial to the great cheeses of Britain, but he also carries amazing selections of American artisan products; French, Spanish, and Italian cheeses; and a gallery of chèvres that will blow your palate way beyond meek Montrachet.

Most cheesemongers store their products in a meat cooler—too cold for a living, breathing authentic product of the land. To do right by these cheeses requires a painstaking process of attending to them in a climate-controlled cooler, respecting their individual idiosyncrasies, and shepherding them till the exact moment when they are at their best before selling them—something that few large stores have the time or inclination to do anymore, but something that is James's point of pride.

If you are interested in knowing everything about the cheese you are buying (and even if you're not but you just want to get the best), you will be completely fulfilled at this exceptional little shop. Look for Neal's Yard Dairy of London cheeses, carried by other specialty stores as well, but available in greater variety here, according to James. Every time I've been in his shop, I've been introduced to something new. The last time, it was an incredible Oregon-produced goat's-milk cheese called Tumalo Tomme from Juniper Grove Farms, which reminded me of *reblochon* from France—a cheese that, it's been said, has a rind as velvety as a deer's antlers and a flavor like filet mignon.

Pacific Food Importers . . . . see Mediterranean

Pike Place Market Creamery

1514 Pike Pl., Stall 3 (in Pike Place Market), Seattle
Phone: 206/622-5029
Hours: 9AM 6PM every day

I'm not saying it was fate, but when Nancy Douty started correspon-
ding with a guy in the McNeil federal penitentiary, it resulted in a
full-service dairy shop in Pike Place Market that is still going strong
after twenty-two years. You see, Nancy somehow fell for the deadbeat
and married him, then watched him run up $36,000 in debt on the
business after he was paroled. She says the bankers told her they

James Cook offers friendly advice.

would never get their money back if she closed, so they were willing to take a chance on her. Since she was raised on margarine and Cool Whip, she had to learn a lot about quality dairy products fast.

She's obviously a quick study because today her shop is loaded with a variety of milk, butter, eggs, whipping cream, cottage cheese, crème fraîche, yogurt, old-fashioned tapioca pudding, locally made mayonnaise, cheese (including vegan cheese), rice and soy milk, and a whole bunch of other stuff. Most stores don't come close to carrying as many different varieties of dairy products as this super-friendly little market does. For instance, they routinely carry eight to twelve kinds of butter, including locally made hand-churned "Danish style" Hansen, Plugra (the bakers' butter), and extra-high-fat, as well as more common brands.

This is the shop to come to if you have to have ostrich or emu eggs to share with a dozen of your closest friends. It's also a source for duck, goose, turkey, quail, and auracana chicken eggs (which are a lovely pale blue) as well as other seasonal eggs. Be wary if buying uncommon varieties, though. It could have been an isolated occurrence, but I had the unhappy experience of dealing with a less than fresh goose egg from the shop.

Quality Cheese
1508 Pike Pl. (in Pike Place Market), Seattle
Phone: 206/624-4029
Hours: 9AM–6PM every day

Quality Cheese has prospered in Pike Place Market for over twenty years by offering friendly service and the best prices in town. They have a fine, if limited, selection of "fancy" cheeses, but you can't beat this shop for prices on everyday cheeses for the average person. The bargains draw loyal customers from all over the city and beyond. (Expect to pay about $2 or $3 less per pound than at DeLaurenti, also in the Market.) Quality also sells Sally Jackson's plain and aged goat cheese, a Washington-made classic. Besides that, look for pâtés, olives, olive oils, and cheese accoutrements, again all very reasonably priced.

The Spanish Table . . . . see Mediterranean

NORTH

Brie & Bordeaux

2227 N 56th St., Seattle
Phone: 206/633-3538
E-mail: brbordeaux@aol.com
Hours: 11AM–7PM Tuesday–Saturday; 11AM–3PM Sunday; closed Monday

Karin Collins, the resident cheesemonger at this pretty little bistro-cum-wine and cheese shop, works hard at pampering her charges. Ripening cheeses to their point of perfection requires energy. It's worth it, though, especially to anyone who has endured nasty cheese that tastes only of the plastic it was wrapped in.

Ripening cheeses is only one of Karin's tasks. She's also a whiz at helping put together cheese trays, selecting wines that are perfect foils for those cheeses, and enthusiastically disseminating her considerable knowledge to any interested parties. She's got about 175 of some of the best cheeses in the world to choose from, all displayed in mouth-watering fashion on the counter and in the refrigerated case.

Because of the shop's name, the staff has been asked more than once if they specialize in Bordeaux wines. While they carry their share, the name is really about combinations—wine and food pairings that work and make eating special. Because it's such a small space, they buy only wines that they really like and that are drinkable right now: not collector's items to be shown off by wine snobs and then hidden away, but hand-picked wines that really work with food. Currently they have a bias for Rhône wines, which are very food-friendly and a great value. I was also pleased to see a good selection of half-bottles, which are very nice for the single diner.

Besides the cheeses and wine, B & B carries olives and pâtés, proscuittos, and high-quality salamis from Molinari. Owner Alison Leber also offers popular bimonthly classes on wine, cooking, and cheese.

At the time of writing, the shop is being sold and its future is somewhat open. It is worth calling before making the journey.

Market Street Wine & Cheese...... see Wine and Beer

EASTSIDE

Capri International Foods

317 Bellevue Way NE, Bellevue
Phone: 425/454-7155
Hours: 10AM–6PM Monday–Saturday; closed Sunday

This longtime Eastside business has had its ups and downs in recent years. There were grumblings when DeLaurenti owned it. Some vowed never to set foot inside again after it was bought by someone who seemed determined to convert it into a convenience store. Then Gary Kunz took over. Gary has zero retail experience, but he's smart enough to defer to his longtime manager, Franck Mossanta, whom he describes as having "a perfectly calibrated nose." And he's been willing to sink a lot of money into creating the best cheese, deli, and specialty grocery on the Eastside.

Capri's cheese counter is a dream. With over 160 cheeses to choose from, any taste can be satisfied. For example, I've recently become interested in Spanish cheeses. On my last visit, Capri offered vivid, nearly purple-veined *cabrales*, smoky *idiazabal*, denominacíon-controlled *roncal*, raw-milk *tronchón*, *mahón* from Minorca, artisan manchego, *zamorano*, and *castellano*. Whew! I found a sublime, nutty, four-year-old aged Appenino Parmigiano-Reggiano. Made from the milk of red cows that give a very low yield of high-quality milk, it's more suited to eating at the table than grating.

The shop also carries *jamon Serrano* (Spanish ham), six kinds of proscuitto (including one aged for five hundred days), authentic Italian mortadella (only recently allowed to be imported to this country), pâtés, salamis, sliced deli meats, olives, cornichons, caperberries, and more. The wine section has been upgraded and has an interesting selection of mostly Italian wines. The special grocery selection is also being upgraded in an ongoing way. Look for *Spinosi* pasta here. Many consider it the best egg pasta, hand-made in the Marches, a coastal region of Italy. If your idea of heaven is a simple dish of pasta with garlic and olive oil, or pasta with a few perfectly ripe, chopped tomatoes and a handful of basil leaves, then you'll want the pasta to be extraordinary. *Spinosi* fits the bill.

chocolates, candies, nuts, and ice cream

Chocolates scream, "I love you"—or at least good chocolates do. Bad chocolates scream, "I'm leaving you." Unless you've got an earnest kindergartner excitedly clutching her offering, you wouldn't want to waste your money on anything but the real thing. And when it comes to chocolate, the real thing is minimal and costly: cocoa beans from South America and Africa, the finest vanilla, pure sweet butter and cream, the freshest nuts and fruit pastes from around the world—simple ingredients where perfection really counts.

Something about chocolate appeals to our animal nature, stirring feelings of passion, love, and ecstasy. In the film *Like Water for Chocolate*, the youngest daughter, doomed to care for her ailing mother, escapes by cooking, releasing her sorrows and longings into the food and infecting all who eat it. It's a magical, mystical metaphor.

Chocolate does contain phenylethylamine, a naturally occurring chemical in the human brain responsible for the euphoric feeling associated with being in love. It's also got caffeine, although in much lower quantities than coffee or tea. And newer research suggests that chocolate contains phenols, chemicals believed to help prevent artery damage, as well as catechins, substances with antioxidant properties that may help fight cancer and heart disease. So don't worry—that luscious piece of chocolate you are about to indulge in is good for your body and your soul.

As with fine wine and great coffee, the chocolate scene in Seattle began to change in the 1970s. Whereas before that our taste buds were drawn to flimsy cardboard boxes of overly sweet chocolate and cream fillings with weird chemical flavors, we now entered the chocolate truffle era. While we still had some old-style institutions such as Baker's Candy Co. making confections that will never go out of fashion, the homegrown foodie explosion was getting ready to reinvent chocolate.

In 1977 Dana Davenport, a member of the third generation of a candy-making family, opened a small café selling European style premium chocolates and espresso—Dilettante Chocolates. Their creations were a shock to the taste buds of people used to milk chocolate and heavily sugar-based confections. Dark chocolate, which is what Dilettante specializes in, is just barely on the sweet side, with complexity and nuances that flood the palate and then recede, leaving a profound sense of pleasure.

By the time Fran Bigelow returned from the Bay Area and opened the tiny Fran's Patisserie in 1982, all of Seattle was ready to sit up and take notice. Fran, who is widely regarded today as one of America's best chocolatiers, is a true Washington treasure. Although dozens of Seattle stores sell fine chocolate nowadays, Fran remains, for good reason, the city's indisputable queen of chocolate.

Whether your chocolate is made right here in Seattle or flown in from Switzerland or Belgium, fresher is better. With highly perishable fillings such as cream and butter, most chocolate is better eaten within a week. Well-wrapped plain dark chocolate, on the other hand, can be kept much longer, eighteen months or more. In fact, certain chocolate connoisseurs feel that aged chocolate improves like fine red wine and is more rich, mellow, and suave the older it gets. Within the realm of indulgences, chocolate, even the high-end premium stuff, is an affordable luxury on a piece-by-piece basis. After tasting my way through dozens and dozens of samples for this chapter, I, for one, have sworn by a new tradition—one champagne truffle a day.

CENTRAL

The Cow's Meow

1835 Queen Anne Ave. N, Seattle
Phone: 206/285-3532
Hours: 1PM–9PM every day

My father-in-law believes that ice cream comes in only one flavor: vanilla. Leave the chocolate, strawberry, and cookie dough to others. To him the true benchmark of excellence is plain old vanilla. What would he think of the Cow's Meow? Katherine Beck conceives of ice cream as a "condiment" to be planned around a menu.

It's not surprising, then, that she's created over 130 decidedly fanciful flavors. She's still getting requests for the honey lavender, which she created for a catered wedding. During berry season, she lets go with local strawberries, raspberries, blueberries, and marionberries. Dad might also raise his eyebrow at some of the sorbets, such as the pomegranate pepper or prickly pear. And heaven forbid I should bring home the cardamom ice cream, which Katherine points out is perfect on warm apple pie.

Her ice cream is intense, rich and creamy with not a hint of stabilizers or emulsifiers—just BGH-free fresh cream, sugar, and eggs. She makes her own chocolate paste from pure cocoa powder, extracts flavors from a chai blend she concocts, purees local fruit for bold flavor, and purchases the freshest whole spices from World Merchants.

Try the Danish sweet cream. It is the essence of ice cream, tasting of fresh cream, innate sweetness and goodness, and little else. The flavor is so clean that Katherine says you can clearly tell by the taste when the cows' diet has changed in the spring.

Dilettante Chocolates

416 Broadway E, Seattle
Phone: 206/329-6463
Hours: noon–midnight Sunday–Thursday; noon–1AM Friday and Saturday

1603 First Ave. (in Pike Place Market), Seattle
Phone: 206/728-9144
Hours: 10AM–6PM Monday–Saturday; 11AM–5PM Sunday

Internet: www.dilettante.com

Cow's Meow is the place to be on a sunny day.

Dana Davenport forever linked happiness to eating chocolate when he introduced Seattle to premium European-style chocolates at his Broadway store in 1977. Using top-of-the-line ingredients, no hydrogenated fats or artificial flavors, lively concentrated fruit pulps in the centers rather than cooked jams, and premium cocoa beans, Dilettante delivers chocolates that provide maximum titillation to the taste buds.

The bittersweet dark chocolate Ephemere truffle is the signature item. A crisp, dark, barely sweetened chocolate shell snaps when you bite it to reveal a dense silken ganache center with 67 percent cocoa solids—intensely flavored, the way all great chocolates are. The milk chocolates use an especially assertive cacao bean to perk up the more placid flavors of that genre. All in all, the chocolate line includes about thirty different pieces. Dana, the creative mind behind the operation, is now working on developing a line of chocolate drinks and baking chocolate.

Note: All Dilettante chocolates are strictly kosher.

Gelatiamo

1400 Third Ave., Seattle
Phone: 206/467-9563
Hours: 7AM–6PM Monday–Friday; 11AM–6PM Saturday; closed Sunday

Maria Coassin could have gone home to her family in the Friuli region of Italy. She could have joined the family bakery, started by her ancestors over two hundred years ago. But instead, she chose to come to Seattle almost five years ago and open an authentic gelateria and bakery. She brought the family recipes; hired a young American culinary school graduate, Erinn Zavaglia, who will soon be her co-partner; and proceeded to knock the socks off Seattle.

The gelati and sorbetto naturally are the focal point for Gelatiamo, and they are splendid. Since gelati are much lower in fat than American ice cream, without air whipped into them, they taste as if you'd taken the most intensely concentrated essence of fruit and dropped it into a blender. That's it—no artificial flavorings, water, or excess sugar to mar the perfect balance of solids, liquids, and sweetness.

The flavors change with the seasons. In winter, try the ethereal blood orange gelato. Its pale pink color doesn't do justice to the explosion of tart-sweet citrusy flavor. Classics are always given their due here, too. I have a thing for lemon ice; something about its tartness makes it the ultimate thirst-quencher, at once frothy and bright with flavor. Look for high-quality Italian cakes, cookies, turnovers, and the like, many based on *pan di Spagna*, Italian sponge cake soaked in rum.

This extremely likable shop envisions itself as a classic gelateria and eventually hopes to stay open in the evenings to serve the after-symphony crowd and families out for the evening, just like its counterparts all over Italy.

Holmquist Hazelnut Orchards

Pike Place Market Daystalls
University District Farmers Market
Columbia City Farmers Market
West Seattle Farmers Market
Redmond Saturday Market
Phone: 800/720-0895
Hours: Vary seasonally; call for hours

Holmquist hazelnuts are distinguished by two characteristics. First, the guy who grew them—who pruned, fertilized, and watered the trees, then harvested, sorted, and roasted the nuts—is almost certainly the guy who is offering you a sample. That's Brian Holmquist, who, with wife Vickie, father Gerald, and brother Richard, is the sixth generation of the family currently living and working together at Holmquist Hazelnut Orchards. The second thing to keep in mind is that Holmquist hazelnuts just plain taste better. Holmquist grows mostly "long" nuts, or, more properly, DuChilly hazelnuts. They've found that their customers prefer the taste over the more common "round" nuts sold at most supermarkets. Holmquist nuts are milder and sweeter and, most importantly, much fresher than most store-bought hazelnuts.

Holmquist has fifteen different items in the product line. The most popular is the lightly salted, but they listen to their customers and are always developing new flavors. All are first prepared by the family, taste-tested, and then heavily sampled at the farmers markets to determine whether they will become keepers. Holmquist also sells hazelnut flour and hazelnut butter and oil. Ask for Vickie's hazelnut zucchini bread, or her hazelnut cookie, both sold at their stands. She dreams of conquering the world with them.

Procopio

1501 Western Ave., Suite 300 (on Pike Street Hillclimb), Seattle
Phone: 206/622–4280
Hours: 9AM–6PM Monday–Saturday; closed Sunday

Faced with the cornucopia of flavors of gelato and sherbets at Procopio, most people react with the uninhibited glee of eight-year-olds. And when they're offered multiple tastings to help narrow the selection, pure sensual greed can rear its ugly head. Brian Garrity has been creating exciting combinations unlike anything else on the market for the last sixteen years. He steeps black pansies in a traditional Italian-style ice for dramatic color. He mixes roses and elderflower for a powerful infusion of floral essence. Lavender gelato is made using a recipe from Jerry Traunfeld of Issaquah's world-renowned Herbfarm restaurant.

Nothing at Procopio is too rich or heavy. The gelato is much lower in milk fat than regular ice cream (about 6 percent, versus 16 to 20 percent for premium ice cream), and the fruit ices are completely nondairy. Since there's no cream to mask them, the fruit flavors sparkle and are gorgeously on target in color and clarity.

Located on the steps of the Pike Street Hillclimb, Procopio draws a mix of locals, who are open to the more unusual offerings, and tourists, who tend to prefer traditional American flavors. They all leave satisfied. Ultimately, Brian dreams of making true Italian-style gelato as popular in America as it is in Italy. His gelato is sold in many high-end restaurants, and he plans to expand that facet of his business. If you're having a dinner party and are looking for an easy intermezzo course, consider the grapefruit or lime ice for a refreshing palette cleanser.

See's Candies

1518 Fourth Ave., Seattle
Phone: 206/682-7122
Hours: 9:30AM–6PM Monday–Saturday; 12PM–5PM Sunday

520 Northgate Mall, Seattle
Phone: 206/363-4567
Hours: 10AM–9:30PM Monday–Saturday; 11AM–6PM Sunday

10212 NE 8th St., Bellevue
Phone: 425/455-1019
Hours: 9:30AM–7PM Monday–Saturday; 12PM–5PM Sunday

Internet: www.sees.com

When See's opened their first Seattle location across from Frederick & Nelson in 1964, they were mobbed. It was the busiest opening day ever in the company's history—a record that still stands today. Seattle obviously loves See's Candies. Is it the nostalgia factor deliberately reinforced by the simple black-and-white motif and old-fashioned crisp white uniforms? Or is it because everyone can find something here to love? According to the company, their bestsellers in Seattle, in descending order, are the pecan buds, peanut crunch, Bordeaux, Scotch kisses, and caramels. With such variety, even the most finicky sourpuss can find something to smile about.

The folks who make the decisions at See's now know they have to tread lightly before tampering with anything. A couple of years ago, they made the mistake of changing the formula for the chocolate butter Easter eggs, and they were overwhelmed by a tidal wave of protest. Needless to say, they beat a hasty retreat; the old, beloved chocolate butter egg is back, exactly the way Mary See created it back in 1921.

See's products are mass-market chocolates, not quite in the same league as pricier European-style varieties. The chocolate flavor isn't quite as pronounced, and the look isn't quite as elegant. But at half the price of some high-end brands, they more than hold their own.

Teuscher's Chocolates of Switzerland

410 University St., Seattle
Phone: 206/340-1747
Hours: 7AM–6PM Monday–Friday; 10AM–6PM Saturday; closed Sunday

If you've got a chocolate addiction, you do what you have to do to take care of it. For at least one Teuscher's customer, that means a daily ferry ride from Bainbridge Island to indulge her cravings. Even worse, she has infected her young kids with her obsession. Now they spurn Hershey's and demand Bailey's Irish Cream truffles from Teuscher's instead. "This isn't extravagance," she insists. "It's so sublime—it kind of spoils you."

For the last six years, Will Deeg, who owns the Teuscher's shop here and one in San Francisco, has flown a weekly shipment of Teuscher's intricately designed Swiss chocolates to our part of the world. Dolf Teuscher and his descendants have perfected the art of truffle and praline making over almost sixty years. The story is that amid the chaos and upheaval after World War II, Dolf was looking for a way to make a living and solve a dilemma that had vexed generations of previous chocolate makers—how to create a chocolate confection that perfectly marries layers of flavor from a soft center outward to a hard shell—the difficulty being akin to frying a ball of cream. Looking up from the family table, Dolf spotted a bottle of Dom Perignon champagne and—Eureka!—the first chocolate truffle was born: Teuscher's champagne truffle. The signature tri-toned champagne truffle (still infused with Dom Perignon) nicely solves the eternal dark chocolate/milk chocolate dilemma by enrobing a layer of each over the ivory-colored champagne ganache center.

You must try the marzipan here as well. It will forever erase any ill will you may have for that confection. And any of the *gianduja*, ground hazelnut fillings, are a wonderful complement to the chocolates. Eating Teuscher's chocolates is such an intense experience, it *is* worth scheduling your life around a ferry.

Turkish Delight—The Oldest Candy in the World

Turks like to think of Turkish delight as one of the oldest sweetmeats in the world. Actually, that is its name only in Western countries; the Turkish name is *rahat lokum*, which means "giving rest to the throat." It's a popular confection all over the Middle East, mostly imported here, with quality and freshness varying considerably. While the Pacific Northwest boasts several superb chocolate makers, I wasn't aware till now that it's also home to a top-quality lokum maker, Huseyin Bayazit and his Bayco Confectionery.

Lokum is a delicate but gummy jelly made by cooking a mixture of syrup and cornstarch slowly for several hours, after which the mixture is poured out, left to set, and cut into cubes, which are rolled in icing sugar. Recipes are generally closely guarded family or trade secrets. Lokum is often flavored with lemon or orange juice and can incorporate nuts, creams, dates, or mastic, and rose water or orange-flower water. Think of it as a very soft, very fresh gummy bear, without the acrid artificial fruit flavor—instead tantalizingly spiced with the flavors of the Middle East. Although lokum is usually very sweet, I found Huseyin's version to be less so. The pistachio-flavored variety was especially exquisite.

Huseyin has traveled throughout the Middle East, sampling and deconstructing different versions of the candy. He found that many workshops had at best marginal hygiene, at least by Western standards, and determined to do better. Since he's an engineer with his own computer company in Vancouver, B.C., he was able to design and build equipment to partially automate, and thus modernize, this ancient process.

Look for a complete selection of Huseyin's lokum at Turkish Delight in Pike Place Market as well as on his Web site, www.turkish~delight.com.

NORTH

Baker Candy Co.

12534 Lake City Way NE, Seattle
Phone: 206/365–1888
Hours: 7AM–3PM Monday; 7AM–8PM Tuesday–Thursday; 7AM–9PM Friday
and Saturday; 8AM–8PM Sunday

The manager at Baker Candy Co. looked shocked when I asked whether they planned any changes in the future. "Why change anything when you've got a good tradition?" he responded. This is the kind of old-fashioned sweets parlor your grandma has been going to since before the War. The soda fountain is straight out of a '40s or '50s madcap romantic comedy, with its red banquette seating and flocked Empire wallpaper.

The homespun chocolate is dreamy comfort food at its best. Go for the Platypus Patties—dark or milk chocolate and sweet pecans held together with a thin layer of caramel. Or regress to a happy childlike trance with a paper bag full of fruit strings, in flavors such as orange and raspberry, covered in creamy chocolate. Almond butter crisps are Baker's version of Almond Roca, and they're divine.

Bottleworks . . . . see Wine and Beer

CBM Creative Chocolates

102 N 36th St., Seattle
Phone: 206/548-0828
E–mail: Kathy@cbmchocolates.com
Hours: 9AM–5:30PM Monday–Friday; closed Saturday and Sunday

Your best friend is having a bridal shower and you need to provide the party favors. Make it easy on yourself and call CBM. They might suggest custom-filled chocolate fortune cookies. Or perhaps one of their hundreds of molded chocolate figures might do the trick. If all else fails, you can hand out the signature item here, a chocolate slug.

The nice thing is that CBM starts with high-quality Guittard chocolate, and they pay attention to the details when it comes to packaging, so everything looks beautifully put together and fresh. Skip anything with white chocolate, though; it's waxy tasting and loaded with cheap, partially hydrogenated vegetable oil, an unfortunately far too common practice not limited to this shop. (The best-quality white chocolates are made with just cocoa butter, milk solids, sugar, and flavorings.)

The Confectionery

4510 University Village NE, Seattle
Phone: 206/523-1443
Hours: 9:30AM–9PM Monday–Saturday; 11AM–6PM Sunday

Jan Thal has been pleasing Seattleites with her mouthwatering confectionery at the University Village shopping center for almost twenty years. The Confectionery carries hundreds of kinds of penny candies, chocolates, and nuts, all rapidly turned-over and exceedingly fresh. Some are standard items you can get anywhere, but what this shop is really known for are the blasts from the past: the stuff you grew up with and haven't seen in years. The staff says if it's out there, they'll track it down and get it for you. They do a booming business in wedding and party favors, too.

If you love licorice, be prepared to choose from among forty different kinds. Chocolates and chocolate-covered pretzels, Cabernet cherries, turtles and truffles, individual flavors of jelly bellies, Jordan almonds and candied violets and roses—the selection of sticky, crunchy, sweet, and scrumptious is totally wicked. They also have one of the largest selections of sugar-free chocolates and candies that I've seen. Just don't make the mistake of coming before a major holiday. It's sheer bedlam.

Fran's Chocolates

2594 NE University Village, Seattle
Phone: 206/528-9969
Hours: 9:30AM–9PM Monday–Saturday; 11AM–6PM Sunday

10305 NE 10th St., Bellevue
Phone: 425/453-1698
Hours: 10AM–7PM Monday–Saturday; closed Sunday

Internet: www.franschocolates.com

Robert Linxe, the famed owner of La Maison du Chocolat in Paris, met Fran Bigelow years ago and passed on a message she's held onto since. Yes, absolutely, she could do it, he said. Don't get too complicated; just open up, and the customers will tell you what to make.

And tell her they did. Since Fran opened her little café in Madison Valley in 1982 (since relocated to University Village), virtually the whole of Seattle has come to admire her exceptional craftsmanship. How does she do it? Like all perfectionists, Fran stays on top of the details. That commitment to quality and single-minded devotion to the craft of chocolate makes hers the standard by which all others are measured. Fran's chocolates tend to the European style: not-too-sweet Belgian Callebaut or premium Venezuelan El Rey dark, milk and bittersweet chocolate give her creations a smooth complexity and deep dark flavor.

Many people have such a single-minded devotion to Fran's chocolates that they think nothing of indulging in one, or maybe two, every single day. The signature GoldBar, created to combat the traditional summer lull in demand for hand-dipped chocolate, is a positively celestial bar of caramel and almonds or macadamia nuts wrapped in dark chocolate. The champagne truffles are delicately brushed with edible gold leaf. Fill a handmade washi paper box (modeled after a Japanese tea box) with them to give to your sweetie, and I guarantee she will be eternally yours.

Fran's ice creams are also to scream for. Go for the tried and true, such as raspberry or lemon. On the other hand, there's the unbelievable turbinado burnt sugar caramel (like eating essence of crème brûlée), or ginger lime, with its kicky infusion of both fresh ginger root and candied Australian ginger puree.

A Chocolatier Is Born

Seattle is known as the birthplace of several national food trends. We reinvented specialty coffee and microbreweries, and now I think we're on to a new one—fine chocolate. Trends start with a trickle, and at some point they reach a critical mass. Fran's and Dilettante Chocolates have already established a reputation outside the Pacific Northwest, and now a second generation of players is furthering our chocolate reputation. Heavenly Chocolates is one of these promising up-and-comers. I'm betting that you'll soon be hearing plenty more about this little business with the magic touch for truffles and all sorts of other decadent chocolate candies. How does anyone decide to open a chocolate business in a town boasting so many already established standouts? Elizabeth Peckham likes to think of her product as unintimidating chocolate. The truffles are composed looking, perfectly fresh and artfully packaged, yet they have a whimsical, fun feel. Her customers have told her they don't think twice about buying her chocolates for themselves as well as for their friends. The taste is more subtle than Fran's truffles—not quite as intense and probably more accessible to the average chocolate lover. Try the raspberry truffles flavored with Framboise liqueur. I loved the snappiness and silky berry taste. She also offers a simple two-toned version of her truffle filling, with layers of lemon-flavored white chocolate and raspberry ganache, that is just this side of oversweet, and simply delicious.

Elizabeth is entirely self-taught as a chocolatier. In fact, she's trained as an architect and also has a master's degree in family therapy. She and her husband were big truffle eaters before she opened the business. Since both come from big families, they decided to give homemade truffles as Christmas presents one year. That was a big hit, and pretty soon the demand from family and friends snowballed to the point where she could see a tangible outlet for her artistic and culinary fantasies, and Heavenly Chocolates was born. (She now teaches chocolate-making classes at Sur La Table and the ASUW Experimental College.)

The business has been growing steadily in the five years of its existence. Elizabeth plans to expand to more local stores, and ultimately go national. Right now, you can find Heavenly Chocolates at PCC stores and the Confectionery in University Village as well as a few smaller shops.

Heavenly Chocolates

Phone: 206/547-0070 for mail order

SOUTH

Gosanko Chocolate Art

24700 Military Rd. S, Kent
Phone: 253/839-1147
Hours: 8AM–5PM Monday–Friday; 9AM–1PM Saturday; closed Sunday

Artistic expression takes many forms. Gus Gosanko's genius is in carving whimsical representations of flowers and animals, kitschy figures, Northwest symbols, company logos, and anything else anyone could possibly dream of, all in solid chocolate. He uses top-grade Guittard chocolate, domestically produced in Burlingame, California. With such large blocks of chocolate, though, flavors tend to be a little one-dimensional and sweet.

Gosanko Chocolate Art is known as something of a leader in chocolate fish. Need a fifty-pound solid milk chocolate king salmon? No problem. Or three-quarter-ounce fingerlings, baby cohos, orcas, bass, trout, halibut, silver- or gold-wrapped sand dollars, dolphins on a stick, clams, or mussels? Call them up. Many figures are foil-wrapped and have startlingly lifelike details. There are almost 1,000 in-stock items to choose from, and if that isn't enough, you can ask them to custom-design your own special mold (although you will need to order a minimum amount for custom-design work).

Note: At the front of the store is a fascinating educational exhibit. All the steps of chocolate making are clearly laid out, with examples of cocoa at different stages of processing. Ronnie Roberts, Gus's son-in-law and the president of the company, told me that this is the first stage of a dream for them. They eventually would love to have a full-fledged chocolate wonderland where they could lay out the whole story of chocolate. "It's the best way I've seen to share happiness with people. Everybody loves chocolate," he said.

EASTSIDE

Chocolates by Bernard Callebaut

128 Central Way, Kirkland
Phone: 425/822-8889
Hours: 10AM–6PM Monday–Saturday; 11AM–5PM Sunday

Belgian Callebaut couverture (bulk chocolate) is used by the best chocolatiers around the world. Bernard Callebaut split with the family business and moved to Calgary, Canada, in 1982 to make small, fine quality individual chocolate. He uses the highest grade of Callebaut couverture, custom-blended to his own specifications, to make exceptional Belgian-style chocolate. (Belgian-style generally denotes a heady, strong chocolate flavor.) Bernard Callebaut chocolates have a very high percentage of cocoa butter, the cream-colored fat of the bean. Combining more cocoa butter than is naturally present in the chocolate, with bitter, dry cocoa powder is what makes his chocolate ultra-rich. The result is "chocolate that will elicit audible gasps of pleasure," according to the *San Francisco Chronicle*.

Chocolates are produced and shipped weekly from the Calgary plant. They are highly perishable because their fillings are based on lashings of pure crème fraîche along with the various spirits, nuts, and fruits. The truffles are all wonderful—well balanced, with exceedingly creamy textures. Bernard Callebaut chocolates recently won first place in a *San Francisco Chronicle* taste test against some formidable competitors.

Far Far's Danish Ice Cream

660 Front St. N, Issaquah
Phone: 425/392-2777
Hours: 11AM–10PM Monday–Thursday; 11AM–11PM Friday; noon–11PM Saturday; noon–10PM Sunday

I made the mistake of sampling the durian ice cream first when visiting the not-so-old-fashioned ice cream parlor owned by Chin and Kheng Ung. (Durian's the one that smells like stinky socks, and tastes, according to its fans, ambrosial.) Kheng told me that my taste buds were ruined for the moment and I wouldn't be able to distinguish the subtleties in any of the other fifty-some flavors she churns.

Chin and Kheng are a Chinese couple from Cambodia. They bought Far Far's, the last shop in a once popular Washington franchise, eight years ago, then went back to Asia to learn to make traditional ice cream. They say that American cream is better than Asian, but that Asians like to use fresh fruit in their ice cream. They've combined the best of both worlds; they process and cook the fruit themselves before combining it with fresh cream. Like all old-fashioned ice cream, Far Far's isn't as creamy as the super-premium brands. Instead, the fruit flavors come through vividly, with no hint of gums or stabilizers to dull the taste.

The Ungs cater to the American palate with dynamite flavors such as rum raisin, fresh banana and pineapple, pistachio, and my favorite—mandarin chocolate chip. But it's the more unusual offerings targeting Asian-American taste buds that keep attracting new customers. Jasmine–green tea, ginger, lychee, sour plum, taro, roasted sesame seed, red bean, and the aforementioned durian all tell you: Dorothy, you're not in Kansas anymore.

Oh Chocolate!

2703 76th Ave. SE, Mercer Island
Phone: 206/232-4974
Hours: 10AM–6PM Monday–Friday; 10:30AM–6PM Saturday; closed Sunday

What has made Oh Chocolate! a Mercer Island institution since 1986? This plain-Jane little storefront operation has countless devoted followers who eagerly drool over the handmade chocolates. Look for flavors such as Tiger Butter (a combination of white chocolate and peanut butter) and MI Latte (coffee flavored, naturally) as well as a very, very sweet strawberry truffle. The truffles are big here, with great, overstuffed mousselike centers that redefine sinful indulgence. (They're a little too buttery for my tastes.)

Typically, anywhere between thirty and forty-five varieties of chocolate are made behind the counter by the salespeople/candy makers in between waiting on their customers. These are old-fashioned candies, with recipes created by the shop's former owner, Gertie Krautheim. She died in 1996, and no one has yet been foolish enough to tamper with her formulas. Her husband, Kurt, still owns the store, but he leaves the chocolate making to the friendly, helpful staff. Janet, behind the counter, thinks "paying attention to proportions and cooking temperatures, and using lots of fresh heavy whipping cream, explains why the chocolates are so yummy."

WEST

Husky Deli . . . . see Prepared Food and Deli Items

coffee, tea, and spices

There's a learning curve that comes with moving to our wet, cool climate. Along with a working knowledge of top-to-bottom Gore-Tex, and the realization that anything that stays still long enough is bound to grow an emerald green moss rug, comes a deep appreciation for true specialty coffee—the kind that is the antithesis of the preground canned brew courtesy of Maxwell House.

Hot, steaming, full-bodied coffee is the specialty of the small local roasters found in this chapter. Our leadership role in this little cultural renaissance means that we have had our pick of the best coffee in the country. While Starbucks has conquered the world and raised the quality bar for everyone, it's the small businesses scattered throughout the city, with their idiosyncrasies and passion and care, that more closely define Seattle's character.

The micro-coffee stampede seems to have originated in the late '70s, when the Wet Whisker on Pier 70 and B & O Espresso on Capitol Hill opened, with fresh roasted coffee beans for sale and coaching on making good drip coffee. Today there isn't a neighborhood in Seattle that doesn't have a coffeehouse, outdoor cart, or drive-through espresso stand. The majority of these buy their coffee already roasted, and many choose one of the micro-roasters listed here. Given the fact that there are a wealth of businesses I could have focused on, I've chosen to include only coffeehouses that roast their own beans and have stayed relatively small and committed to their communities. (By the way, it's amazing to see the rocks, nails, straw, cloth, chunks of dirt, and other detritus that typically arrive in a bag of unroasted coffee beans.)

Storing coffee is a necessary evil. Ideally, you would roast your coffee, grind it, and use it within a couple of days. Since most people don't have the resources to do this, the trick is to find the freshest coffee at a store that has rapid turnover, and use it as soon as possible, preferably within a week or two. Anything that you can do to maintain freshness will give you a better cup. Once you buy it, store coffee in an airtight container at room temperature. I always thought coffee should be stored in the refrigerator or freezer, but every coffee roaster I talked to shuddered at the thought. Freezing and refrigeration may make coffee last longer, but they alter the natural aging process and can add some funky flavors to a very porous product.

Although we've been drinking great coffee for a long time, the same isn't true for fine tea. Market Spice in Pike Place Market was a lone voice in the wilderness for a long time. For too many years, tea has been proclaimed as the next big thing-to no avail. But lately, change is in the air; not a day seems to go by without a new report extolling the health benefits of tea. Serious teahouses, such as Teacup on Queen Anne and Teahouse Kuan Yin in Wallingford, remain destinations, and new ones, like the fabulous Blue Willow, are opening.

For years, the only choice when it came to spices and herbs were those high priced, dusty bottles at your local supermarket. With the exploding interest in ethnic cuisines and healthy eating, however, Seattleites have embraced herbs and spices as a low-calorie way to add flavor. Our best spice merchants go to great lengths to make sure their spices are impeccably fresh. Whether they air-freight small quantities to guarantee freshness, buy directly from the growers, or turn over their merchandise so fast that nothing sits on their shelves longer than a month or two, you can bet that their products will be fresher than anything you'll buy in a supermarket. By the way, if you're looking for low prices, any of the Indian grocery stores in town offer incredible savings, although you might have to buy in larger quantities than you need.

CENTRAL

Beans & Machines

1121 First Ave., Seattle
Phone: 206/625-1482
Hours: 7AM–6PM Monday–Friday; 11AM–6PM Saturday; noon–5PM Sunday

I realized the folks at Beans & Machines knew what they were talking about when I overheard them discussing the pros and cons of the La Gaggia and La Marzocco espresso makers. La Marzocco is a commercial machine that is considered to be the ne plus ultra of the espresso world. For most home baristas who don't want to pay upwards of $4,000 for the Marzocco, La Gaggia is as good as it gets, and Beans & Machines is their source for this extremely well made residential machine.

The shop currently stocks over twenty-five different espresso machines, from basic $49 versions to the fully loaded $2,800 La Gaggia, which requires its own separate plumbing lines. Each can be demonstrated and discussed knowledgeably by any of the salespeople. In addition, look for a full line of natural-flavored syrups and whole bean coffee as well as a good tea selection. Interestingly, when the shop first opened about five years ago, they sold their coffee beans for around $5 a pound but got few takers. When they raised the price, sales zoomed. It seems there's a perception that high price equals high quality, and people just won't believe otherwise.

Tea Cupping with a Professional

Tea cupping, or professional tasting, is a serious business, with its own arcane rules and rituals. If you're like me and don't know oolong from Darjeeling, it's doubly perplexing. Still, I was thrilled when Frank Miller, the owner of Blue Willow Teahouse, invited me to "cup" with him as he sampled new lots of Darjeeling that he was preparing to bid on. Estate-grown Darjeeling is considered the champagne of tea—the finest, most complex example of the second most consumed beverage in the world.

Frank takes a professorial approach to tea cupping, so as I noisily slurped sample after sample, and breath-warmed and sniffed my way through about fifteen different lots, I picked up some useful nuggets of knowledge. Frank pointed out that tea is the yin-yang beverage of the modern world. It is used to both rev up and induce a state of serenity in a body. Tea imparts a sensuality and an atmosphere of calm while physiologically giving the sipper a mental recharge. "You're never jangled by tea," he opined.

A lot of attention is being paid to tea these days. People are interested in embracing a "lifestyle" epitomized by the rituals and soothing effects of tea drinking. All kinds of health benefits are attributed to this remarkable beverage, further fueling the buzz. Tea sales in this country have risen from $1 billion in 1990 to over $5 billion today. While that's a drop in the bucket compared to coffee sales, it makes people like Frank very happy.

Taking its cue from the teahouses of Asia, but with a Seattle sensibility, Blue Willow Teahouse, the retail arm of the import company, is planned to open in late 2001. A sunny, futuristic interpretation of a tea emporium, it will be located in the mezzanine of a completely remodeled 1920s building, in a lavish and sunfilled space with huge glass windows and a handsome teak bar. Salespeople will prepare and dispense oolongs from Taiwan, Japanese tea grown by the eighth or ninth generation of a family outside of Kyoto, and tea from places as diverse as Sri Lanka, the Cameroon Highlands, and a Malaysian estate planted in 1929 (and still run by the founder's granddaughter). Over sixty varieties will be offered. In addition, a computer kiosk will allow research on tea and its culture, and tastings and educational material will be readily available. All pretty impressive stuff for a nice Jewish boy from New York who joined the Peace Corps and went to India in his twenties, discovered Asia and Buddhism in the process, and learned to keep his sight lines open to both the East and West.

Blue Willow Teahouse

1024 E Pike St., Seattle
Phone: 206/325-5140
Hours: phone before visiting
Internet: www.bluewillowtea.com

Caffé D'Arte

2000 Second Ave., Seattle
Phone: 206/728-4468
Hours: 8AM–5PM every day

You wouldn't order chicken cordon bleu in a restaurant without expecting the chef to put all the ingredients together in a final dish. Likewise, says Mauro Cipolla, when making espresso, the emphasis should be on blending coffee beans to create a consistent signature recipe for a roasting house, rather than roasting a single variety (for example, Colombian or Kona). Because you're dealing with nature, coffee beans vary from field to field, country to country, and producer to producer. A skilled roaster should be able to note the characteristics of each coffee bean and mix the beans in differing proportions to emphasize the good qualities and reduce the bad ones. The idea is to give people everything they like in coffee—richness, flavor, strength, aroma, body, mild acidity, and a pleasant aftertaste —without negative aspects such as bitterness or sourness.

Surprisingly, Mauro, like most coffee roasters in Italy, doesn't care whether he is using arabica (which are considered to have more subtle and rich flavor potential) or robusta beans. That's because he's more interested in the quality of each individual bean than in its so-called reputation. He routinely samples up to twenty different beans to find just the right characteristics, before individually roasting batches of each one and then hand-blending to create Caffé D'Arte's traditional roast. As would be expected from this resolutely Italian roaster, the product line is heavily weighted to *espressi regionali Italiani*. Each region, from north to south, is represented by its own signature blend, from the mild Northern Italian Firenze to the dark, brooding Taormina from Sicily. Note that the fiercely opinionated Caffé D'Arte also doesn't believe in vacuum packaging; they say it lulls people into a false belief that they can keep their coffee for months and months. Buy your coffee more frequently but in smaller amounts, they advise, and you won't be disappointed.

Caffé Vita

1005 E Pike St., Seattle
Phone: 206/709-4440
Hours: 6AM–midnight Monday–Friday; 7AM–midnight Saturday and Sunday

2621 Fifth Ave., Seattle
Phone: 206/441-4351
Hours: 6AM–5PM Monday–Friday; closed Saturday and Sunday

813 Fifth Ave. N, Seattle
Phone: 206/285-9662
Hours: 6AM–8PM Monday–Friday; 7AM–8PM Saturday and Sunday

Internet: www.caffevita.com

Mike McConnell and Michael Prins are so passionate about coffee that they didn't hesitate before opening their coffee roasting business in this latte-saturated town about six years ago. Tasting and drinking their coffee, I was reminded again of how small, dedicated businesses can find success and happiness even when facing down some pretty big competition.

Mike showed me around the new roasting facility at the Pike Street location, and I was bowled over. Peek through the windows between the café and the roasteria to view the 1930s-era German roasters. The operators are tuned in to every squeak and grunt of the machines. They love working with these well-crafted, rebuilt antiques that are still able to churn out perfect batches of roasted coffee beans. Before they get to the roasters, though, the green coffee is stored in a temperature-controlled basement area, another extra step Caffé Vita takes to maintain that critical freshness.

Caffé Vita sells about five blends of coffee for espresso. The Caffé del Sol, with its chocolaty notes, was perfect with a pitcher of steamed milk for my morning café au lait. They also sell two or three single-origin estate varietals. Look for the excellent La Torcaza from the Baru region of Panama or the Guatemalan Genuine Antigua, which is not organically certified but is nevertheless totally organic.

The Crumpet Shop . . . . see Bread

Punchinello performs his highwire act at Caffe Vita.

Espresso Vivace Roasteria

901 E Denny Way, Seattle
Phone: 206/860-5869
Hours: 6:30AM–11PM every day
321 Broadway E (sidewalk coffee bar), Seattle

Espresso Vivace makes an ideal espresso, honey-thick with a pure red-brown *crema*. This is coffee that tastes exactly like it smells, rich and exotic with a buttery power that wraps around your tongue like velvet gloves and stays long after you've swallowed. It's coffee as made by an artist with an uncompromising and singular pursuit of excellence.

David Schomer is the genius behind this operation, and one whiff of the air inside the Denny Way store will confirm his devotion to coffee. Piles of unroasted coffee beans from all over the world lie in burlap bags surrounding the roasting room, waiting for master roaster Dan Reed's touch. Coffee here is roasted daily and never sold more than four days after the roasting date, which is printed on every bag. Actually, they wait for two days before they sell, because coffee gives off gases immediately after roasting that need to dissipate first.

Espresso Vivace makes just two blends of coffee: the Vita, a heavy-bodied blend ideal for cappuccinos and lattes, and the Dolce, a sweeter, earthier blend meant to be enjoyed without milk. I have to fight the impulse to bestow a "best this" or "best that" label, but my goodness, they come close.

Be sure to stop and admire the mural at the back of the store by the artist Kurt Wenner. Its subject matter is intriguing—and somewhat controversial, I would imagine.

Market Spice

85A Pike St. (in Pike Place Market), Seattle
Phone: 206/622-6340
Hours: 9AM–6PM Monday–Saturday; 9AM–5PM Sunday

"You have to be crazy to love being at the Market, and I love it," says Marie Naland, the manager of Market Spice, a business that has been doing things right since 1911 by selling fresh, high-quality tea, coffee, spices, and accoutrements. The business has changed hands and names several times and is now owned by an individual who prefers to remain in the background.

Customers have been coming to this store for generations. Marie told me that she's had more than one person reminisce about sitting on the rickety red stool by the counter while their moms or grandmas shopped for spices. When she got rid of the stool, people were really upset. The owner most people remember is Ruby Ratelonis. She developed Market Spice tea, a concoction of tea, cinnamon, orange oil, and spices that is the shop's signature blend. (It's okay if you like that sort of thing, but personally I prefer my teas unadulterated.)

Market Spice has a most incredible selection of teapots, ranging from ye olde English flower and chintz, to wacky contemporary decoratives in animal shapes, to high-grade *yi xing* Chinese clay pots. There are seemingly hundreds to choose from. In addition, over three hundred different bulk spices and spice mixes are for sale, guaranteed to have high turnover so you know they're fresh, along with fifty-five kinds of coffee, including flavored and more standard blends. I was happy to see Typhoo and PG Tips, two English tea brands that make a good, strong "cuppa char."

Marie Naland might be crazy, but she's one smart cookie—the entire inventory control system for the store is kept in her head. No computer tracking here!

Curried Chicken with Homemade Mild Curry Powder

My cousin, Charles Chitayat, is a spice importer in Montreal, Canada, and is always experimenting to find the "perfect curry powder." He's also a superb, practiced cook. This is his tried-and-true recipe. Serve it with fluffy basmati rice and your favorite vegetables.

Serves 4, with extra curry powder left over for your next dish

Curry Powder

- ¾ tablespoon black peppercorns, ground
- ⅔ tablespoon cayenne pepper
- ⅔ tablespoon celery seed, ground
- 5 tablespoons coriander seed, ground
- 2 tablespoons cumin seed, ground
- 1 tablespoon fenugreek seed, ground
- 1 tablespoon ginger powder
- 1 ⅓ tablespoon mustard seed, ground
- 2 ¼ tablespoons turmeric

Marinade

- 1 cup yogurt
- 3 tablespoons vegetable oil
- Cayenne pepper to taste (optional)

Chicken

- 1 pound boned, skinless chicken breast, cut into bite-size pieces
- 5 tablespoons vegetable oil

2 medium onions, coarsely chopped
4 cloves garlic, coarsely chopped
½ pound mushrooms, sliced
2 large tomatoes, peeled, seeded, and diced
Salt and pepper to taste
Sliced almonds, toasted (optional)

Combine all curry powder ingredients, increasing or reducing proportions of each spice according to personal taste. Store in airtight container in a dark and cool place.

In a medium bowl, combine marinade ingredients and 2 tablespoons of the curry powder. Add chicken pieces and thoroughly coat. Cover and refrigerate for 2 to 3 hours.

Prepare all remaining ingredients before starting to cook.

In a large frying pan, heat 2 tablespoons of the oil and fry onions until translucent and golden. Add garlic and continue cooking on low heat for another 2 to 3 minutes, just to provide some extra flavor. Remove from pan and set aside.

Add 3 tablespoons of the oil to pan and fry mushrooms until just wilted. Add chicken, scraping in yogurt mixture, and simmer on medium-low heat. Do not let sauce come to a boil, as yogurt will curdle. When chicken is half cooked, add tomatoes, salt, and pepper. Cook covered on low heat, stirring occasionally, until chicken is cooked through.

Sprinkle with toasted almonds and serve.

Teacup

2207 Queen Anne Ave. N, Seattle
Phone: 206/283-5931
Hours: 9AM–6PM Monday–Saturday; 10AM–5PM Sunday
Internet: www.tearanch.com

Brian Keating, the owner of Teacup, doesn't stand on ceremony. Any way you like to drink your tea is okay with him. From a bag, out of a paper cup, on the run, iced, flavored, decaffeinated—it's all right when it comes to tea. He sells over a hundred fifty varieties of loose tea from all over the world, including some of the finest and most exclusive teas and tisanes around. On any given day, you'll find the standard black, oolong, and green teas, along with many other unusual varieties.

Teacup carries most of the legendary Dammann teas, the only shop on the West Coast to do so. Dammann, the oldest tea broker in France, is known for its scented teas using real oils, fruit or spice essences, and pungent botanicals. Try the Gout Russe Douchka, an Earl Grey of their own formulation with just a hint of tangerine and lime. I also took home some whole-leaf, silver-tipped Ambootia Organic, from the premier estate in Darjeeling. Exquisite. It's an exclusive here on the West Coast for Teacup; you'll have to travel to the Ambootia tea counter at Harrods in London to get a larger selection. There's a thriving market in counterfeit Darjeeling, so the best estates have started to trademark themselves; given the price of some of these teas, it's no wonder.

Torrefazione Italia

320 Occidental Ave. S, Seattle
Phone: 206/624-5847
Hours: 6AM–6PM Monday–Friday; 8AM–6PM Saturday; 8AM–5PM Sunday

1310 Fourth Ave., Seattle
Phone: 206/583-8970
Hours: 6:30AM–6PM Monday–Friday; 9AM–5PM Saturday; closed Sunday

622 Olive Way, Seattle
Phone: 206/624-1429
Hours: 6:30AM–5:30PM Monday–Friday; 8AM–5PM Saturday; closed Sunday

701 N 34th St., Seattle
Phone: 206/545-2721
Hours: 6AM–6:30PM Monday–Friday; 7AM–6PM Saturday and Sunday

Torrefazione has a special spot in Seattle's heart, being one of the first fine coffee roasters in town. They serve their coffee in lovely Deruta ceramic china in all the cafés, making for a very civilized latte break. While they almost don't qualify as a micro-roaster, with nineteen stores in their chain, they've had a great reputation among true aficionados, and I was curious to know whether they've been able to maintain their quality since changing ownership.

The company has mythologized their history and markets the story on all their slick packaging. In 1986, founder Umberto Bizzarri came to Seattle from Perugia, Italy, with his family's recipe and opened the first Torrefazione, in Pioneer Square. Since then, he's sold the business to a holding company that also owns Seattle's Best Coffee. The two companies are completely independently operated, and Torrefazione is striving to preserve that original quality while operating under this corporate umbrella.

I give them a mixed report card. While the general quality of the beans has slipped, all of the eight blends, including one decaf, still make a very acceptable cup of coffee. These are all Italian-style coffees using 100 percent arabica beans. Whether brewed in an espresso machine, a drip brewer, or a French press, they are all full-bodied and roasted to a pleasing mahogany brown, with no oils on the surface of the beans from overroasting to mar the finish. I'm most partial to the Roma, which brews beautifully in my French press at home.

World Merchants

1509 Western Ave., Seattle
Phone: 206/682-7274
Hours: 10AM–7PM Monday–Saturday; noon–6PM Sunday
Internet: www.worldspice.com

Tony Hill used to travel around the world as a consultant in the high-tech business. In his spare time, he would explore markets in out-of-the-way places. He observed that spices are the "glue food" that everyone, no matter what their ethnicity, uses. Coming back to Seattle, he mused aloud with friends over dinner about how to combine his love of ethnic cuisine and his fascination with the ancient and honorable spice trade. A suggestion was made, and *ba-da-boom*, World Merchants was born.

Tony has made a conscious decision to stay small and to control every aspect of quality and education for himself and his customers. The shop buys directly from growers 90 percent of the time and air-freights the purchases, so that nothing stays on the shelves for more than three months. In fact, they shoot for a six-month ticker from the *moment of harvesting* till a spice heads out the door with a customer. If that isn't reason enough to root through your spice drawer and replace ancient, long-dead purchases, I don't know what is.

Silly me, before I walked into World Merchants, I thought paprika was paprika. The shop carries four different kinds of paprika, including a smoky Spanish *pimentòn* with an earthy and smoky sweetness that is simply wonderful—not just for use as a garnish, but as a dominant and vibrant fire-roasted flavor component. The shop specializes in custom-blending whole or ground spice mixtures, including ten curry blends, barbecue rubs, jerk seasonings, Creole mixes, and an intriguing Kyoto seafood rub that worked beautifully in my kitchen rubbed into a fillet of steamed salmon served over soba noodles.

The other, equally large part of the business is loose-leaf tea sales. The selection changes with the seasons but always includes a huge variety of green teas from China and Japan in addition to the usual black, oolong, and herbal tisanes. The staff will patiently explain how to use everything you buy in the store, and besides that, you can get a geography and ethnography lesson with every purchase.

Kyoto Salmon with Soba Noodles

World Merchants makes an intriguing Kyoto seafood rub (containing green tea, black sesame seed, sea salt, and a hint of wasabi) that I thought would work beautifully with salmon. My experimentation led to this recipe. Serve it with a good pot of green tea.

Serves 4

Dipping Sauce

> 1 bag instant dashi (Japanese soup stock)
>
> 2 cups hot water
>
> 1/4 cup mirin (sweet cooking rice wine)
>
> 1/4 cup soy sauce
>
> 1 teaspoon sugar
>
> 1 cup brewed green tea

Salmon

> 1 pound salmon fillet, in one piece
>
> 2 tablespoons Kyoto seafood rub from World Merchants
>
> 1 tablespoon peanut or other vegetable oil
>
> 2 tablespoons additional oil
>
> 12 ounces Japanese buckwheat noodles (soba)
>
> 1 medium or 1/2 large cucumber, split lengthwise, peeled, seeded, and roughly sliced into julienne
>
> 2 green onions, finely sliced crosswise

For dipping sauce, steep dashi in hot water in saucepan for 5 to 10 minutes. Add mirin, soy sauce, and sugar. Bring to a boil over medium heat. Remove from heat and discard dashi. Add tea; allow to cool.

Slice salmon on a diagonal into 4 equal pieces. Rub Kyoto mixture into fish portions evenly on both sides. Dribble with the 1 tablespoon oil and let stand for 5 to 10 minutes.

Heat the 2 tablespoons oil in nonstick skillet over medium-high heat. Add fish, skin side up, and cook until golden brown, 2 to 3 minutes. Turn and cook the other side, another 2 to 3 minutes. Set aside and keep warm.

Cook noodles according to package directions. Drain and divide between 4 soup bowls.

Top each serving with cucumbers, then a piece of salmon. Garnish with onions. Serve immediately with dipping sauce on the side.

NORTH

Caffé Appassionato

4001 21st Ave. W, Seattle
Phone: 206/281-8040
Hours: 6AM–7PM every day
Other locations scattered around town

Every coffee roaster has their own slant on why their coffee stands out in a crowded field. Appassionato sees themselves as one of the early players, arriving at just the right moment and staying just small enough to maintain quality, kind of like a Napa Valley boutique winery on a bit larger scale.

A lot of people in Seattle consistently rate Appassionato as their favorite brew. The key to the coffee is the roasting process, says vice president Tucker McHugh. All coffee in its original state is highly acidic. By roasting it, you break down that acidity. Of course, the differences come down to the skill of the roaster, since the duration and temperature of the roasting significantly affect the final taste. Low temperature with longer time and more air flow adds up to the lower-acid coffee that is Appassionato's trademark. If you're prone to upset stomach from coffee, then this one's for you.

This roaster sells about fifteen different varieties, equally split between single-estate varietals and blends. Try the Appassionato Bluff, named after the Magnolia Bluff, where the owners live. The Morning Passion is my favorite—a consistently snappy brew well suited for that first cuppa. The roasteria at Fishermen's Terminal is a lovely spot to while away an afternoon, with the enormous roaster in plain view.

Lighthouse Roasters

400 N 43rd St., Seattle
Phone: 206/634-3140
Hours: 6:30AM–7PM Monday–Saturday; 7AM–7PM Sunday

Lighthouse roasts to what they call "full city," which they describe as a degree of roastedness with maximum flavor and minimum bitterness, akin to Italian or French roast coffee. They carry three different blends and about eight or nine single-origin coffees. Cognoscenti give high marks to this little business that has been open since 1993. In fact, many people feel that along with Espresso Vivace and Caffé Vita, it's the best of the micro-roasters in town.

Early one Friday morning I chatted with roaster Eric Anderson while he worked. He's been roasting for about three years and says that as he's learned about roasting, the process has become more about reacting to the coffee beans than manipulating them. Each batch comes with a certain moisture content, woodiness, bean size, and other variables. A good roaster's job is to draw out those qualities that will give consistency to the beans. Of course, you have to start out with good-quality beans, and this is where a micro-roaster has it all over the big boys. Despite what they say, Anderson feels that it's just not possible for mega-corporations to buy enough superior-quality coffee to feed their operation. Many small-scale farmers can't or won't sell to Starbucks and their ilk because they either don't have enough to supply them or don't want to put all their eggs in one basket. That's why there's always room for small players like Lighthouse.

Note: There is no connection between this business and the Lighthouse Roaster out of Port Townsend whose products are sold in some area supermarkets.

Teahouse Kuan Yin

1911 N 45th St., Seattle
Phone: 206/632-2055
Hours: 10AM–11PM Sunday–Thursday; 10AM–midnight Friday and Saturday
Internet: www.teahousechoice.com

Miranda Pirzada's shop in Wallingford has been a home away from home for tea lovers throughout Seattle for over ten years. Starting with a degree in South Asia studies, a good tea palate, and the belief that tea makes a far more complex and interesting beverage than coffee, she traveled extensively through Asia looking for suppliers. This fiercely independent woman has always operated with one uncompromising principle—she deals only with traders who care about their tea.

The inventory is not exhaustive. For example, there aren't fifteen kinds of Darjeeling, only one or two of the best examples. I tried the Namring Upper Estate Darjeeling, from an estate where Miranda personally knows the manager and has picked his best lots at auctions two weeks apart. It's delicate and flowery, without a lot of background tannin, so it's easy to drink. This staunchly purists' shop doesn't sell tea bags because they're made using low-quality dust with color but no aroma. The house Earl Grey goes easy on the bergamot because Miranda wants people to taste the pure tea flavor. They hand-blend herbal teas here with soothing names such as Haiku, Wu Wei, and World Peace. You can also pick up fine-quality teapots, all of which are designed for use and not to be merely decorative. Beautiful handmade batik tea cosies as well as an assortment of accoutrements are available.

Zoka Coffee Roaster & Tea Co.

2200 N 56th St., Seattle
Phone: 206/545-4277
Hours: 6AM–midnight every day

Zoka Coffee reminds me of a college student union; the place seems to always be humming with young student types sprawled around tables with computers, books, and book bags heaped nearby. There's a roasting machine at the back of the room, and owner Tim McCormick does the roasting in plain sight, in small batches several times a day. He used to work for Starbucks and Caravali in their quality control departments, so he is focused on finding the finest grades available.

Zoka likes to seek out coffee from small, high-elevation farms, some of which have been in operation for more than a hundred years. Their growers are concerned with promoting sustainable agriculture, and the store likes to emphasize the individual characteristics of each of their coffees and blends. Their organic coffees include a mild Mexico Oaxaca, fair trade–certified shade-grown Guatemalan, and Sumatran from the highland forests of Gayoland. They are constantly on the lookout to expand the line with beans that meet their standards.

Zoka also carries a variety of loose tea, but it doesn't seem to be as much of an emphasis. Service is friendly, if occasionally uninformed.

SOUTH

Imperial Tea Court . . . . see Asian

Tim McCormick of Zoka Coffee checks for a perfect roast.

fish It isn't hard to persuade people in Seattle to eat fish. After all, we live in a piscatorial paradise blessed with an abundance of marine resources. Because we have a lot of experience, we demand top quality and freshness. And we have some extremely knowledgeable and dedicated retailers who work hard to provide a reliable supply of seafood in an unpredictable business.

When I first arrived in Seattle, I remember being absolutely astounded at the selection of salmon. Where I come from, shopping for salmon is fairly simple. You have a choice of "baby" or Atlantic farmed salmon. That's it. Today in the Pacific Northwest, even ordinary supermarkets will offer more than one or two types. Going to a specialty seafood market will give you access to the best of this extraordinary product. Whole or filleted salmon, caught wild, lovingly handled, and rapidly delivered to these markets, is a top-quality food that fully deserves its revered status in Northwest culture. Farmed salmon, which have steadily improved in quality and are available year-round, are a less expensive alternative.

Most area fish markets typically offer an eye-popping parade of pristine, locally grown or caught fish and shellfish. Oysters during the height of the season can be had in more than a dozen varieties. Littleneck or Manila clams, Penn Cove mussels, Dungeness crabs, Hood Canal spot prawns—the names reflect local fishing grounds. We tend to take this selection for granted, but few other areas in the country can offer this variety and freshness so consistently. No wonder tourists at Pike Place Market are goggle-eyed and more than a little envious.

The Northwest has a long history of appreciation for smoked fish, of course. In the course of the research for this book, I talked with native Indian fishermen; small, almost backyard smokers; large, internationally marketed brand-name producers; and everyone in between. Hot alder-smoked salmon is as emblematic of the Pacific Northwest as Dungeness crab, and many people wouldn't dream of a holiday or celebration without it. Again, we have a lot to choose from. Whether your tastes run more to traditional, heavily smoked fish, salt-and-sugar-cured gravlax, or garlic-flavored smoked mussels, someone here in Seattle is making and selling it.

The fishing industry in the Pacific Northwest is undergoing dramatic changes these days. Supplies of some traditional favorites are in jeopardy, while other species are more abundant. Fishing boats are having to range farther afield to chase after fewer and fewer fish. The business is in a state of flux. Whether to compensate for the uncertainties or because our palates are more adventuresome, one of the biggest changes in the retail end involves air-freight delivery of fresh fish. Fish from all over the world, but especially from Hawaii and the Pacific Islands, can be caught and thrown into the refrigerated belly of a commercial airliner to arrive at your local market within a day or two of catching.

With all these choices, and since fish is a commodity where freshness and safety is paramount, a trustworthy source is absolutely critical. Here's where we are also extremely fortunate. We have a handful of totally committed markets dedicated to bringing us the best selection and, given that fish is no longer cheap, the best value around.

Should I Trust My Fish Market?

In a fish market, appearance is 90 percent of the game. It isn't everything, because some places put a lot more emphasis on fixtures and expensive display cases, while others are more focused on a "get 'em in, get 'em out" fast-and-furious approach. Still, ask yourself these questions when you walk into a market.

What does it smell like in there? You should be greeted by a wonderfully briny sea smell that instills confidence. Any shop permeated with a strong "fishy" smell may be less than ideal. That doesn't necessarily mean it's no good, but be on your guard.

Look at the care and handling of the fish. Are the fillets sitting in pools of liquid? The flesh of fillets or steaks should look moist—not dry, but not exuding a lot of liquid either. Be aware that some fish markets routinely spritz their fillets with water to create that lovely, glistening appearance. Is there sufficient ice cover? Do the refrigerated cases look clean? Is the fish protected from sunlight, dirt, and flies? Is the store busy enough to give you confidence that stock is turned over rapidly?

Look at the live fish tanks. The water should be relatively clean and well aerated, and the less crowded the better. The fish should be lively enough. Any fish that die in the tanks should be promptly removed. Are the lobsters missing claws? Do the fish have open wounds or skin lesions? Obviously you'll want to avoid those establishments.

When you've found a retail market that you like, ask them questions. They should have answers. Where does this fish come from? Is it wild or farmed, fresh or frozen, and is it properly labeled as such? How should I cook it? One incredibly helpful service to customers that a good fish market provides is lots of recipes and educational leaflets about their products. Of course, you should give them feedback too. Let them know when you like something and what your preferences are. You'll both be happier for it.

Finally, once you have found a fish market that you trust, be willing to listen to their recommendations. Put yourself in their hands. Their livelihood depends on it. After all, they are only as good as their last customer says.

Grilled Fish with Mediterranean-Style Salsa

This is a simple dish that works best with firm-textured fish such as halibut or swordfish. Both of these fish are firm and usually quite lean, so marinating is helpful. Also, it is really important not to overcook them so they don't dry out.

Note: If you don't want to charcoal-grill the fish, you can easily pan-fry or cook them under the broiler.

Serves 4

Salsa

> *1 large tomato, sliced in half and cooked in iron skillet till blistered and soft, then peeled and diced*
>
> *1 lemon, peeled and chopped*
>
> *½ cup chopped cilantro*
>
> *1 or 2 anchovy fillets, minced*

Cooked crab at Wild Salmon Seafood Market.

> *8 to 10 kalamata olives, pitted, then smashed and chopped*
> *1 tablespoon capers, chopped*
> *¼ cup extra virgin olive oil*
> *Salt and pepper to taste*

Fish

> *3 tablespoons olive oil*
> *1 tablespoon soy sauce*
> *A few fresh thyme leaves*
> *Salt and pepper to taste*
> *4 halibut or swordfish steaks (6 ounces each)*

Combine all salsa ingredients in bowl. Let stand for 1 or 2 hours so flavors can develop.

In small bowl, combine olive oil, soy sauce, thyme, salt, and pepper; mix well. Place fish in single layer in glass or porcelain dish. Pour marinade over fish, massage well on all sides, and refrigerate for 1 hour.

Prepare charcoal for a medium fire in barbecue, or preheat a cast-iron skillet on medium-high heat. Lightly oil grill or skillet. When coals glow red and are covered with ash, place the fish on grill or in pan. Cook just until fish begins to turn opaque but has a thin pinkish line in the center (no longer than 3 minutes per side if the steaks are ½ inch thick).

To serve, place a steak on each plate. Top with a generous serving of salsa and serve immediately.

CENTRAL SEATTLE

Pike Place Market
First Ave. and Pike St., Seattle

A great market reveals itself over the course of many visits. My favorite time to visit Pike Place Market is early in the morning, before it's open. There's a sense of anticipation, a purposeful bustle in which all the players are rushing to get ready, akin to the theater in the last minutes before the curtains are raised. Color and smell, noise and taste—all are props carefully laid out to draw the visitor in. Fish here may look as if it's casually heaped, but make no mistake. Many a tourist has been lured by a prized king and left the Market wondering how to wrestle that travel pack into the overhead bin to get it home.

City Fish Co.
Midway through the covered arcade
Phone: 206/682-9329; 800/334-2669
Hours: 9AM–6PM every day

Jon Daniels was buzzed, even though he was hobbling around on one leg (mountain biking accident), when I stopped in to talk to him. An energetic young man who's spent his whole life around fish and fishermen, he's got lots to say about the business. Jon grew up in a fishing village in Alaska, spent time as a commercial fisherman, sold smoked fish in retail kiosks in malls throughout the Northwest, and finally bought this shop in 1995.

City Fish was established in 1917 as a city-run fish market, the first in Pike Place Market. Being one of the smaller seafood outfits in the place, the folks here don't try to compete in the fish-tossing competition. They buy in smaller quantities every day, so they feel their fish is fresher. "Good attitude coming out, good product, good price" is Jon's motto.

Roasted Salmon with Proscuitto and Herb Butter

I got the idea for this dish from a recipe in the San Francisco Chronicle and have made it many times since. I find it to be very rich, particularly when made with king salmon, so I can get by with using less fish.

Serves 3 to 4

Herb Butter

> *1 teaspoon chopped basil*
>
> *1 teaspoon chopped parsley*
>
> *1 teaspoon chopped chives or scallions*
>
> *4 tablespoons butter, softened*
>
> *Juice of ½ lemon*
>
> *Freshly ground pepper to taste*

Roasted Salmon

> *1 pound salmon fillet (preferably king), skinned; ask for thick end*
>
> *1 teaspoon salt*
>
> *Freshly ground pepper to taste*
>
> *4 thin slices proscuitto (no need for expensive imported proscuitto; domestic is fine)*

For herb butter, mix chopped herbs with butter, lemon juice, and pepper. Set aside.

Preheat oven to 500 degrees F.

Rinse salmon and pat dry. Cut crosswise into 4 equal pieces. You should end up with 4 very skinny, long strips of fish. Remove as many pin-bones as possible using tweezers or needle-nosed pliers. Lightly salt and pepper the fish.

Roll fish around itself with skinned side on outside. Smear herb butter on top of fish roll, then wrap proscuitto around roll. (It doesn't have to be neat, just as long as it is a nice self-contained bundle.) Smear a little extra butter on top of proscuitto.

Place fish rolls in buttered, heatproof dish. Bake until firm to the touch, about 5 or 6 minutes.

Serve immediately.

Jack's Fish Spot

In the Sanitary Market
Phone: 206/467-0514
Hours: 7:30AM–6PM Monday–Saturday; 7:30AM–5PM Sunday

Three things distinguish Jack's from the other fish stores in Pike Place Market. First, they're across the street from the main action, so you don't have to wade through hordes of tourists or risk being clobbered by a flying fish. Second, they're the only market with live fish tanks. They've got an elaborate system for keeping the shellfish ultra-fresh in running-water tanks, and with seafood, fresher is always better. Lastly, they have a seafood bar, with oysters on the half-shell and a fine cioppino that sells by the cauldronful every day. The recipe is a bastardized version of one served by El Pescador in Del Mar, California. It's loaded with shrimp and other goodies, with a nice balance of spice and garlic punctuating each spoonful.

Pike Place Fish

By Rachel the Pig
Phone: 206/682-7181
Hours: 9AM–6PM every day

You have to push your way past the crowds at this raucous market. The philosophy here is to have fun and to send the customers on their way with more than just fish. "We want our customers to leave in a better frame of mind than what they came with," was the answer when I asked about the guiding philosophy of this store. And so the antics include throwing a twenty-pound salmon over the heads of the crowd, or scaring some poor unsuspecting soul with a well-timed tug at the prominently displayed giant monkfish. It is all in good fun, and the crowd eats it up, although it's probably not the best way to treat a princely Copper River salmon.

The specialty of the house is Northwest fish, fresh and smoked, almost entirely from Alaska. It is always impeccably fresh and top quality, albeit pricey. Once when I walked by with a purchase of alder-smoked fish from the "other" fish market, they called me over and insisted on a side-by-side taste test, *mano a mano*, theirs against ours. I have to say that this market won hands down, with a deeper, more assertively salmon flavor in a soft, lightly smoked piece of fish. The secret, they told me, was that they use only wild caught salmon, rather than farmed fish, for all their smoking.

Pure Food Fish Market

Midway through the covered arcade, near the Athenian Inn
Phone: 206/622-5765
Hours: 9AM–6PM every day
Internet: www.freshseafood.com

Irving and Saul Amon have been the owners of this market since 1956. Many of their staff seem to have been there almost as long. Irving told me that the secret to their success is their reputation and relationships with their suppliers. As with the other shops in Pike Place Market, all of whom have to cater to a mix of locals and tourists, the selection here is heavily weighted to the classic Northwest. This means that, through the seasons, you'll find a range of enormous whole salmon, as well as translucent, beautifully pale halibut, all begging to be grilled, poached, steamed, or smoked. Oysters, crab, Alaskan spot prawns, local mussels and clams, squid, smoked fish—all the usual suspects are tidily set out and can be packed for long-distance travel.

Totem Smokehouse

1908 Pike Pl.
Phone: 206/443-1710; 800/972–5666
Hours: 9AM–6PM every day
Internet: www.totemsmokehouse.com

Say you've got an aunt in Pleasantville, Iowa, and you've got to get her something—fast. Hustle over to Totem Smokehouse, where they specialize in mail order (75 to 80 percent of their business is to out-of-towners). Everything they make is packaged for travel and postal delivery. The fish itself is premium, wild-caught king or sockeye, lightly smoked with a semisweet flavor. The taste isn't assertive; it's designed to appeal to people who may or may not like smoked fish, so you know you can't go wrong. Go ahead, surprise Aunt Sally with a bit of the Northwest.

Mutual Fish Co.

2335 Rainier Ave. S, Seattle
Phone: 206/322-4368
Hours: 8:30AM–5:30PM Monday–Saturday; closed Sunday

Say you've decided that you're going to do an oyster tasting and
you've got to have a dozen varieties of the Pacific Northwest's finest.
Do you panic, or do you rush down to Mutual on Rainier? Naturally,
you rush down to this great fish market. Although there's no guarantee that they'll have a dozen different types, they'll likely come closer
than just about anyone else in the city. The live fish tanks here are
home to an incredible rotating selection of the finest oysters, live
spot prawns, crabs, lobsters, and mussels. Mutual not only carries
fish from the Northwest but also air-freights it in from all over the
world. You name it, they have it—or they can get it if it's to be had.

Mutual Fish is the domain of the Yoshimura family, which is now
in its third generation in the retail/wholesale fish business. Harry
Yoshimura took over from his dad, who founded the business some
fifty years ago, and his son Kevin is now working with him. Harry is
astute, funny, and completely gracious with his time and knowledge.
His basic message is that you get what you pay for. Quality, particularly in the seafood biz, costs money. Sure, you can get it cheaper in
a supermarket. But do you know how the fish has been handled and
where it came from? Harry does—he has long-standing, carefully
nurtured relationships with all his suppliers. He also likes to experiment with his product mix, so you're as liable to find New Zealand
yellow-eyed snapper and Hawaiian opah as you are king salmon and
halibut. The store draws a variety of ethnic groups, as well as a huge
wholesale business, so Harry can offer a range of products that will
be snapped up by knowledgeable cognoscenti.

Wong Tung Seafood . . . . see Asian

Talking to a Native Indian Smoker

Most people heading north on Highway 305 barely notice, as they barrel off Bainbridge Island, that they're passing through the Suquamish Indian reservation (except over the Fourth of July weekend, when it's a popular place to stock up on fireworks). And most probably miss Willie Pratt's faded sign, on the left side of the road about a mile past the Clearwater Casino, advertising his smoked salmon. Compared to the other fish markets in this chapter, Willie is small potatoes; he's just trying to get by, "value adding" to what he can catch in his Kingston to Vashon fishing grounds. He's a soft-spoken, quiet man. A Suquamish Indian, he's been fishing these grounds all his life, and it's getting harder and harder. He finally came to the conclusion that to survive, he needed to branch out. That's when he got into the smoked salmon business.

"It's my grandmother's recipe," he told me when I asked him how he got started. "I messed around for about two years till I got the recipe right. In the old days, before the white man came, we didn't use salt. We just dried it real hard. Now I use alder or maple to smoke it heavier than most. I call it 'overcooked barbecued salmon with extra sauce.'"

Willie used to give his friends samples of his smoked salmon, and they encouraged him to sell it. So he does—on the honor system. He's got two or three refrigerators and a lock box on the side of the road. Take what you want, and put the money in the box. From about August through November, there's also fresh salmon in there. He's now got about two or three hundred customers, and his reputation is growing.

The younger, more athletic Suquamish have stumbled onto a far more lucrative livelihood than smoking fish: fishing for geoduck. About five or six years ago, some of them sat up and took notice of what the Canadians were getting for geoduck in the overseas market—about $5 to $6 per pound. Geoduck clams are found in the intertidal zone in bottom beds eighteen to seventy feet deep. The tribe is allowed to harvest 2.7 percent of the known biomass, counted annually, and they do it by diving with surface-supplied air tanks and wearing eighty-pound lead weights. Once they've located the clam beds, they use high-pressure hoses to liquefy the sand and pry the clams loose. A good diver can pull up anywhere from 300 to 1,000 pounds a day. A lot of this hard cash has been funneled into tribal social programs.

NORTH

The Fresh Fish Co.

2804 NW Market St., Seattle
Phone: 206/782-1632
Hours: 9AM–7PM Monday–Saturday; 9AM–6PM Sunday

I had passed by this store for years on my way to Shilshole Bay before I realized that it was a serious fish market. After all, it's a store within a convenience market, and it just doesn't look as if it could possibly have much to offer. Surprise! This is an excellent, full-service store that offers the best of Alaskan seafood.

Joan Stafford and her husband were in the fish processing business on the Oregon coast for years before they went up to try their luck in Alaska. In 1986, they came back down to the Lower 48 and bought a small seafood market, which eventually became the Fresh Fish Co. Their contacts in Alaska and Oregon allow them to deal directly with the suppliers, instead of going through a level of distributors, so they can offer very competitive prices and top quality. They sell a great homemade cioppino base here; all you've got to do is add your fish. And the crab cakes are packed full of Dungeness crabmeat, with a little bit of mayo and mustard and red pepper and just enough bread crumbs to bind them. The store is also in a perfect location, by the Ballard Locks, making it convenient for tourists to stop in and pick up fish to take home.

Jensen's Old Fashioned Smokehouse

10520 Greenwood Ave. N, Seattle
Phone: 206/364-0880
Hours: 9AM–6PM Monday–Saturday; closed Sunday

Mike Jensen, the owner of this smokehouse, has a reputation for being a straight-shooter who caters to his customers. He has slowly and steadily expanded his operation, but his niche is custom-smoking fish for sport and commercial fishermen. While I waited to talk to him, I chatted with a guy who'd brought in some king salmon he'd caught on a fishing trip. He told me he's been coming here for a while and likes what he gets: a quick turnaround and a warm welcome from the staff every time.

Jensen's makes a range of smoked fish products. They use only wild caught fish, lightly brined and smoked in accordance with contemporary tastes, which now emphasize flavor more than preservation. "In the old days, people preferred a much saltier, drier fish," Mike says. "Now they like it soft, they're looking for new flavors—maybe garlic or cracked pepper." He gave me a sample of the shop's newest product, his salmon jerky. Sometimes salmon jerky can be overly dry and leatherlike, but not Mike's; it has just enough chewiness and flavor to make you keep nibbling till it's all gone.

Sandy's Sea Foods

10528 Greenwood Ave. N, Seattle
Phone: 206/362-6868
Hours: 11AM–5PM Tuesday–Saturday; closed Sunday and Monday

The giant Pop-art salmon made of two steel drums on the roof of this store, right next door to Jensen's, is your first clue that Sandy is not your normal shopkeeper. She definitely has a free-spirited approach to her work. Since she recently had a baby and naturally is head over heels in love, this means that her store is not always open during its posted hours. Between her baby talk and her nonstop chatter, I left with my head spinning.

What Sandy sells is simply high-quality fish, nothing else. Well, that's not quite true. Sandy also sells pickled herring, made from her mother's secret recipe, which they've been selling since about 1950. I tried it and, as promised, it was a treat. There wasn't a lot else to choose from in the store's case, but that could be because Sandy puts out only what is absolutely fresh. The smoked salmon here, made for the store elsewhere, is a little less salty than Jensen's.

Seattle Caviar Co.

2833 Eastlake Ave. E, Seattle
Phone: 206/323-3005
Hours: 10AM–5:30PM Tuesday–Friday; 11AM–5PM Saturday; closed Sunday and Monday
Internet: www.caviar.com

Everyone's got a caviar story. Maybe because the stuff is so expensive, every occasion where it's served is memorable. Dale and Betsy

Sherrow, the owners of this off-the-beaten-path shop on Eastlake Avenue, love to tell a few tales about their customers. Like the one about the Metro accordion-bus driver who stopped his vehicle right in the middle of Eastlake, passengers and all, and rushed in to buy some caviar. Or the Seattle meter maid who pulled up in front of the shop and caused everyone inside to scatter back to their cars to feed their meters. She only wanted some caviar.

Caviar is one of those foods that people either don't get, or love with a passion that goes beyond reason. For those who must indulge, this shop is a real find. They specialize in Russian "black pearls" from the female sturgeon of the Caspian Sea. Dale used to be a seafood broker, but around 1989 he realized that the culinary scene was changing and Seattle was ready for a product that has always been associated with sophistication and luxury. He started off wholesaling to the best restaurants in town and in 1997 expanded to the retail shop. "The key to making this business more diverse is education. We've always sold to Iranians, Russians, and others who are familiar with caviar, but now we offer tastings every Saturday to educate people about the nuances between caviars. We carry beluga, sevruga, and osetra from Russia, as well as farmed domestic caviar from the Sacramento River delta and from the Yellowstone River in Montana."

Business in money-rich Seattle has been great. Besides caviar, champagne, and foie gras, fresh truffles from Italy and France are available in season. Dale told me that recently, in a tit-for-tat feud with the European Union, 100 percent tariffs were slapped on truffles. Even at about $1,600 per pound, he told me straight-faced, that still translates to *only* about $100 per serving.

University Seafood & Poultry

1317 NE 47th St., Seattle
Phone: 206/632-3700
Hours: 10AM–6PM Monday–Friday; 9:30AM–5:30PM Saturday; closed Sunday

"I don't sell anything that I don't eat myself, and I sell nothing but the best," Dale Erickson replied when asked what makes his fifty-five-year-old store so special. "Almost all my salespeople have been with me at least fifteen years, and they are all good cooks. They know what they're selling." His shop keeps a low profile given the amazing breadth of its offerings, and Dale likes it that way. He enjoys being just off the Ave in the University District. It keeps him on his toes, and what with the university nearby, people from all over the world are his customers.

University Seafood & Poultry is a small storefront. But once you enter and start looking around inside, like peeling layers off an onion, you'll see more and more of just about any fine comestible you can imagine. Dale used to go to the waterfront to pick up fish, but now he spends a lot of time on the phone talking to both coasts. He grabs what's best out there and brings it to his customers almost immediately. I picked up some fresh Oregon white shrimp, for instance. They were utterly delicious, plump and succulent without that weird, chemical taste and mushy texture that frozen shrimp so often have. Dale also sells Argentine beef, which comes from a very different creature than the American cow. Argentine cattle are fed on grasses rather than the high-carbohydrate grains given to American cattle, so their meat has a distinct flavor.

The friendly folks at University Seafood & Poultry know their stuff.

Wild Salmon Seafood Market

1900 W Nickerson St. (at Fishermen's Terminal), Seattle
Phone: 206/283-3366; 888/222-FISH
Hours: 10AM–6PM every day

I love the fact that this market makes a huge effort to educate their customers. They have excellent information sheets, telling you the ins and outs of all their specialties and giving lots of simple recipe ideas. Obviously, wild salmon is a focus here, and it's available year-round, fresh during the season and high-quality "fresh-frozen" at other times.

The oyster selection is vast. The last time I bought Kumamoto oysters (my favorite) here, they were huge (by Kumo standards). As far as I'm concerned, absolutely nothing beats a half-shell oyster with a squirt of lemon or, almost as good, with some garlic butter at a beach barbecue. Cocktail sauce lovers should note that this shop makes a kick-ass sauce to go with those oysters.

Fishing on the *Papa George*

There is a certain romance of the sea, an idea that the finest, most sparkling-fresh fish should come directly from the fishing boats as they dock and unload their catch. In Seattle, Fishermen's Terminal is home port to the huge Alaska-bound commercial fishing fleet. Unfortunately, the dreary reality is that when they return after several months at sea, virtually all of those boats deal only with wholesale brokers and factory processors. A poor soul who wanders down to the docks in search of a squeaky-fresh, still flopping fish is bound to be disappointed.

But at least for several weeks of the year, usually in the early fall through Thanksgiving, Fishermen's Terminal is the place to come down and make a connection with the folks who work so darn hard to bring the catch in. They're down there every day selling what's in their hold, which is anything from albacore tuna to chum salmon.

The signs were large and hard to miss, along Nickerson and entering Fishermen's Terminal: "Blast and bled, sashimi-grade, flash-frozen tuna." The *Papa George* was the first in a small cluster of boats docked at the western edge of the Terminal. She's a tidy boat skippered by Stephen Lovejoy, with his crewmate Holly Huntress, for nine months of the year off the California and Hawaiian coasts. Stephen and Holly fish primarily for albacore. In years past, they would sell directly to the Japanese-bound market. But in 1998 the bottom dropped out of the wholesale albacore business, and they had the choice of selling their catch for next to nothing or seeing what they could do on their own at the dock. Holly, a lovely and lively woman clearly starved for social interaction after six months at sea, thoroughly enjoys the opportunity to meet and greet people.

Stephen and Holly are troll fishermen, called "swivelnecks" in the business because they're constantly turning their heads from side to side to check their lines. They believe their processing technique results in a top-quality frozen fish that is far superior to a "fresh" fish that has been squished and bruised in the hold of a ship for two weeks before returning to port.

The tuna is hooked, sixteen lines per side plus three in the stern, and reeled on board, where it's swiftly dispatched with a thump to the head. When the gills are cut off, the still-beating heart pumps out most of the blood. Holly then positions the fish on a small wooden trough just above the freezer hatch, gives it a good rinse, and drops it into the hold. The fish is frozen rock solid to 28 degrees within twenty-four hours and stacked like so many pieces of bug-eyed, gleaming silver cordwood for the months at sea.

Buying a ten- to fifteen-pound frozen-solid tuna does present some problems for the home chef. If your family is the size of mine, it can be a little too much of a good thing all at once. Luckily, Wild Salmon Seafood Market, in the retail area of the Terminal, will cut and vacuum-pack the fish into more manageable sizes for a small fee. It's worth it, and even with that extra cost, and the waste from buying a whole head-on fish, you'll still save significantly compared to buying tuna in a market. Plus you'll have the fun of coming down and visiting the *Papa George*.

EASTSIDE

Ohana Seafood Market

168 Lake St. S (in Kirkland Waterfront Market), Kirkland
Phone: 425/576-1887
Hours: 9AM–6PM every day
Internet: www.fish2go.com

Marshal Caluya, also known as the Saint because he's a sweet and innocent Catholic boy, is proud of his Hawaiian roots. He says his store has the true aloha spirit. That means you'll get friendly service and lots of smiles. They have a good selection of popular fish and shellfish. The quality is excellent, and the fish is properly iced and displayed. Ohana is located in the downtown Kirkland Waterfront Market, next door to Washington Harvest Farms, which makes for convenient one-stop shopping. The emphasis on old-fashioned service and the care these two markets take with appearances goes a long way to win them the loyalty of many of the new condominium residents in downtown Kirkland.

World-Class Northwest Smoked Salmon

Gerard & Dominique Seafoods' owner, Dominique Place, doesn't mince words. "I'm French. Good food makes me happy. And good salmon is like fine wine. The best has lots of flavor and a clean taste. You want to enjoy it now, not taste it for hours afterward." Anyone who's tasted really funky smoked fish knows what he's talking about.

Dominique and his former partner, Gerard Parrat (of Relais fame), are chefs who came up through the old-style, hierarchical French apprenticeship system, first in France and later in Seattle. Give the French credit: they are sticklers for quality. And the two chefs didn't like the smoked salmon they tasted here. At first they fooled around in their kitchens, jerry-rigging a homemade smoker and adjusting temperatures and spice mixtures and smoking times, till they came up with a product they were satisfied with.

About ten years ago, they decided to get serious and went commercial. They started off with three customers. Today, Gerard & Dominique sell their products in Japan, in Puerto Rico, and all over the United States. Their salmon is served in the first-class cabin by a major airline, and they sell to restaurant kitchens all over Seattle and beyond. And they've expanded the product line to include smoked trout, seafood sausage, oysters, scallops, mussels, and several kinds of chowders and soups. Gerard retired from the business, but his name lives on. Today, Dominique and his charming wife, Chouchou, are the forces behind this extremely successful high-end smoker of seafood.

The key to G & D's smoked salmon, and the reason they are considered by many to have the best smoked salmon in the country, is simple. They use only tagged no. 1 grade, troll-caught wild king salmon, as well as high-quality farm-raised whole fish caught and processed within a couple of hours. Troll-caught is preferred because the fish doesn't bruise and lose oil and moisture the way it would if it were flopping around in a net. The kings are perfect specimens, silver blue with nary a blemish—caught by Bruce Gore, a highly respected Alaskan fisherman who pioneered the flash-frozen-and-handled-with-kid-gloves salmon fishing business.

King salmon has the perfect fat content for hot smoking. The fish emerges from the smoker sweet and soft, but not as soft as some, with a mild flavor. "Like eating candy," says Dominique. For the lox-style cold-smoked fish, Dominique prefers coho. It's leaner and takes well to his process. A key difference in his style of smoking is that he doesn't use a brine. Instead, the fish is dry cured with a mixture of spices, salt, and sugar, then washed and slowly smoked over fruitwood. The result is silkiness and buttery richness that melts on the tongue.

The business of smoking fish is the result of a peculiar alchemy—part science, part art, part instinct, and part ferocious attention to detail. There is no lack of practitioners of the art of smoking here in the Northwest, but for world-class salmon, you need look no further than Gerard & Dominique.

Gerard & Dominique Seafoods

P.O. Box 1845, Bothell
Phone: (800)858-0449
Internet: www.gdseafoods.com

Smoked New Zealand Green-Lip Mussels
with Pesto Sauce
Gerard & Dominique Seafoods

Serves 4

Dominique suggests serving about 6 mussels per person, as an appetizer.

   1 cup bread crumbs

   1 to 2 ounces olive oil

   1 tablespoon chopped parsley

   1 to 2 cloves garlic (optional)

   1 tablespoon pesto

   Freshly ground black pepper to taste

   24 Gerard & Dominique smoked green-lip mussels

   2 tablespoons freshly grated Parmesan

In a small stainless steel bowl, combine bread crumbs and about 1 ounce of the olive oil. Stir till oil is absorbed. Add parsley, garlic, pesto, and pepper.

Place mussels on a baking sheet. Dab about a tablespoon or so of the mixture on top of each mussel. Sprinkle with a little Parmesan.

Broil 2 to 3 minutes. Watch them carefully so they don't dry out. Serve immediately.

meat and poultry

It is no secret that the art of the butcher has been going the way of the spotted owl in recent years. Without intensive, loving patronage, the old-fashioned butcher with his skilled cutting, knowledgeable advice, and superb service will be history in not too many years.

With most people buying their meat in supermarkets these days and Tyson putting a mediocre chicken in every pot, the dedicated carnivore must search carefully and insistently for quality ingredients. Luckily for us here in Seattle, there are a number of quality purveyors of meat and poultry: Ones who know where their meat is raised and butchered and can discuss the fine points of prime versus choice grade; who can offer us chickens that spent their lives roaming at liberty, scratching for their own secret morsels and free of antibiotics, rather than caged and drugged; who still take the time to dry-age their meats on the premises; and who know how to swiftly transform a hanging carcass of meat into neat, usable cuts. Good butchers will cut meat to order and freshly wrap every purchase so that it is not sitting in a pool of blood and liquid, tightly encased in plastic, like meat from the supermarket. Small differences maybe, but well worth the trouble and the slightly higher expense.

More and more chickens of various types are turning up in markets these days. Free-range and organic chickens are readily available, and there is no doubt in my mind as to their superiority. Free-range chickens have more flavor because it takes longer for them to grow to full size. They reach about three pounds in seven to eight weeks, while commercial chickens take only about five weeks. The added time allows their muscles to develop more fully, resulting in more flavor. Of course, you can find free-range chickens in most supermarkets these days, but a specialty market will still give you the best. They will usually cut poultry up for you if required, and their selection of birds can run the gamut from the diminutive poussin to the opulent turkey.

Meat, and especially beef, consumption in this country has been steadily dropping for years. But in a millennial twist, even though we are eating less of it, when we do, we are demanding the best quality. More than one butcher told me that his customers are coming back to him after eating supermarket meat because they want taste and are tired of watery, bland meat with the texture of fuzzy slippers.

A final menace to meat was pointed out long ago, in the eighteenth century, by English actor David Garrick when he wrote: "Heaven sends us good meat, but the Devil sends cooks." In other words, buy the best of the best, don't mess around with it too much, and you won't go wrong.

Meat and Poultry Labeling Terms

What does it mean when a bird is labeled free-range or natural? Does "natural" mean raised without hormones? There is a hodge-podge of labeling terms out there, making it difficult to be certain what you are getting. Here is the USDA's own glossary of meat labeling terms.

free-range: Producers must demonstrate to the USDA that the poultry has been allowed access to the outdoors.

halal and Zabiah halal: Must be handled according to Islamic law and under Islamic authority if prepared in federally inspected meat packing plants.

kosher: May be used only on the labels of meat and poultry products prepared under rabbinical supervision.

natural: Containing no artificial ingredients or added colors and only minimally processed (in a way that does not fundamentally alter the raw product). The label must explain the meaning of the term "natural" (i.e., "no added colorings or artificial ingredients," "minimally processed").

no antibiotics added (red meat and poultry): May be used on labels if sufficient documentation is provided to the USDA by the producer demonstrating that the animals were raised without antibiotics.

no hormones (pork or poultry): Hormones are not allowed in raising hogs or poultry. Therefore, the claim "no hormones added" cannot be used on the labels of pork or poultry unless it's followed by the statement "Federal regulations prohibit the use of hormones."

no hormones administered (beef): May be used on labels if sufficient documentation is provided to the USDA by the producer demonstrating that no hormones have been used in raising the animals.

organic: Has not yet been defined by the USDA. Until a definition is approved, the USDA is permitting certain meat and poultry products to be labeled "certified organic by [name of certifying entity]." The certifying entity must have standards that define what constitutes an "organically produced" product and a system for ensuring that products meet those standards.

CENTRAL SEATTLE

A & J Meats & Seafood

2401 Queen Anne Ave. N., Seattle
Phone: 206/284-3885
Hours: 10AM–7PM Tuesday–Friday; 9AM–6PM Saturday; 11AM–5PM Sunday; closed Monday

A & J is the gold standard for butcher shops in Seattle. It is at the top of the heap in terms of quality and service. Its prices can be stratospheric, though; if you have to ask how much a steak costs here, you probably can't afford it. Just know that you are getting the best. Rick Friar and his dad before him believe strongly that bending over backward to offer the best products and the best service has made their business the success that it is. Their suppliers have relationships with them stretching over fifty years, and they work hard to ensure that they get exactly what their customers demand.

Whole sides of free-range, certified hormone- and antibiotic-free, Charolais beef are dry-aged for a minimum of three to four weeks here, before being split and cut into gorgeous steaks and roasts, stewing cuts, and sausages. They make their own lamb, veal, pork, and chicken sausages and dress them in a thousand flavor combinations. They smoke their own meats and marinate a variety of meats ready for your barbecue. They sell only wild caught fresh fish and beautiful, golden-skinned free-range chickens. In short, they are friendly, knowledgeable, and willing to tell you more than you ever needed to know about the meat you buy.

Don and Joe's Meats

85 Pike St. (next to Pike Place Fish in the Market), Seattle
Phone: 206/682-7670
Hours: 9AM–6PM Monday–Saturday; closed Sunday

Don and Joe's carries a full line of top-quality, beautifully displayed, fresh meat. Their beef is grain-fed Washington grown, and they carry some prime as well as choice cuts. In fact, their display case goes way beyond the usual variety and regularly features items such as lamb's tongues, kidneys, sweetbreads (a euphemism for the pancreas or thymus gland of a lamb or calf), honeycomb tripe, and other offal cuts. Every once in a while I get a hankering for liver and onions, and the calf's liver here is choice: pale pink, creamy, and totally satisfying. No question, this is a guilty pleasure, but a genetic predisposition based on centuries of sitting down weekly to a plate of chopped liver at the Sabbath table does pop up once in a while. Don and Joe's have never disappointed me when I get that urge.

Venetian-Style Liver and Onions

The liver for this dish should be cut into bite-size strips, about ¼ inch wide and 2 inches long. Be careful not to crowd the pan when you sauté them, so they will retain their precious juices rather than steam and turn bitter and gray.

Serves 6

> *One ½-pound calf's liver, cut into slices no more than ¼ inch thick*
>
> *3 tablespoons vegetable oil*
>
> *3 cups onion, sliced very thin*
>
> *Salt and freshly ground pepper to taste*
>
> *2 tablespoons balsamic vinegar*

Remove any gristly, chewy tubes still on liver.

Choose your largest frying pan, preheat it on medium-high heat, and add oil and onion. Cook onion for about 20 minutes, reducing heat to medium-low as onions become limp and nut brown.

Remove onions from frying pan, leaving whatever oil and juices remain in pan. Increase heat to high. When oil is very hot, add half the liver slices, or as many as will fit without crowding pan. Stir-fry rapidly, till liver just loses its raw color, and sprinkle with salt and pepper. Repeat until all slices are cooked, then return all slices to pan.

Quickly return onion to pan. Turn onion and liver once or twice. Drizzle balsamic vinegar on liver, then transfer entire contents of pan to serving platter and serve at once.

Crystal Meats

94 Pike St. (behind Quality Cheese in Pike Place Market), Seattle
Phone: 206/622-5499
Hours: 9AM–6PM Monday–Saturday; closed Sunday

In the old days, there were as many as fourteen butcher shops in Pike Place Market and surrounding area. Nowadays, all that's left are Don and Joe's and Crystal Meats, the latter in operation since 1947. Crystal understands its clientele, some of whom are third-generation customers. They come, some every day, because they can get cuts here that they can't get anywhere else. Brontosaurus-sized cuts of chuck roasts or quarter pounds of ground meat—both requests are given equal attention. And prices are low, perhaps reflecting the more working-class nature of the clientele. Whatever the reason, this is an honest, no-pretensions market selling value and service.

Market House Meats

1124 Howell St., Seattle
Phone: 206/624-9248
Hours: 8:30AM–4:30PM Monday–Friday; closed Saturday and Sunday

When asked to explain the secret of his success, Jack Akrish, the owner of this bare-bones market a block off the freeway, sums it up succinctly: "Our brine is the best in the world." Unlike large-scale commercial processors that use a vacuum tumbler to fast-cure brisket into corned beef, Market House uses top choice brisket that's hung and then barrel cured for a minimum of ten days. The brine is sweet smelling, perfumed with a mixture of peppercorns, coriander, ginger, and other spices, and it is out of this world. (They also pickle tongue in the same way, but I can't say I've had a hankering to try it.) There's not much else to this funky shop, except a row of jars of pickles and sauerkraut sitting on an empty refrigerated case. You can also buy the corned beef at Queen Anne Thriftway and the Butcher Shoppe in Ballard.

Vacuum Packaging and Aging

One of the biggest differences between butcher shops of yore and the majority today is the way they receive their meat. While nowadays most meat comes to the butcher already sectioned and hermetically sealed in polyethylene vacuum packs, long ago it came in great big hanging sides, to be aged and then split into retail cuts. There are markets here in Seattle that still know how to split carcasses, and they are well worth seeking out, if for no other reason than that they will have a far greater variety of cuts.

The meat industry favors the vacuum-packed "box cuts" for several reasons. It doesn't require as much skill and expertise to cut often boneless hunks of meat. It is also a lot easier and requires less education to sell certain cuts, usually the higher-end and higher-profit roasts and steaks that come in vacuum packs. But there is some controversy as to whether vacuum packaging will allow meat to age. The meat industry, for the most part, prefers to age in vacuum packs because less shrinkage occurs and because the so-called aging can conveniently take place as the meat is shipped across the country. For connoisseurs of true dry-aged beef, though, nothing but beef hung upside down till it has lost about 25 percent of its weight, developed almost a coat of mold (which is then cut off), and deepened its flavor and tenderness will do.

NORTH

The Butcher Shoppe

1918 NW 65th St., Seattle
Phone: 206/783-0454
Hours: 10AM–6PM Tuesday–Friday; 9AM–6PM Saturday; closed Sunday and Monday

The Butcher Shoppe is the quintessential neighborhood butcher selling high-quality meat at a fair price. This, of course, is no small claim today. Owner Steve Halbakken is as solid as a half a side of beef, and he's got a warm welcome for every one of his customers. Sadly, he says, young couples don't cook anymore, so he tries to make it easy on them. That means lots of helpful advice and, for those who can't handle even that, all sorts of basic comfort foods already prepared and ready to pop into the oven. The Butcher Shoppe deals in hanging sides of grain-fed Angus and Hereford beef, some of which is dry-aged, and they augment this with some boxed meats. Lamb is reared locally. There is an in-house sausage-making business, Seattle Sausage Co.

CasCioppo Brothers Italian Meat Market

2364 NW 80th St., Seattle
Phone: 206/784-6121
Hours: 9:30AM–6:30PM Monday–Saturday; 9:30AM–5:30PM Sunday.

So I was in New York the other day, in Katz's Deli for a pastrami sandwich. What I really wished for, I whined to whoever would listen, was a real sandwich, a Katz's kind of sandwich, steamed, thinly sliced meat stacked high on rye bread, slathered with spicy mustard, a half-sour pickle on the side—in Seattle. "Seattle? *Fuhgedaboutit!!!*" was the chorus. Well, let me tell you. It's here . . . and it's good, darn good. CasCioppo Brothers built their name on Italian sausages— honest-to-God, juicy, garlic-laden noblewursts. They're still there in the meat case, along with steaks (dry-aged on the premises), cheeses, and Boar's Head deli meats. But the pastrami sandwich is king here— rich and warm and tender, slightly salty but also slightly sweet, with just enough fat clinging to the meat to keep it juicy. Oh yeah, the guy who stocks their wine case (I know . . . wine is an oxymoron in an authentic New York deli) is Gus Froyd and he's been in the business forever and he really knows his stuff. Everything in the wine section has been hand selected.

Straight Talk from an Expert

Bruce Aidells is known as the Sausage King. He's also an authority on meat, with several books to his credit, and is a chef who knows lots about taste. Taste, of course, is entirely subjective and is affected by a whole range of variables: the animal's breed, its food, and how it arrived at market. In the case of beef, whether it was dry-aged or wet-packed is crucial. To Bruce's mind, beef develops an intense mellow flavor with dry aging, whereas wet-aged meat sits in its own blood and develops a funky flavor with a watery rather than a juicy taste. Finally, cooking time is really important. Overcooking, particularly with the leaner beef bred today, can dry out a fine piece of meat.

The beef industry hasn't been as effective in educating customers about lesser cuts, the homely second-quality meats that require patient braising to bring out their succulent flavor. Markets almost exclusively use polyethylene vacuum-packed "box cuts" featuring tidy boneless steaks and roasts because that is what the customer wants. With less choice, it's almost impossible to find bone-in chuck roast in meat markets these days, for example. And good cooks know that the bone is what contributes flavor and unctuousness to a stew. Statistics from the National Beef Association show that 50 percent of all usable parts of the cow are processed into ground beef, an acknowledgment of the reality that time and traditional knowledge are the real luxuries these days.

One bright spot, in his view, is that the small, independent butcher shop today is in a better position than it has been for a long time. As the big supermarkets consolidate, there is less and less choice for the consumer: fewer butchers at the supermarket counters having less knowledge, and fewer neighborhood butchers around to answer any questions. This is where the endangered neighborhood butcher, if he can distinguish himself with better service and quality, has a future. The best butchers are able to use clever marketing and work continuously to educate and inform their customers by offering tastes, giving information and recipes, and taking the time to explain why things are the way they are.

Continental Spices & Halal Meat . . . .

see Indian and Pakistani

Fremont Fresh Market

3601 Fremont N., Seattle
Phone: 206/ 633-3663
Hours: 7AM–midnight every day

This small independently owned market is a full-fledged, mini-super-market. It offers some of everything: produce, packaged goods, a fine deli, and an excellent wine department. But best of all, it offers Morrey Eskenazi. Morrey, who was previously found under a revolving cow on the roof of his butcher shop in White Center, closed shop and tried retirement in 1999. He lasted a few short months. This is a guy who lives in kibitzing with his customers, who doesn't feel happy unless he's got a butcher knife in one hand and a sample of something to offer in the other. When owner Ross Angeledes of Fremont Fresh invited Morrey to come out of his self-imposed retirement and pre-side over the market's butcher case, he didn't need to ask twice.

Morrey's specialty is the highest quality meat, impeccably trimmed and handed over to his customers with real devotion. "I love what I do. Everyone who comes through is my friend," he says. The meat itself is immaculate, with nary an excess bit of fat or gristle. As he puts it, "What do they think? People aren't going to notice if they get home and find lousy meat on the underside of the package?" No fear here. The other proof of Morrey's genius is his smoked meats. He makes an awe-inspiring Chinese barbecued pork loin so good that it will make you reconsider ever setting foot in an authentic Chinese barbecue joint again. Everything he smokes (except the pork—by law) is nitrite free, and is lightly if at all salted. This way, the pure flavor, overlaid with just a hint of alder smoke, comes through. Try the beef jerky. It's so thick and succulent you might as well be eating a fresh-cooked slab of steak.

Where's the Organic Beef?

In my roaming around, I continually asked whether markets sold local, organically raised, hormone- and antibiotic-free meat. The answers were always "no" closely followed by "too expensive" and "not enough of a market." Why aren't there any sources for local, organic beef, especially since consumers have clearly shown that there is a market for organic products?

I got some answers when I talked to a Lopez Island farmer by the name of Henning Sehmsdorf. Henning farms about fifty acres of land and about twenty-five head of cattle on the island. He is involved in Community Supported Agriculture (CSA) programs, and raises his beef and pork on a grass-fed diet that is certifiably organic. Until recently, though, he was not allowed to certify his meat as organic. Instead, he could call it "natural," "pasture-raised," "hormone-free," "antibiotic-free," "humanely raised," or "environmentally raised."

The USDA now allows meat to be labeled as certified organic, but as a small farmer, Henning has had to deal with other road-blocks. When it comes time to slaughter the animals, he arranges for an off-island custom butcher under state authority to come into his field, kill the animals, and then take them off-island to be cut, wrapped, and frozen before selling them directly to individuals. Henning can't sell to a retail market because he can't label his meat "USDA-inspected." And he can't get USDA-inspected because he can't get a USDA-certified processor to inspect his meat. He's too small—just like virtually every organic beef farmer that I talked to. But he's working to change that, at least in the San Juans. In a farmer-driven project that should be up and running in the next year, a mobile USDA meat processing facility will come directly to small-scale farmers throughout the San Juans, making it possible to purchase locally grown organic beef in retail shops.

Henning points out that while it is possible to buy free-range beef, it is usually prohibitively expensive and aimed at the luxury market. What he is producing is whole carcasses (including less desirable cuts) that will be marketed at a reasonable cost. His project is a model being watched carefully by small-scale farmers throughout Washington.

Seattle Exotic Meats

17532 Aurora Ave. N, Seattle
Phone: 206/546-4922
Hours: 10AM–6PM Monday–Saturday; noon–4PM Sunday
Internet: www.exoticmeats.com

This is definitely a niche market. It appeals to people who are interested in the novelty factor; without question, the options here challenge the most imaginative palate. It also draws people who have health concerns. All the meats inside Seattle Exotic Meats are farm raised, fresh frozen, and certified to contain no chemicals or growth hormones. Choose from buffalo, ostrich, and wild boar. Alligator, snapping turtle, and rattlesnake might also hit the spot—or venison medallions from New Zealand, kangaroo steaks, and antelope. If you're the kind of shopper who was hoping for a visceral experience of wading through blood and guts and great big fleshy hunks of meat, this might not be the best spot, though. It's a rather sterile-looking place, with everything neatly cut and vacuum packed in freezer cases.

University Seafood & Poultry . . . . see Fish

SOUTH

Bob's Quality Meats
4861 Rainier Ave. S., Seattle
Phone: 206/ 725-1221
Hours: 10AM–7PM Monday–Friday; 9AM–5PM Saturday; 11AM–4PM Sunday

James Ackley and his son, Abraham, bought their family business in 1998 knowing that a full-service butcher shop in this dizzying era of Internet shopping and humongo-retailers is akin to the old-fashioned milk delivery truck. Still, they reasoned, their loyal customers have been shopping with them since James's dad first opened his place in West Seattle in 1963, later moving to Columbia City in 1979. And the family has done business with the same farmer who raises their beef outside of Yakima since Grandpa Ackley's days. Of course, to meet the demands of a changing neighborhood, they now sell an Ethiopian scrub-pastured beef called *siga*. They also make fabulous link sausages, paying special attention to the flavor preferences of their largely Southern constituency. Creole-style white *boudin* with allspice, parsley, pork, and rice, or Texas red-hot pork links, with cilantro, onion, and a mess of peppers (including chipotle), are just two of the flavors that have met with favor. The spices are mixed from scratch so you can ask them to add a little extra sage or hold the chili peppers, as you wish. They dry-cure their own excellent ham and bacon here so that you can taste real meat and not watery, insipid flesh.

Wagyu Beef Explained

Imagine the richest, most sinful cut of meat in town—one that is so well marbled that it is almost white and, when cooked, slides ever so luxuriantly down your throat. There is such a phenomenon, and it is known as Kobe beef, from the *wagyu* breed of cattle in Japan. Kobe cattle are pampered beyond belief, gratified with hand massages and daily beer rations. Balducci's, in New York, sells the meat for an incredible $125 per pound. In Japan the prices are even higher, and Japanese gourmets say it is well worth it.

Wagyu beef has always been an expensive curiosity in this country—till now. Washington State University has a pilot project to breed, raise, and export it back to Japan. The herd has been growing for some time, without the massage and the beer, and the beef is now available in retail markets here in the Pacific Northwest. I was intrigued when I saw it for sale at Uwajimaya, and since the price was comparable to that of other steak cuts, I snapped it up and rushed home to experiment.

The wagyu cows at the WSU farm are well looked after, no doubt. Theirs is not the same four-star existence as their Japanese compatriots, though. For one, they roam their pasture, unlike Kobe cows, which do little more than stand and be cosseted. The result is a meat that is well marbled but doesn't come close to the Kobe version, sort of like the difference between a World Wrestling Federation champ and a sumo wrestler. WSU's meat was nicely marbled and flavorful, but according to my Japanese friends it doesn't bear much resemblance to real wagyu. Still, for those who are interested, Uwajimaya sells "Japanese-style" wagyu beef in a variety of cuts at prices ranging from $5 to $15 per pound.

Mondo's Meats

4225 Rainier Ave. S, Seattle
Phone: 206/725-1565
Hours: 8AM–4:30PM Monday–Friday; closed Saturday and Sunday

The name brings to mind the big hapless brute from the old Mel Brooks movie *Blazing Saddles*, and the place itself doesn't have a lot of what you'd call atmosphere. In fact, its utilitarian setting might make you feel as if you're shopping inside a refrigerator. Mondo's Meats is principally a wholesaler that opens its doors to the public. But don't let that stop you. What I tasted would fit right into A & J

Meats' case, with one important exception: it's a lot cheaper. I paid half of what I would have at A & J for some beautiful tenderloin that was as good, if not better, than A & J' s wares.

Lew Banchero and his son are working a family business that began in the early '30s. What they're selling is grain-fed Texas long-horn beef that's free-range and certified antibiotic/hormone-free, hung and aged on the premises, and cut to order. Longhorn beef is a leaner product, touted as a more "heart-healthy" choice, significantly lower in calories and cholesterol than regular beef. No display cases here, but call ahead and they will have anything you want. They also make Mario's Italian sausages; I would have tasted them but my sons got to them first, so I guess that means they were good. Plans are to open a proper retail shop next door in the near future.

EASTSIDE

Fischer Meats

85 Front St., Issaquah
Phone: 425/392-3131
Hours: 8AM–6PM Monday–Saturday; 10AM–6PM Sunday

Another longtime Eastside butcher shop, Fischer first opened its doors in 1910. Its present owner, Chris Chiechi, took over from John Fischer about ten years ago. The great thing about this market is that they have everything. Since they hang and split their own sides of beef, they will custom-cut anything you want to ensure freshness. My family is partial to a cut of beef called hangar steak that is just not available at most butcher shops. It's a deeply flavorful, somewhat tough cut, intensely bloody and almost liver-flavored, that makes perfect steak frites. This is one of the few shops in town that can get it (at very reasonable prices). They also make their own corned beef, sausages, beef and turkey jerky, and delectable, spicy pepperoni that didn't make it out of the car on the ride back home.

Golden Steer Choice Meats

15255 NE Bel–Red Rd., Bellevue
Phone: 425/746-1910
Hours: 9AM–6PM Monday–Friday; 8:30AM–5:30PM Saturday;
10AM–4PM Sunday

Al and Norma Dick have been owners of this business since 1968. Their son John, who also works in the shop, wanted to be sure I knew how proud of them he is. Norma makes all the sauces and dressings they use, and Al is the guy behind the counter providing great customer service. In fact, many of their customers are the third generation of a family doing their meat purchasing here. The coarse, garlicky, wine-flavored sausage was excellent; the breakfast links cooked up succulent and meaty (no fillers used here). They also sell a host of Bavarian Meat products. Only the tenderloin disappointed me a little, having a funky, somewhat mushy texture.

Carniceria Zacatecas . . . . see Latino

prepared food and deli items

I am a person who hates to eat take-out food (except for Chinese out of a box). I figure if I'm going to pay someone to prepare my food, I'd like them to also serve it to me and do the dishes afterward. But the truth of the matter is that I buy prepared food to go all the time. Sometimes it's a time issue. Often it's because someone does something a lot better than I could ever do, and I don't mind paying for the labor involved. So when I buy gourmet take-out, I'd like it to be as good as great restaurant food. And while gourmet take-out is expensive (though not as expensive as eating in a restaurant), I want to feel that I'm getting good value.

Seattle is not an exceptional take-out town. Sure, we have Pasta & Co., which has set the standard for close to twenty years and is a first-rate resource for many a harried or inexperienced cook. And scattered throughout town are a handful of good-quality shops with a singular point of view. But for a metropolitan area of this size, we have precious few idiosyncratic shops specializing solely in take-out and bearing the unique stamp of an owner's perspective.

Take-out food is a huge category. Virtually every restaurant in town sells their food packaged to go as a sideline of their business, although it may or may not be a significant portion of their overall sales. Then there are the superstores—Larry's, Whole Foods Market, PCC, Thriftway—which offer extensive selections of prepared food, big catering departments, and all manner of help in putting together a meal. Both of these kinds of businesses fall outside the scope of this chapter, which focuses on a third kind: the small take-out shops or delis that specialize in preparing food, whether individual portions or party platters, for eating at home or at the office. Because they are often small and independently owned, they consistently offer unique food and specialized service. These are the businesses that I love to patronize.

Take-out food often looks a lot better than it tastes. The truism that you eat with your eyes is obviously a mantra that all take-out shop owners must fall asleep reciting every night. Beautiful oversized platters, tantalizing garnishes, and mouthwatering descriptions make it easy to buy more than you intend. That's okay—just be sure to ask for a taste before you buy. And make sure you get instructions on how best to reheat the food. I love what Pasta & Co. does with their shopping bags: clearly printed on each and every one are idiot-proof directions for reheating the food. Finally, it goes without saying that you expect the food you buy to have been freshly prepared that day. There is no excuse for buying food that has sat in a refrigerated case or under a heat lamp for too long.

CENTRAL

Cucina Fresca
1904 Pike Pl. (in Pike Place Market), Seattle
Phone: 206/448-4758
Hours: 9:30AM–6PM every day

A lot of prepared foods look great but fall flat when it comes to taste. When I want a casual take-out dinner that looks gorgeous *and* tastes as good it looks, I head to this stylish shop in Pike Place Market. Its owners, Jessica and Jay Beattie, are fervent about food. In fact, Jessica is about the most exuberant proselytizer for the Market and the touchy-feely/know-your-purveyor school of food shopping I have encountered. "Shopping here appeals to those people who want the whole experience. They want to be able to see their food, smell it, hear it being made. They want to have a relationship with their purveyor," she rhapsodizes.

And they do. Virtually everything sold here is prepared in front of customers in the recently remodeled kitchen. The staff is friendly

Pasta & Co. sets the standard for fresh pasta.

and quickly gets to know their regulars' favorites. The emphasis is on Mediterranean-inspired food, pasta, roasted meats, lovely salads and side dishes, focaccias, desserts, and a few of Jessica and Jay's favorite condiments.

As I spoke with Jessica, she was transported by memories of pasta shops she'd visited in Italy. "I'd love to be able to produce artisan pasta here, ultra-thin sheets hand-rolled and hand-cut, maybe with fresh herbs or flowers layered in the dough. I'd send it home wrapped simply in a white envelope with a blue sticker, like they do in a certain shop in Rapallo, in Liguria. So beautiful," she sighs. The ravioli she does make are resilient little envelopes that, while more prosaically packaged in freezer bags to feed two, are very tasty indeed. Mix-and-match fillings and sauces, with standouts such as the snappy Gorgonzola walnut ravioli, or the more subtle wild mushroom-stuffed version, or the heavenly asparagus-filled ravioli, are available seasonally.

Grilled and Pickled Fennel
Cucina Fresca

This recipe is an excellent addition to any antipasti assortment. It also makes a wonderful summer side dish with grilled meat.

Serves 6
   6 fennel bulbs
   Olive oil
   4 cups water
   2 cups white wine vinegar
   ½ cup sugar
   1½ teaspoons salt
   2 teaspoons pickling spice
   8 garlic cloves, halved

Preheat grill to medium high.

Trim stalks of fennel till only bulbs are left. Remove outermost layer of bulbs if they seem too discolored or tough. Wash bulbs and pat dry.

Slice bulbs in ¼-inch pieces. Lightly toss with olive oil and grill. You need only grill one side, but be sure it is well marked.

Bring water, vinegar, sugar, salt, pickling spice, and garlic to boil in a stainless steel pot. Add fennel pieces and bring back to the boil. Boil for additional 2 minutes. Put in a large, shallow pan to cool.

Refrigerate and allow to "pickle" for at least 24 hours.

DeLaurenti. . . . . see Mediterranean

King's Barbecue. . . . . see Asian

Pasta & Co.
2109 Queen Anne Ave. N, Seattle
Phone: 206/283-1182
Hours: 10AM–8:30PM every day

815 E Pike St., Seattle
Phone: 206/322-4577
Hours: 7:30AM–7:30PM Monday–Saturday; 7:30AM–7PM Sunday

2640 NE University Village, Seattle
Phone: 206/523-8594
Hours: 9:30AM–9PM Monday–Saturday; 9:30AM–6PM Sunday

10218 NE 8th St., Bellevue
Phone: 425/453-8760
Hours: 9AM–7:30PM Monday–Friday; 9AM–6PM Saturday; 9:30AM–6PM Sunday

When Marcella Rosene opened Pasta & Co. in 1981, she single-handedly elevated fresh pasta and ravioli from out-of-reach-to-all-but-a-few-ethnics-or-obsessives to the realm of the everyday in Seattle. Her superb pasta and take-out food, along with her three cookbooks, have made her an icon of food retailers in the Pacific Northwest. Marcella recently sold majority ownership of the business to a venture capitalist, but intends to stay on as spokeswoman, food consultant, and resident guru.

. . . and something sweet from Pasta & Co.

These days many markets prepare the same dishes as Pasta & Co., but few can claim to be as reliable and have such consistently great recipes. The shops have a three-pronged approach to their business. They teach their customers how to cook, with classes, newsletters, and the finest ingredients for cooking from scratch. Or they send them home with ready-to-heat meals that require nothing more than boiling water or programming a microwave. Or they teach them to fake it. Let's be honest—more than one customer (including yours truly) has shamelessly hidden the telltale boxes and sprinkled on a bit of this and a dash of that to put together a "home-cooked" meal for guests.

Personally, I think fresh pasta can be overrated because too often it ends up as a mushy, waterlogged mess. Not so at Pasta & Co. The fresh and frozen pastas and sauces are the linchpins of the business for good reason. They're flavorful and well textured, and they hold up to the shops' hearty sauces. The ravioli are uniformly superb and, best of all, generously stuffed with their fillings. And the aforementioned sauces are assertively seasoned, without the nasty, acrid, dried herb flavor and unbalanced sweetness predominant in so many store-bought sauces. Try the Moroccan, which adds chunks of eggplant and spices to the basic marinara.

The other useful dish at Pasta & Co. is roast chicken. The skin isn't as crispy as I'd like, but the meat is tasty and juicy, redolent of spices and garlic. One of these little puppies can supply at least a couple of nights' worth of food for my family.

Mama Lil's—The Best Peppers You're Likely to Taste

Back in the days when Howard Lev was a screenwriter, he started including a jar of his pickled peppers with all his submissions. Invariably, the response would be something like "Good script, but I really loved those peppers." As is the lot of many a writer, he also drove a cab on weekends to make ends meet. Picking up customers coming out of restaurants, he'd offer them a taste of his peppers. After selling quite a few jars out of the back of his cab, it dawned on him that he had a golden goose in those peppers. That's when Mama Lil's Pickled Peppers were born.

Howard's mom always put up peppers back home in Youngstown, Ohio. Even after he moved to Seattle to go to school,

Mama Lil's boy—Howard Lev.

she'd send him care packages of her pickles. While visiting the Yakima Valley one day, he stopped off at Kruger Pepper Farms, a U-pick farm for tomatoes, peppers, and grapes. To his everlasting joy, he tasted those same Ohio peppers, aka Hungarian goathorns. Only here, they were much better—gloriously red-ripe and perfectly balanced between sweet and hot. The conditions in Yakima, it turns out, are perfect for these peppers: hot days and cool nights. (In Ohio, in contrast, because of the heat, by the time the peppers start to redden they have turned soft, so invariably they are picked green and don't have the crispness, elusive warmth, and gorgeous rosy color of the Yakima ones.)

Later, back East and wandering through Amish country, he tasted a batch of pickled peppers at a roadside stand. After wheedling the recipe out of the Amish farmwife, he couldn't believe the amount of sugar in it, so he started fooling around till he developed his own version. The key difference is his labor-intensive process of first hand-cutting and pickling the peppers for twenty-four hours, then draining them thoroughly dry, before roasting them in a mixture of canola and olive oil.

You get a twofer with these peppers. First, the peppers themselves are silky and butter-soft, with an unmistakable heat that blooms in your mouth. In addition, the spicy oil is useful in and of itself. You can dispense with any other flavored oils in your pantry; the oil from Mama Lil's peppers is as deeply flavored and gutsy as you'll ever need. Use it as a bread dip, a salad dressing, or a marinade, or add it to anything that could benefit from a spoonful of punchy flavor.

The best thing about these peppers is that they just don't taste like a commercial product. They do indeed taste like they've been made by Howard's mom (or my own). Howard also makes a variation of his grandma's mustard pickles, Mama Lil's Peppalilli. Matt's in the Market, a seafood bar tucked away in Pike Place Market, uses it as a condiment for their wasabi-hot tuna sandwich. Smart folks would use it on sandwiches of all persuasions. Also recently introduced are Hot Peppas in sweet brine, which are simultaneously sweet (with maple syrup), mildly spicy, garlicky, and mouthwateringly good.

Howard is refreshingly candid about his business. He says it's disheartening that his products haven't been picked up by any huge accounts. After all, he's selling a locally grown, handmade artisan product that has won awards at the Fancy Food Show, a national gathering for the specialty foods industry, and garnered a lot of raves from anyone who's ever tasted it. As he puts it, "No one else is foolish enough to do what it takes to get [the peppers to market]. During production season, I'm sorry to say, I've lost good friends. I get pretty crazy." During the rest of the year, you can meet Howard at the Redmond Saturday Market, find his peppers at area supermarkets and fancy food shops, or mail-order them directly from him.

Mama Lil's Fine Condiments

Phone: (206)322-8824
Fax: (206)726-8372
E-mail: mamalils@zipcon.net

Mama Lil's Peppers and Pasta

Serves 3 to 4

> *3 ripe tomatoes*
> *1 small red onion, quartered and thinly sliced crosswise*
> *2 garlic cloves, minced*
> *Handful of fresh basil leaves, torn into bits*
> *½ cup Mama Lil's peppers, including oil*
> *2 zucchini, sliced ¼ inch thick, brushed with olive oil and broiled or grilled*
> *2 ounces mild goat cheese*
> *Salt and freshly ground pepper*
> *12 ounces fusilli or penne*
> *Dash balsamic vinegar*

Dice tomatoes and place in large bowl, along with onion, garlic, basil, and peppers. Slice zucchini into finger-size widths and add to tomato mixture. Crumble in goat cheese.

Bring a large pot of water to boil. Add salt to water and cook pasta until al dente. Drain pasta, add to vegetables, and toss well. Add salt to taste, season with lots of pepper, and add a splash of balsamic vinegar. Serve immediately.

Note: Meat eaters can include a few slices of soppressata salami, cut in the same shape as the zucchini.

Lucky Palate

307 W McGraw St., Seattle
Phone: 206/352-2583
Internet: www.luckypalate.com

Sometimes even putting your shoes on and dragging your sorry, beat-up body out the door to pick up a to-go meal is too much. That's when Lucky Palate's home delivery meal service starts to sound good. If you're interested in earnestly healthy, completely vegetarian and almost vegan food, it'll sound even better. For me, though, the bottom line always comes down to one question: What does the food taste like?

Normally, cooking that involves a long list of don'ts and thou shalts doesn't appeal to me. But I tried a package of Lucky Palate's chile and cheese tamales, served with ancho chile salsa, and darn if it wasn't delicious. Warm and earthy with fresh corn, along with masa, cheese, and mild green chiles, it was a no-brainer meal that perfectly hit the spot.

Intrigued, I examined the menu for the week: Cuban bean and veggie stew, veggies with marinara sauce, miso-tamarind dal, gazpacho, spinach-poppyseed pasta salad, curried chickpeas and potatoes. This is food that spans the globe with an ever-changing interplay of flavorings such as citrus, herbs, chiles, and spices. If you absolutely can't face cooking on a regular basis but are committed to eating healthy, then this service might work for you. Sign up for delivery by Thursday of the prior week for delivery of all your week's meals on the next Tuesday. Prices are reasonable and quality is generally high. My only quibble was with the verbena-flavored lemonade—it was nasty and tasted medicinal.

Note: Lucky Palate sells their tamales at the Columbia City Farmers Market.

Pecos Pit BBQ

2260 First Ave. S, Seattle
Phone: 206/623-0629
Hours: 11AM–3PM Monday–Friday; closed Saturday and Sunday

Debra and Ronald Wise are two of the most modest cooks in Seattle. They're born-again Christians who waited and prayed for two years before opening, unsure of what the Lord had in store for them, knowing only that they wanted to work together. Ronald grew up deep in barbecue country, in Pecos, Texas, so he knew a thing or two about smoky pig parts. They decided to do what he knew best and what didn't seem available in Seattle: Texas-style barbecue.

For the last twenty years, their funky take-out spot nestled alongside First Avenue has drawn customers like an open soda bottle draws bees on a Texas summer day. It's a varied crowd—truckers, dot-commers, suburbanites, and carpenters. And it's the smoky brisket, not the décor, that draws them in. This is classic Texas barbecue, smoldered slowly over wood for twelve to fifteen hours. The true secret is in the smoke that comes from the meat juices dripping onto the wood. As Debra says, "You have to cook it forever and slow.

Brisket is lean with no gristle or fat, so if you don't cook it right, you'll end up with a pretty cut of meat that's as tough as a saddle."

Texans like beef as much as pork for barbecue, and Pecos obliges with both. And it dishes out the rarest of rarities for a barbecue joint—baked beans that are actually good. It's all served with an unusually sophisticated sauce, not too sweet and available mild, medium, or hot. Believe them when they say hot—its zing *will* set you on fire. Order sandwiches to go, or call twenty-four hours ahead and order a few pounds of unsliced meat and sauce to take home. You and your guests will bow your heads in prayer just as the Wises always do before tucking in, thankful for the substantial pile of meat on your plate.

Piroshky Piroshky

1908 Pike Pl. (in Pike Place Market), Seattle
Phone: 206/441-6068
Hours: 8:30AM–6PM Monday–Friday; 8AM–6:30PM Saturday and Sunday

Oliver Kotelnikov claims to be the first (and the best) to bring piroshky to Seattleites' hearts and appetite. Peek your head in the window, or wedge yourself into the shoebox-sized shop to see what he's talking about. His able staff rolls and stuffs dozens of these hefty Russian turnovers, which are stuffed with the contents of a traditional Slavic larder and swaddled in a moist yeast dough or flaky puff pastry. Grab a classic cabbage or potato or mushroom, or go luxe with smoked salmon pâté. Vadim, the baker, insisted that I try his favorite, the cherry and cheese rolls. Studded with cherries and oozing with cheese and cherry juice, these reminded me of nothing so much as tender, yeasty, delectable blintzes. For a classic Seattle experience, do as many do: grab a couple of piroshky and head to Victor Steinbrueck Park for an al fresco lunch.

R & L Home of Good Bar-B-Que

1816 E Yesler Way, Seattle
Phone: 206/322-0271
Hours: 11AM–9PM Tuesday–Saturday; closed Sunday and Monday

The meat coming out of Mary Collin Davis's kitchen is barbecue at its truest. Big, meaty alder-smoked ribs, tender brisket, and hot links appeal to true barbecue folk who want to taste the meat, not the sauce. You can smell the delicious aromas a block away. After the tender, smoky meat emerges from the oven, it's doused in plenty of tangy, natural-tasting barbecue sauce. Choose from three degrees of fire, and have your meat wrapped to go, either as sandwiches piled on soft white supermarket bread for sopping up all the juices, or in dinner platters, or by the pound to reheat in a low oven. On weekends, Mary puts up a mean pot of greens, and her peach cobbler and sweet potato pie aren't half bad either. While you're waiting, get a chuckle out of the attitudinal signs pinned around the restaurant.

Saigon Deli . . . . see Asian

Salumi. . . . . see Mediterranean

Turkish Delight
1930 Pike Pl. (in Pike Place Market), Seattle
Phone: 206/443-1387
Hours: 11AM–5PM every day; in summer, 10AM–7PM every day

Owner Semra Yavuz says the secret to her incredibly crispy and delicious baklava is that she puts in two layers of nuts and uses a light hand with the butter for a greaseless and chewy sensation. She and her husband Ahmet regularly bake at least four kinds of baklava and cigar-shaped *surina*, including pistachio, almond, walnut, or pecan-almond. Trolling around her refrigerated case, you might discover borek with that same flaky phyllo dough, or whole wheat pastry crust *talas* stuffed with chicken or veggies. It's not a bad idea to make a meal of these, along with one or two salads. The salads are entirely satisfying, many based on roasted veggies, cracked wheat, or yogurt and loads of garlic.

Doner kebab, a standard at any Middle Eastern take-out stand, can range from cheap-eats heartburn special to earthy opulence. The version here is uncommonly good. Turkish Delight doesn't use a premarinated commercial meat mixture for the doner; instead, they rub the meat with a secret blend of spices and garlic before hand-shaping it around a giant skewer and slow roasting it. Look for *lokum*, or Turkish delight, made by the Yavuzes' friend Huseyin Bayazit (see Chocolates, Candies, Nuts, and Ice Cream).

According to Semra, the best part of her job is the friends and "family" she's made at Pike Place Market. While she misses her hometown of Bosphorus, Turkey, she says, "I love being here. It makes me feel like I'm home. It would be very hard to think of anything bad to say about my life at the Market."

NORTH

CasCioppo Brothers............see Meat and Poultry

Scandinavian Specialty Products .... see Scandinavian

SOUTH

Salumeria on Hudson..............see Mediterranean

EASTSIDE

The British Pantry
8125 161st Ave. NE
Redmond
Phone: 425/883-7511
Hours: 10AM–5PM Sunday–Tuesday; 10AM–9PM Wednesday–Saturday; closed Monday

British food has gotten a bad rap in this country. Unjustifiably so, says Mavis Redman, the owner of British Pantry, a bakery, grocery, and gift shop in the heart of Redmond's commercial strip. Before I encountered the British Pantry's meat pies and pasties, even I, married to an Englishman, also regarded most British food as stodgy swill with all the appeal of nursery food. But her meat pies have caused me to reconsider. These pies are packed dense with meat and gravy and have a satisfying richness (but not fattiness) that can come

The Union Jack stands proud at The British Pantry.

only from long hours of cooking. The pastry crusts are all made the traditional way, with lard (gasp), so they're exceptionally flaky yet still have substance. Your cardiologist might wring his hands, but then again, give him a pork pie and he too might be hanging out in Mavis's shop. The pies and pasties come in various shapes, some in the traditional chimneypot form, some in enormous crescents or rolls, and each a hefty single serving. Take a few home with some pints of stout and you might just rethink your opinion of the Brits' claim to gastronomic fame. I also recommend the sweet pastries, especially the mince pies and Eccles cakes.

Note: There's a great selection of English sweets—with such classics as sherbet fountains, walnut whips, and Cadbury 99s, which all English schoolchildren will instantly recognize—as well as other foodstuff and gift items and an eatery, Neville's Restaurant at the British Pantry.

Another note: My husband was extremely disappointed that this review did not go on to extol the wonders of British cuisine as a whole, but alas, meat pies and puddings do not a great cuisine make.

3 Pigs BBQ

1044 116th Ave. NE, Bellevue
Phone: 425/453-0888
Hours: 11AM–8PM Monday–Saturday; closed Sunday

What is barbecue? That depends where you come from. Because we don't have a tradition of barbecue, in Seattle expectations aren't so ingrained that only one style counts. But in the South, barbecue connects people deeply and immediately to their homes and their past. Whether you grew up in Memphis, Kansas City, or Texas totally defines your taste in that hallmark of soul food.

Here at 3 Pigs, brothers John and Todd Harrell coat whole pork shoulder, ribs, or brisket with a seasoning rub that probably includes a ton of garlic, cayenne, paprika, and black pepper. They cook it slow and low over indirect heat, using mesquite wood for a strong, smoky flavor, for twelve to fourteen hours. Then they shred it and coat it to order, with a molasses-based sauce, before piling it on white bread. John says, "That's what I know from growing up in Atlanta—barbecue Southeast style." John adds scornfully that some barbecue places, which he mercifully refuses to name, actually mince and dress the meat with sauce ahead of time and then let it sit on a steam table till the orders come in.

The Harrell brothers have been barbecuing out of this tucked-away spot in the middle of a Bellevue strip mall for fourteen years. They've got a wall full of ribbons and trophies to attest to their prowess as barbecue champs. They're happy to take their show on the road by hauling their barbecue trailer rig to feed you and your nearest and dearest 200 to 500 friends. Or stop in and pick up barbecue by the pound.

Note: The Harrells sell their barbecue sauce in area supermarkets. The story goes that they entered two sauces in a contest at the

Puyallup Fair in 1988, one sweetened with honey and the other (the restaurant version) with molasses. The honey version won first place, and the molasses second. So they diversified: they now sell the honey-flavored sauce in supermarkets under the Harrell Brothers label and continue to use the molasses-style sauce in the restaurant.

WEST

Husky Deli

4721 California Ave. SW, Seattle
Phone: 206/937-2810
Hours: 9AM–9PM Monday–Saturday; 10AM–7PM Sunday

Jack Miller says that with twenty-two grandkids in the family all living within one mile of the store, there are a lot of hands ready and willing to work at the business his grandfather Herman Miller started in 1932. Herman sold ice cream cones to the Seattle public schools through a business then known as "Edgewood Farms—home of the husky ice cream cone." By the end of World War II, Edgewood Farms was no more and the Husky Deli had opened. The ice cream, though, still plays a big role in the business. It's made in-house with a little less fat than true premium ice cream, and comes in forty or so flavors. Kids have been dragging their parents to Husky Deli for eons to sit at a stool in the front of the store and lick great gobs of chocolate Swiss orange or blackberry, seasonal favorites such as pumpkin-eggnog, and a rainbow of other flavors.

The uninhibitedly greedy will find a hoard of other toppings and sweets here to satisfy them. Look for chocolates by Dilettante, Fran's, and Joseph Schmidt of San Francisco. Herds of turtles, peanut clusters, haystacks, creamy chocolate sauces, and cordials all inspire a madness that can wreak havoc on constricted grown-up ideas of eating. Husky is also famous for its ample meat and cheese trays, gargantuan sandwiches, and classic hors d'oeuvres, all adequately prepared but less than inspiring. They use high-quality Boar's Head meats, charge low prices, and mostly prepare everything from scratch.

produce and farmers markets

Food fashions come and go. Fashion in fruits and vegetables says as much as anything else about us at the turn of the millennium. As I write this, I flip between a 1960s edition of *The Joy of Cooking* and *Chez Panisse Vegetables* by Alice Waters, published in 1996. Without belaboring the obvious, it is interesting to note that both books, written some forty years apart, have essentially the same message. To preserve the true, delicate flavors of fruits and vegetables, it is important to shop wisely and ask questions: How was it grown, when was it harvested, and how long did it take to get into my shopping basket? When you can answer some of these questions, then the final step, the cooking, becomes the simplest. Most fruits and vegetables are at their best when the least is done to them.

These days, there are many ways to shop for fine fruits and vegetables. Some are new variations on old concepts. Online purchasing of organic vegetables is a new way of doing business, for instance. But home delivery of those same vegetables, coupled with the intimate service provided by a little business such as Pioneer Organics, harks back to the days of the milk and egg man delivering to your back door. Another example: I asked City Greens market owner Chris Bounds about the produce he carries and got the answers I wanted to hear. He knows the farmers who are growing his food and has developed relationships with them. Heck, he even farms with them. When the head honcho of a market can answer such questions, you know this is an old-fashioned, new way of doing business.

During the local growing season, the finest food to be had is at area farmers markets. Many farmers come to certain markets season after season, setting up their stalls in the same place every week. Such markets are a great opportunity to get to know farmers and give them your feedback. They will become a steady, dependable source of ingredients for your family's meals.

Farmers are handling living food, open to variations and taste all along the way, so the best strategy is to head to the market with an open mind. Unlike when you stock up on staples, it helps to shop at a farmers market *before* you decide what to make for supper. That way you can be inspired by whatever's freshest that day. And chances are, when you bring it home, you won't have to beg anyone to eat their vegetables.

Several other trends have affected produce in this new millennium. The push to eat food that is grown in ecologically sound ways, along with increased concerns about health, has resulted in a tremendous increase in the availability of organically grown produce. For me, as I suspect for many others, the issues come down to taste as much as anything. "Organic" doesn't mean much if the produce is yellowed, wilted, bruised, or just plain old. When "organic produce" meant a few vegetables lurking in a sad pile at the back of a health food store, I said no thanks. More and more, though, an infrastructure exists to get organic food to a greater number of people, meaning that availability and quality have increased as prices have decreased.

The other monumental change is the general availability of what was considered exotic or just plain weird in the olden days (that is, just ten years or so ago). But minds are gradually changing, and Seattle is finally shedding its reputation as a city with great regional products but limited cuisine. Fruits and vegetables that immigrants to Seattle once had to import here specially are now readily available almost everywhere—either grown locally or brought here expediently courtesy of new methods of shipping and handling.

The best produce markets in Seattle today are those where fruits and vegetables, ripe and seasonal and treated with respect, are the stars. They are the ones here to stay.

CENTRAL

Pike Place Market

First Ave. and Pike St., Seattle
Phone: 206/682-7453

The first day I moved to Seattle, I was awake and wandering around downtown at an absurdly early hour. Drawn to Pike Place Market, I attended roll call, then watched the highstallers and farmers and craftspeople setting up their elaborate tables. I was enchanted. To this day, early morning when the Market slowly comes to life is my favorite time.

Like all great institutions, the Market has evolved piecemeal over the years to satisfy the wildly different needs of its inhabitants. Tenants and farmers must meet some pretty stringent requirements. The daystall tenants change according to a complicated formula based on seniority and who got there first. Farmers occupying the daystalls must have grown or gathered everything they sell, with some specific exemptions. They can employ other salespeople but must personally be at their stalls at least once a week.

Once upon a time the highstallers, the folks operating the permanent stalls that are at the Market day in and day out all year long, grew all the food they sold on their own farms. No longer. For the most part, they buy from wholesalers, just like any other greengrocer in town. The biggest difference between Market produce stalls and other greengrocers is their lack of storage space. They have to sell everything they put out every day. That means you can be guaranteed freshness.

The Market sponsors Organic Shopping Days on Wednesdays and Sundays during the local growing season. It's a wonderful reason for us to return to the Market, which is sometimes perceived as being too much of a hassle to shop at. Anyone who has an interest in the Market agrees that for it to survive, it has to remain true to its origins as a farmers market serving Seattle, rather than a tourist tchotchke destination.

Note: There is one hour of free parking at the Public Market Parking Garage on Western Avenue, the best enticement yet to shop at the Market.

The highstallers all have their niches—things they are known for that draw their particular fans. I've listed the stalls as you encounter them heading south, first down Pike Place and then through the covered arcade.

Corner Produce: This is the first glimpse many people get of the Market as they round the corner of First Avenue and Pike Place, and it's an enticing one. Along with a few designer lettuces and fancy mushrooms, you'll find basics such as collard greens, plain old lunch-box apples, and iceberg lettuce.

Frank's: Frank's is one of the real old-timers, the only highstaller that still has a farm. They carry pineapples and papayas along with farm-grown produce.

Jordan Village: This all-organic stall sells produce from the Love Israel commune in Snohomish, supplemented with California-grown produce in the off-season. While it's a little pricier than nonorganic, it's still reasonable.

Manzo Bros.: These are the folks who broadcast loud and clear, "Pleeza no squeeza." Displays look as if they have been laid in place, one fruit at a time. Take one down and the whole towering edifice will fall. Break past those off-putting signs, though, and you'll get friendly service.

Lina's: Next door to Manzo Bros., Lina's is a good, reliable source for basic produce. Lower rent than Sosio's without sacrificing high quality.

Mai Choy: A welcome addition that specializes in Asian vegetables. Marvelous greens, herbs, root vegetables, and tropical fruits, augmented with some Asian groceries, make this stall stand out. During the season, they grow their own produce on a family farm.

Sosio's: This is the place to shop for wild mushrooms. On a given day, you'll find neat displays of wild-picked chanterelles, shiitakes, trumpet's ears, chicken of the woods, oyster mushrooms, lion's mane, and anything else that's in season. If you're feeling particularly flush, they occasionally carry fresh cèpes, or porcini mushrooms. Beyond that, all of the produce here is impeccably fresh, though a tad pricey.

Mario & Luigi's: How come Mario always manages to find a deal? Three pounds of bananas for a buck, or a five-pound bag of oranges for a buck, make a visit to this stall worthwhile. Admittedly, you'll find a few spots and maybe a soft one here or there, but at these prices, who's complaining?

NORTH

Big Apple

155 NW 85th St., Seattle
Phone: 206/789-5440
Hours: 8AM–8PM every day

Not so long ago, most urban centers were dotted with markets like this one: neighborhood produce markets adding their color and life to the city. Most are long gone, and the ones hanging on have to have a unique shtick. Big Apple succeeds by selling fruits and vegetables at bargain prices. But that's not all. Unlike the produce markets of old, Big Apple carries some really unusual designer produce, such as the *manzano*, an apple-banana, or the babáco, a rather strange-looking papaya from Belize. This is definitely not your mom's produce stand.

Owner John Paul Calamaras used to be a commercial fisherman, and he still knows enough to carry some great house-smoked salmon. I tasted some chokingly fiery salmon jerky that brought me to my knees, as well as a tamer teriyaki salmon jerky that was excellent.

Baked Squash with Apples

Michele Catalano, the coordinator for the Pike Place Market Basket CSA, contributed this simple recipe. She says it can be used with any type of winter squash, although smaller varieties such as acorn, delicata, sweet dumpling, or festival work best, as they make a nice single serving when cut in half.

Serves 2

> *1 winter squash, cut in half lengthwise, seeds removed*
> *1 apple, any variety except Delicious, chopped*
> *1 teaspoon lemon juice*
> *¼ cup brown sugar*
> *½ teaspoon cinnamon*
> *2 tablespoons butter*

Preheat oven to 350 degrees F.

Place squash cut side down in greased baking dish and bake for 30 minutes. Meanwhile, combine apple, lemon juice, brown sugar, and cinnamon.

Turn squash and fill with apple mixture. Add ¼ inch of water to baking pan. Dot each half with butter and continue baking for another 20 minutes.

City Greens

1120 NE 45th St., Seattle
Phone: 206/675-1221
Hours: 7AM–10PM every day

In its three years of existence, City Greens has established a unique niche for itself while surrounded by some stiff competition. The phenomenally successful University District Farmers Market is nearby, and several major supermarkets are within a five-minute drive. What's the key to City Greens' success? Owner Chris Bounds says he has relationships with growers that stretch back over years. Since he himself is a farmer in the Skagit Valley, for instance, he's got contacts that help him sell over 200,000 tulips in season (at lower margins than everyone else, so he can pass the savings on).

In the fall, the air at City Greens is sharp and ripe with the aroma of over one hundred varieties of apples. Chris thinks he has more varieties than anyone else in the nation. Sometimes he can get only one case of a particular kind, the yield from a single tree. The big chains wouldn't—let's be honest, couldn't—give the time of day to a farmer who showed up with one case of a doomed apple varietal, but City Greens is happy to take it.

Produce, year-round, is the heart and soul of this operation. Beyond that are a smattering of grocery, deli, meat, wine, and other gourmet and natural food items, most fairly ordinary.

Farmers Markets

Way back in the culinary Dark Ages of 1993, a small neighborhood farmers market opened in the University District with a handful of farmers selling mostly what they had grown themselves. Today the U-District Farmers Market is Seattle's biggest, most successful farmers market (outside of Pike Place), has spawned a couple of little siblings in Columbia City and West Seattle, and is an inspiration for all other urban markets in the area.

Chris Curtis has been the organizer, volunteer coordinator, and all-round den mother to this thriving institution from the beginning. She told me that although initially there was no clear vision for the market, one has evolved over the years. The key to a successful greenmarket is a focus on farm-grown products. That means no craftsy tchotchkes, no flea market tables, only 100 percent vendor-grown products. The market has to work hand in hand with both farmers and customers in education and in supporting small-scale agriculture.

How successful is the U-District Farmers Market? On a busy Saturday morning, an average of 4,000 to 5,000 people come out to buy from about fifty different vendors selling berries, vegetables, organic produce, eggs, mushrooms, bouquets of colorful flowers, fruit from eastern Washington, herbs, nuts, and nursery stock. In addition, there are stalls selling freshly baked breads, honey, cheeses, fresh pasta, preserves, and thirst-quenching apple cider. The average farmer sells about $800 worth of products each Saturday, with some earning as much as $4,000 to $5,000—chump change compared to an Albertson's or QFC, but an opportunity for survival for a small-scale farmer.

Will you save money by shopping at a farmers market? Probably not. Small farmers are fighting overwhelming challenges: competition for dwindling land resources, higher labor costs due to smaller-scale and often organic growing methods, and, not least, the vagaries of nature. They have to charge more just to stay alive. What you will get is access to the best, most flavorful farm products, along with an irresistible opportunity to meet the farmers who grow your food, find out how it's grown, and learn the best ways to prepare it. It is a quintessential Seattle shopping experience to visit the U-District market in prime season and wade into the human swirl of tie-dye, Gore-Tex, flannel, hipsters, and moms and dads, all in search of the best seasonal produce grown by local people.

Shopping at a farmers market is a refreshing experience, but don't automatically assume that the fruit or vegetables you buy there are going to be of prime quality. I've purchased my share of mealy, bland, tasteless fruits and veggies at farmers markets (just as I have at supermarkets). Too much or too little rain, too much sun or no sun, a cold spell at the wrong time—all these can spell disaster for the ripening produce. As in everything else, some farmers are simply better than others at what they do. As always, use your senses: taste with your eyes, nose, and mouth before you buy.

Bainbridge Island Farmers Market
Saturdays, 9AM–1PM
April–mid-October
Ace Hardware Lot, High School Road and Route 305, Winslow

Columbia City Farmers Market
Wednesdays, 3PM–7PM
June–October
Columbia Plaza, 4801 Rainier Ave. S, Seattle

Fremont Sunday Market
Sundays, 10AM–4PM
April–October
N 34th St. and Fremont Ave. N, Seattle

Pike Place Market
Every day, 9AM–6PM (organic days Sundays and Wednesdays)
Open all year
First Ave. and Pike St., Seattle

Redmond Saturday Market
Saturdays, 8AM–2PM
May–October
7730 Leary Way, Redmond

University District Farmers Market
Saturdays, 9AM–2PM
May–November
NE 50th St. and University Way NE, Seattle

West Seattle Farmers Market
Sundays, 10AM–2PM
June–October
SW Alaska St. and California Ave. SW, Seattle

What's Fresh Now?

Puget Sound Fresh is a program sponsored by the King County Agricultural Commission to showcase farm produce grown, raised, or harvested right here in our local communities. To enable consumers to better plan their menus around seasonal produce, the program has published a quick reference guide showing what products to look for at various times of the year. The following chart is reprinted with their permission.

	JAN	FEB	MAR	APR	MAY	JUN	JUL	AUG	SEP	OCT	NOV	DEC
Apples												
Asparagus												
Basil												
Beans												
Beets												
Blackberries												
Blueberries												
Boysenberries												
Broccoli												
Brussels Sprouts												
Cabbage												
Carrots												
Cauliflower												
Celery												
Cherries (pie)												
Cherries (sweet)												
Christmas Trees												
Corn												
Cucumbers												
Currants												
Dill												
Eggs												
Flowers												
Fruit (Yakima)												
Garlic												
Gooseberries												
Herbs												
Honey												
Kale												
Lamb												
Lavender												
Lettuce												
Loganberries												
Marionberries												
Melons												
Nursery Stock												
Nuts												
Onions												
Peas												
Peppers												
Plants (Bedding)												
Potatoes												
Pumpkins												
Quinces												
Raspberries												
Raspberries (Fall)												
Rhubarb												
Spinach												
Squash												
Strawberries (June)												
Strawberries (Everbearing)												
Tomatoes												
Zucchini												

Rising Sun Farms & Produce

6505 15th Ave. NE, Seattle
Phone: 206/524-9741
Hours: 8AM–8PM every day

If Whole Foods Market is the yin of the produce business, then Rising Sun must be the yang. Whereas Whole Foods specializes in cosseted, high-priced organics, Rising Sun, just down the street, draws in their many customers by promising high volume and low, low prices. The last time I drove by, oranges were selling for 19 cents a pound, romaine lettuce was two for a buck, and the bagged, dried fruits and nuts were almost half the price as at Whole Foods.

The produce looks fine, although occasionally a little wilted. The nuts are sweet and fresh-tasting. This is probably not the best place to get unsulphured, unadulterated dried fruit, though. Still, Rising Sun has to be doing something right. They've been in business longer than just about any other produce market in town.

The freshest daikon still has its leaves.

Skunk Bay Mushroom Farm

Lion's mane mushrooms have a flavor and texture similar to crab-meat and can be used as a seafood substitute in vegetarian dishes. These mushrooms make a wonderful addition to many egg, pasta, or vegetable dishes. Just cut or tear the mushrooms parallel to the icicle-like growth in ¼-inch-thick slices, and sauté them in olive oil until they turn a light golden brown. They can be layered in your favorite rice, pasta, or quiche recipe. Their flavor and digestibility improves with cooking, so they should not be eaten raw. Don't be afraid of experimenting with lion's mane. Look for fresh mushrooms that feel firm but not dry and that exude a mild sweet fragrance.

This recipe comes courtesy of Skunk Bay Mushroom Farm, a grower of exotic mushrooms based in Kitsap County. Look for Skunk Bay Mushrooms at Pike Place Market and the University District Farmers Market.

Lion's Mane Mushroom Quiche

1 pastry shell, either homemade or frozen

1½ cups grated mild cheese

1 medium onion, diced

½ pound lion's mane mushrooms, sliced

1 tablespoon butter

1 tablespoon olive oil

Salt and pepper to taste

3 eggs

1 cup milk

2 tablespoons flour

¼ teaspoon dry mustard

Preheat oven to 375 degrees F.

Cover bottom of pastry shell with cheese.

Saute onion and mushrooms in butter and olive oil until softened. Place mushroom-onion mixture on top of cheese. Add salt and pepper to taste.

Beat together eggs, milk, flour, and dry mustard and pour over mushroom layer.

Bake for 45 minutes or until center is firm.

Hint: Use mushrooms at their peak, when they are white and firm.

Sunset Hill Greenmarket

6405 32nd Ave. NW, Seattle
Phone: 206/784-7594
Hours: 8AM–8PM Monday–Friday; 9AM–8PM Saturday; 9AM–7PM Sunday

If you want food and booze and don't want to haul up and down the aisles looking for your fixins, a small neighborhood store—where, as the song goes, "everybody knows your name"—might be the answer. Residents of Sunset Hill in Ballard have supported this cheerful little market for the last four years and give it raves for super-friendly service, commitment to local products, and competitive prices.

Kathleen Hayes and Mary Toutonghi have a background in the restaurant business, so they foolishly thought it might be easier to operate a grocery store instead. The produce is exceptionally fresh. I found a basket of first-of-the-season peas that were so tender and sweet that they didn't need cooking at all. Mary and Kathleen come along every few minutes to baby and coddle their little charges, just as you would your own precious first-born. Wines are generally fairly priced and meant for everyday drinking. They also stock high-quality grocery items, but told me they didn't want to be labeled a gourmet or natural food store—just "a small community-minded store, not only a convenience store."

SOUTH

MacPherson's Fruit & Produce

4500 15th Ave. S, Seattle
Phone: 206/762-0115
Hours: 8AM–6PM every day

Greg MacPherson is loud. He's the kind of guy who hates, really hates, to be taken advantage of. And he's not afraid to say that his customers really care what they pay for their food. So he takes care of them. He takes care of his suppliers too: pays cash, moves their products (even if it kills him, he told me), and puts together a lot of deals. Sometimes he charges so little, he might as well give it away.

His Beacon Hill market on a weekend is jammin'. Raucous music spills out onto the parking lot. Women in *burkas*, Latinos, African

Americans, Asians, Caucasians—you name it, they're all here. I confess that MacPherson's is my greengrocer, one that I have frequented hundreds of times. It's my favorite for one simple reason: its utter lack of pretension. Employees are invariably respectful yet cheery and joking with the regulars; customers trade opinions over the kiwifruit; it has the feel of a slightly scruffy, old-fashioned neighborhood bazaar. Besides, fruits and veggies are so abundant and cheap here that I can take home bags of them while hardly paying more than a twenty note.

Community Supported Agriculture

I have a soft spot in my heart for farmers. Anyone who can grow a bounty of fresh-as-can-be produce while overcoming the vagaries of weather, perform back-breaking labor for low wages, and deliver an overflowing basket of the tenderest, sweetest fruits and vegetables practically to my doorstep throughout the summer deserves all my support. Community Supported Agriculture (CSA) is a program that enables me, and others like me, to "subscribe" to that farmer for a growing season. We pay in advance for a weekly share of the food he or she grows, which is then delivered to a central point. In addition to receiving beautiful produce, I love the idea that in a CSA, I can help maintain the viability of these farms.

Michele Catalano, who runs the Pike Place Market Basket CSA, is a persuasive advocate of these programs. She grew up in Maine where, she told me, the CSAs seemed to rely heavily on cabbage—weeks upon weeks of it. Happily, the Northwest's beautiful green landscape is much more congenial to growing things. CSA baskets are typically stunners, loaded with an outstanding variety of produce, almost all of it organic, that changes as the season progresses. The Market Basket CSA, unlike some others, has the advantage of including products from many farms throughout Washington.

Michele says that there are some common misconceptions about CSA. It's not a program to subsidize farming, for instance. Customers pay a fair market value up front for products, while the farmer gets a guaranteed market. Michele gets great pleasure from introducing new customers to CSAs, watching them become fervent believers, and seeing them graduate to becoming regular farmers market shoppers (preferably at Pike Place Market, of course).

The customer base at the Market Basket CSA is healthy and growing. The only limiting factor is the diminishing pool of farmers available to supply all the farmers markets and CSAs in this area. It can't be overstated: farming is a precarious occupation, especially for the type of small business farming that is more concerned with growing food for flavor than for the ability to travel well. According to Seattle Tilth statistics, Puget Sound is the fifth most threatened farmland region in the United States.

CSAs aren't for everyone, of course. Those baskets don't come cheap; as in everything, quality costs. They are comparable, though, to organic produce at any supermarket around town. Also, although this isn't necessarily a disadvantage, produce has been preselected; you're stuck with what you're given, even if you haven't a clue what to do with it. (Michele encloses a newsletter in each basket giving simple recipes and news about the farms.) If you go out of town, you have to make arrangements for what should happen to your basket. Many people give theirs to Pike Place Market's Food Bank or, even better from Michele's perspective, introduce their friends to the program by giving their basket to them. CSA baskets are usually designed to feed two to four people. If yours is a family of heavy produce eaters, be prepared to augment with additional purchases.

Michele has dreams for the Market Basket CSA. She'd like to see it extend through to Thanksgiving and possibly have a Christmas basket or even a winter-share basket. Customers have asked for more products, maybe a bread share or cheese, along with value-added products such as shelled nuts and honey.

The following is a list of local CSAs.

The Cabbage Ranch, Carnation	425/333-6969
Full Circle Farm, North Bend	425/831-2151
Goodlett's Farmlett, Auburn	206/722-0508
Growing Things, Carnation	425/788-0480
Holly Park, Seattle	206/978-6372
Jubilee Farm, Carnation	425/222-4558
Longfellow Creek Farmlette, Seattle	206/933-6606
Pike Place Market Basket CSA, Seattle	206/682-7453
Rainier Vista CSA, Seattle	206/978-6372
The Root Connection, Mountlake Terrace	425/774-8844

EASTSIDE

Washington Harvest Farms

170 Lake St. S (in Kirkland Waterfront Market), Kirkland
Phone: 425/889-0335
Hours: 9AM–7PM every day; in summer, 7AM–10PM every day

I was drawn to the huge bin of coconut-sized Fuji apples on the sidewalk in front of this market. It turns out they are locally grown, and the market's owners personally go to the packinghouse and grab them before they're waxed. That's the way they run the operation here: lots of hands-on attention and gorgeous produce. "People buy with their eyes here, so everything has to look great," says manager Damu Maples.

They buy locally when they can too. I like the way they carry lots of Washington-made value-added products. For instance, Woodring Farms fresh apples are here in season, and apple butter from the same farm is here the rest of the year. Pickles, jams, fruit-flavored taffies, exotic produce, and Macrina bread—what more could you ask for?

Pioneer Organics—Home Delivery with a Difference

If you're young and dynamic, want to get into a new business but aren't sure how, and come from a family that's been in the food business for generations, it takes a certain inventiveness to find the perfect solution. Ronny Bell came here from New York several years ago and, in a brilliant flash of insight, neatly crossed cutting-edge business trends with generational rebellion to create a pioneering concept: a year-round home delivery service for certified organic produce. Call it, if you will, building a New Age business the old-fashioned way.

Ronny's family is in the kosher food business (his grandfather founded Hebrew National), and he grew up working for them yet looking for a way to avoid compromising his ideals. Ronny confided, "I was programmed in Long Island and deprogrammed in Madison, Wisconsin." That's where he went to college and was exposed to the writing of Paul Hawken *(The Ecology of Commerce)* and Wendell Berry, a farmer-philosopher who romanticized farmers and their importance to society.

As is the way of many idealistic young people, Ronny

responded by going back to the land, working on a farm outside Madison. He quickly realized, though, that he wasn't cut out to be a farmer; commerce ran in his blood. He started bundling produce and selling it to co-ops in Madison. One thing led to another, and he ended up in Seattle, where he worked for a short-lived organic fast-food chain, then in the wholesale business, and finally had his epiphany.

Ronny began Pioneer Organics on a shoestring with six customers in 1997. Three years later, he has a customer base of seven hundred, with about four hundred regular subscribers. They've all heard about the service by word of mouth, and it's all run out of a bare-bones warehouse in the backwaters of Fremont. Customers come from as far away as Issaquah and Everett, and they all rave about the service. After all, Pioneer is selling a lifestyle: healthy and guilt-free groceries made easy. They're committed to delivering, on a weekly or every-other-week basis, a small, medium, or large box of 100 percent certified organic produce, augmented with organic eggs, bread, and other natural groceries. For those who don't know what to do with the kale or daikon radishes, recipes are included.

Any business must look to the future. Pioneer looks to build as sustainable a business as possible at the cutting edge of environmental, holistic, and health issues. Their dreams include delivery trucks using natural gas, which is a cleaner fuel that is domestically produced, and, ultimately, a full online natural grocery store. Piece by piece, Ronny Bell intends to remain true to both his heritage and his ideals.

Pioneer Organics
102½ NW 36th St., Seattle
Phone: 206/632-3424
Internet: www.pioneerorganics.com

Enjoy your five daily servings of fruits and veggies at MacPherson's Produce.

wine and beer Wine shops are not people,

but they have personalities nevertheless. Some can be challenging, even a little intimidating. Intellectually, you approach them with a little caution, reviewing opinions and palate before checking in at the door. Others are like the affable fellow next door who always greets you with a smile and an invitation to linger and chat, and perhaps offers you a juicy little nugget about a new acquaintance. Maybe it's because wine lends itself to a conversational approach, requiring discussion in such a personal way. Whatever the reasons, the best wine shops are a sum of their owners' passions, reflecting both their own and their customers' tastes as much as the hard-knock realities of the marketplace.

The variables in high-end wine stores are price, selection, and service. Surprisingly, the difference between two stores' prices on a particular wine isn't usually that great. Prices are set by distributors, and all wine shops (and beer shops, for that matter) are given equal access. If there are differences, it's usually because of loss leaders and special markdowns. That said, it is worthwhile to shop around. For example, Pete's Wine Shop is known for having great prices on champagne, whereas joining the Vintage Club at McCarthy & Schiering gives you hefty discounts on every bottle in the store, even sale items.

Some good wine shops are known for having incredible depth in one area or another. If you are a fan of a particular type of wine, it is worthwhile to become a regular at a shop that caters to your tastes, joining the buyers' club, getting on the mailing list, and periodically browsing the aisles. Most serious collectors methodically cruise through at least two or three different stores, searching for value and unusual offerings, on a regular basis.

Most importantly, as many owners repeatedly told me, they need feedback. It helps them hone their selection and, even better, give you, the customer, the service you deserve. Communicating your expectations allows a shop to get to know your tastes and to suggest or alert you to other bottles you're likely to enjoy. Service in the high-end wine business is all about building a relationship with customers and treating them well no matter how much they know about wine.

Much to the dismay of everyone involved, wine seems to have an "intimidation factor," which all wine stores try hard to overcome. Because Seattle is a relatively young market, with no more than twenty to twenty-five years of premium wine drinking under its belt, people are often unsure of themselves and their tastes when they walk into a wine store. Like most people, I find that talk of flavor nuances such as gunmetal and spicy oak with hints of ripe fruit leaves me completely befuddled. Alas, the wine industry does little about this, being content to reinforce the mistaken notion that wine is only for the elite and well off. To paraphrase the classic words of a connoisseur, James Thurber: "It's only a naïve little wine without any breeding, but I think you'll be amused by its presumption." Maybe, but trusting your instincts will always trump the presumption of superiority. Or to put it in plain English, if you like it, drink it.

Washington State Liquor Control Board

It used to be that wine-and-spirits stores were located in back alleys and scuzzy off-the-beaten-track locations, and there was something faintly illicit about shopping in them. Times have changed, and even the Liquor Control Board is jazzing up and try-ing to appear hipper. Steve Burnell is the board's wine program manager, a recently created position. He met me in one of Seattle's newer stores, at Second Avenue and Seneca Street, one he's very proud of. This is a new kind of wine-and-spirits store—a visible location, lots of fine wood paneling, and upgraded premium wines.

The Liquor Control Board operates under strict rules about what they can and can't do. They're not allowed to promote alco-hol or advertise, so they try to focus on value. That means you can get some great buys. They can buy direct from the wineries, directly import some things, and often take lower markups, giving them price advantages they pass on to the consumer. Best of all, the stores are completely self-sufficient and return any profits they generate to the state's General Fund. In 1998, that meant almost $38 million in profits and alcohol sales tax were returned to the fund, and to you and me.

The board tries to promote the Washington state wine industry. They sponsor Washington State Wine Month in September, with giveaways and an expanded selection, and try to take their managers out to visit the wineries. They have the same access to allocated wines as everybody else, though, so you're not more likely to find a rare item here. They do have a nifty service on the Web, www.liq.wa.gov, where you can look up a wine and vintage and find out details about price, availability, and approximate inventory.

The biggest problem with wine-and-spirits stores is that often the staff doesn't know much about the wines they're trying to sell. Some of the hub locations, especially the University Village store, Houghton Market in Kirkland, the Eastgate store in Bellevue, and the 12th Avenue and Pine Street store in Seattle, are staffed with more knowledgeable people, but you're still mostly on your own when choosing.

Pike & Western Wine Shop offers an international selection of wines.

CENTRAL

Champion Wine Cellars

108 Denny Way, Seattle
Phone: 206/284-8306
E-mail: LeTastevin@aol.com
Hours: 11AM–7PM Monday–Saturday; closed Sunday

Champion was the first wine shop to get a retail wine license in Seattle (prior to 1969, wine was available only in state stores). Emile and Stephanie Ninaud bring an Old World, slightly formal sensibility to wine sales. The shop is comfortable, the sort that true wine connoisseurs love to poke around in. Quiet and dimly lit, nooks and crannies overflow with bottles that invite browsing and discussion. Being French, Emile's heart beats much, much faster when he talks about French wines, especially those of Bordeaux. His family owns vineyards in the Blaye region, on the northern banks of the Gironde River, opposite Bordeaux. So he's an enthusiastic proponent of the *vin de Blayais*, which he describes as "not so over-oaked, a little fruitier and more accessible than Bordeaux." What this translates to are some very reasonably priced, perfectly drinkable wines that keep for a day or two after opening (and even improve). The shop also has a fine collection of Sauternes, as well as wines from the Northwest and a selection of other regions.

DeLaurenti . . . . see Mediterranean

Esquin Wine Merchants

2700 Fourth Ave. S, Seattle
Phone: 206/682-7374
E-mail: wine@esquin.com
Hours: 9:30AM–7PM Monday–Friday; 9:30AM–5:30PM Saturday; 11AM–5PM Sunday

Esquin owner Chuck LeFevre dreams of being the undisputed "master of the universe" in the wine kingdom. His goals are simple: "I want to be the center of the wine-buying universe in Seattle." To do that, he intends to have the best selection and the best prices. Since Esquin moved to the enormous Fourth Avenue location, they have tripled their inventory, increased their mailing list to over 10,000 names, and opened an impressive wine storage area, with room for 550 storage lockers that are temperature and humidity controlled. The store is neatly laid out and easy to walk through. Salespeople are reasonably courteous, but my experience is that it's a little hit or miss whether you'll get a lot of attention from them. I did have a happy experience with a friendly staff member whom I later encountered in a restaurant, working his night job as a sommelier. He remembered me and my taste in wine, and since I'm easily impressed, I was pleased.

European Vine Selections

522 15th Ave. E, Seattle
Phone: 206/323-3557
Hours: noon–7PM every day

I had walked by this shop many times before I even noted its existence. My loss. It isn't huge or comprehensive, but as owner Doug Nufer (who also moonlights as a *Stranger* columnist) told me, "The shop is for people who are adventurous and will try anything. We like to focus on wines in the $5 to $20 price range. I don't want to sell trophy wines or explicitly cheap wines. I'm just looking for variety and value." Doug gave me the impression that he is pretty satisfied with things the way they are: stay small, develop a loyal neighborhood clientele, have a life outside the store. Sounds like an excellent philosophy.

European Vine Selections has been at this location for fourteen years. It started life as a "club" for wine lovers in Fremont interested in bringing in little-known wines from Europe (which then meant just about anything). In those days, if you were interested in a wine, say Chateau Lynch-Bage, you'd have to have a bottle sent directly from the winery to the state testing lab to determine the alcohol content, before it could be imported. The lab would take a small pour for its sampling, and the rest went down the drain. Arghh!

Now that the law has been changed, merchants can buy only from licensed distributors, who sometimes have to buy from licensed brokers. A wine may have been "stepped on" four times before it gets to the consumer. While that means we can buy small esoteric labels today that we never had access to before, it also means we're paying significantly for the privilege.

Madison Cellars

4227 E Madison St., Seattle
Phone: 206/323-9333
E-mail: fredmadcel@aol.com
Hours: 11AM–6PM Tuesday–Saturday; closed Sunday and Monday

There is a basement *cave* at the lowest spot this side of Lake Washington that is the perfect location for a wine shop. Madison Cellars has filled that spot for the last twenty years. The outgoing, chatty proprietor, Fred Andrews, has created an atmospheric wine cellar tarted up with faux grape tendrils painted on the walls, solid brick alcoves, and exposed beams. It's all very cozy. The shop is known for having bottles that everyone else has sold out of, and verticals (meaning a run of vintage years) of hard-to-find items, as well as some old Bordeaux, Madeira, and champagnes. Fred says he always likes to hold something special back that he won't sell. I used to work for a longtime specialty grocer that called such items "fixtures"—items designed to impress and get the customers' attention. Admittedly, this practice is a little snooty and pretentious, but it works. Madison Cellars has a loyal clientele that is sophisticated yet price conscious. The shop is uniformly strong in all major wine regions.

Market Cellar Winery

1432 Western Ave. (in Pike Place Market), Seattle
Phone: 206/622-1880
Hours: 11AM–6PM Tuesday–Saturday; noon–5PM Sunday; closed Monday
Internet: www.marketcellarwinery.com

A winery in Seattle? Yes indeed. Tucked in a Western Avenue storefront at the base of Pike Place Market is a winery that has been producing wines since 1996, the Market Cellar Winery. They released their first vintage Cabernet Sauvignon in '96 and a Merlot in '97. The Cabernet I tasted was wonderfully fresh and grapey and easy to drink. This is also the store to come to for all your home-brewing and wine supplies. They carry a huge selection of dried grains, malt powder, bottling implements, hydrometers, barrels, plastic jugs, and whatnot. Just in case you were looking, they say they are the only cork shop in the city. Should you feel that you could make better wine than theirs, you'll find a lot of recipes here for making your own wine and beer.

Pete's Wine Shop

58 E Lynn St., Seattle
Phone: 206/322-2660
Hours: 7AM–9:30PM Monday–Saturday; 9:30AM–9:30PM Sunday

134 105th Ave. NE, Bellevue
Phone: 425/454-1100
Hours: 10AM–8PM Monday–Saturday; noon–6PM Sunday

Internet: www.petesfinewines.com

Pete's are the *über*-wine stores of the Seattle area. They're the Goliath that has a reputation for being unbeatable on price and volume (although that isn't necessarily true). Their salespeople are knowledgeable, and if they don't know, then someone in the stores will. The layout of the Lake Union store is chaotic, though. Some people like the "bumping against each other, wine in the aisles, wine under the produce bins, wine next to the Ben and Jerry's" feel, but it makes me claustrophobic. The Bellevue store, however, is much roomier and easier to shop in. Amazingly, the Lake Union store has about 1,800 different bottles of wine crammed in the middle of a grocery store, and the Bellevue store about 2,000.

Owners of wine stores are an idiosyncratic lot, and their stores bear their own personal imprint. The imprint at Pete's is George— George Kingen, that is, who's been the owner since 1975. I found him, at 8 AM, moving cases of wine like a bullish young man thirty years his junior. When I asked him the reason for his success, he told me, "I'm fair to all my customers. When an item is allocated, I don't mark up any more than I normally would. I try to build loyalty in my customers." George's love is champagne. He says he can drink it with meals, before meals, after meals, in the middle of the morning or the middle of the night. So his stores carry a fantastic selection of champagne, among many other things.

Pike & Western Wine Shop

1934 Pike Pl. (in Pike Place Market), Seattle
Phone: 206/441-1307
E–mail: wines@pikeandwestern.com
Hours: 9:30AM–6:30PM Monday–Friday; 9:30AM–6PM Saturday; noon–5PM Sunday

Michael Teer of Pike & Western Wine Shop.

Michael Teer sees his shop as an ambassador of Washington wines to visitors from around the world. In fact, about 40 percent of the business is Northwest wines. This longtime institution (it celebrated twenty-five years at Pike Place Market in 2000) is committed to supporting both the Market and local producers. Michael sees the future for the Northwest wine industry as unlimited, as long as the wineries can find their own distinct character and not try to mimic California and Europe. He told me that a lot of new wineries have opened in recent years, which has led to some uneven quality and lots of experimentation. It's a pretty exciting time for a relatively fledgling industry. Some of his favorite wineries, such as Chinook, Quilceda Creek, and Andrew Will, are always on hand. Another of his great loves is Italian regional wines, especially the '97 vintage from Piedmont and Tuscany. Other strengths are dessert wines and champagnes, and of course there is a good selection of wines from California, France, and other, more minor wine regions. Most importantly, the philosophy here seems to be to gently educate but not push; since such a broad spectrum of the public walks in daily, there has to be something here that people will recognize, and from there perhaps be lured into trying something new.

Seattle Cellars

2505 Second Ave., Seattle
Phone: 206/256-0850
E–mail: SeaCellars@aol.com
Hours: 11AM–7PM Monday–Saturday; closed Sunday

I was impressed with one service offered by Seattle Cellars that I haven't seen anywhere else: an extensive resource center at the front of the store complete with CD-ROMs, books, and research material, all available for browsing. It's a terrific idea that should be copied by other stores. This Belltown shop, open since 1996, likes to offer service and education with a twist. For instance, every store does in-store tastings. But when Seattle Cellars did a champagne tasting, they used a bottle-opening method perfected around Napoleonic times—severing the whole top of the bottle with a saber. By all accounts, it was a great show.

Owner Dave Woods believes very strongly that not many wine shops can compete with him on service. He's pleased to see all the new residential growth around him in Belltown and regards his store as a neighborhood hangout offering a broad spectrum of wine for every taste and pocketbook. Since all those downtown apartments tend to have very little storage space, the shop also provides a very popular service: temperature- and humidity-controlled storage lockers. In shopping for an inexpensive bottle to serve for dinner that night, I walked out of the store with a great wine label, which got a big chuckle when I got home—"Fat Bastard" 1998 Chardonnay from the Pays d'Oc of France.

The Spanish Table . . . . see Mediterranean

The Stumbling Monk
1635 ½ E Olive Way, Seattle
Phone: 206/860-0916
Hours: 11AM–9PM Sunday–Thursday; 11AM–10PM Friday and Saturday

I'm no beer connoisseur—I'm blown away just by the selection at your typical supermarket beer case. The truth of the matter is that since I know less than nothing about styles of beer, I buy based on bottle design. Like the makers of hot sauces, microbrewers seem to revel in outrageous puns and cool graphic design. The Stumbling Monk (which has its own clever imagery) has enough selection to really spin my head.

Owner Rob Linehan estimates he carries about 400 to 500 different beers. He turns the selection over quickly, unlike a supermarket, where bottles are liable to be forgotten at the back of the case and no one is really paying close attention. For artisan-style beer, unless a bottle is vintage-dated and meant for cellaring, freshness is paramount. "Someone walks into my shop, they're willing to try what they've never had before. It's a great opportunity to introduce them to something new. They go to the grocery store to get the same as always." For instance, Rob helped me sort through the numerous styles of regional Belgian beer to put together a mix-and-match six-pack as a birthday present for a friend. Wow, what a flavor range! Rob grew up in eastern Washington, and he has ferreted out some really interesting microbrewers that you'd have a hard time finding on your own, even with a road map and endless hours behind the wheel.

NORTH

The Ballard Market
1400 NW 56th St., Seattle
Phone: 206/783-7922
Hours: Open 24 hours a day

I had put this chapter to bed—that was it, no more entries—when I started talking to a guy in another wine shop. "You've got to go see

Britt Speakman at Ballard Market—she really knows her stuff," he said. When I heard this from a second source within the same week, I figured they were on to something I had better check out.

Ballard Market is a Thriftway, one of a chain of supermarkets that are all independently owned and operated. They have a lot of leeway within each market to run things as they please, and each individual Thriftway has its own personality. Britt and a young man with an appropriately Scandinavian name, Ole Thompson, now run the wine section here. When I asked them why they do things the way they do, Ole said, "We're not focused on one wine region or another. Wines are always changing, so we might be strong in one area at one time; then a few months later, the whole mix has shifted in another direction. We like to carry what's good." For instance, when I visited, the '97 Zinfandels were fabulous, so they had over sixty different bottles to choose from. They were also beefing up their '98 Rhônes and '97 Italians.

It's a good philosophy to have. While perusing the shelves, I got into a conversation with a lady who comes in every Friday to get a bottle of wine for her Shabbat dinner. She said Britt had never steered her wrong—ever. Anybody who has that kind of record is okay with me.

Best Cellars

2625 NE University Village, Seattle
Phone: 206/527-5900
Hours: 9:30AM–9PM Monday–Saturday; 10AM–6PM Sunday

224 Parkplace Center, Kirkland
Phone: 425/576-0770
Hours: 10AM–9PM Monday–Thursday; 10AM–10PM Friday and Saturday; noon–6PM Sunday

Internet: www.bestcellars.net

I heard grumbling from some wine shop owners when Best Cellars opened up in the University Village shopping center: "Dumbing down . . . mediocre wines chosen by some guys from the East Coast . . ." and so on along those lines. Ouch. While there's some truth in the kvetching, the bottom line is that Best Cellars does a great job of marketing their wines to people who wouldn't know a Chardonnay from a champagne, and certainly haven't a clue what to eat with either one.

The store is graphically laid out for those with short attention spans. Wines are strikingly lined up vertically by color with bold headlines such as "juicy," "fizzy," and "fruity." It's all very unpretentious and easy to grasp. Nothing wrong with that. Best Cellars also keeps the lid down on prices; nothing in the store is over $10. That makes your bottle of wine affordable and easy to drink every day. I wouldn't be surprised if some of those other shops start copying Best's blueprint.

Bottleworks

1710 N 45th St., Suite #3, Seattle
Phone: 206/633-2437
Hours: 11AM–8PM Tuesday and Wednesday; 11AM–10PM Thursday–Saturday; noon–7PM Sunday; closed Monday
Internet: www.bottleworks.com

Join the words "cellar" and "vintage," and beer isn't what immediately comes to mind. But in fact, since February 1999, this Wallingford shop has been encouraging Seattleites to think of beer as a beverage that can be cellared and vintage dated, and that can range from sophisticated and subtle to mindless thirst-quencher. Bottleworks sees itself as a store creating beer knowledge. For instance, the staff told me that the key to selling beer is storing it at the correct temperature, about 52 degrees F. Most grocery stores keep it way too cool. At 32 to 40 degrees, all beers lose their distinctive qualities and become not much more than your basic Bud. Expect to find about six hundred different beers as well as cider, mead, and the largest selection of beer paraphernalia on the West Coast.

Amid all the beer is a lavish display of truffles and pralines from the Belgian chocolate maker Leonidas, flown in weekly. What does chocolate have to do with beer, you ask? "Belgium makes the best beer and the best chocolate in the world," Matt the manager cheerfully told me. Based on my sampling, I can report that I would die a happy woman with one of these chocolates in my hand.

Brie & Bordeaux . . . . see Cheese

City Cellars

1710 N 45th St., Seattle
Phone: 206/632-7238
Hours: 11AM–7PM Monday–Saturday; noon–5PM Sunday
Internet: www.citycellar.com

If you're a neophyte and are curious about fine wines, a good place to begin your explorations would be a shop that doesn't condescend and is run by people who are friendly, young, and energetic. So visit City Cellars, owned and operated by three very approachable young "wine geeks" whose mission in life is to listen to their customers and steer them right, without making them feel foolish in the process. The wines here are carefully chosen and emphasize small producers above and beyond the standard bottles typically carried by supermarkets.

Dig deep into the Italian section. It's an eclectic assortment of regional gems, including some personal favorites such as the 1997 Chianti Classico from Carpineto. The shop also carries a continually changing best-buys shelf that features at least a hundred wines at or under $10. City Cellars has a strong French section, including a great number of champagnes, as well as Spanish, California, and some Northwest wines. My only quibble is that I found some bottles priced just a tad higher than I've seen elsewhere.

La Cantina

5436 Sand Point Way NE, Seattle
Phone: 206/525-4340
Hours: 10AM–7PM Monday–Saturday; closed Sunday

There are wine bores and there are wine geeks. Then there are the *amateurs du vin*, who the French simply call "lovers of wine." Michael Dodson most decidedly is passionately, crazily in love with wine, specifically French Burgundy. He says that he is the best source for Burgundy in Seattle. Since 1979, Michael has been making annual visits to that region, where he seeks out small, idiosyncratic growers and then arranges for a wholesaler to bring their wines in for him exclusively (making them—gasp!—very affordable). Michael describes Burgundy as a "thinking man's wine." It's a hundred times more variable than Bordeaux, and you can't choose one by reputation alone. As he puts it, "What counts is who's in the kitchen."

His customers are the grateful recipients of his legwork. Every single bottle in the store has a story behind it, and the proprietor will be happy to tell you the tale and answer any questions you've ever dreamed of asking about wine. Serious collectors tell me that La Cantina is the zenith of wine stores here in Seattle.

Note: There is no relationship between this shop and La Cantina in Bellevue.

Market Street Wine & Cheese

5424 Ballard Ave. NW, Seattle
Phone: 206/297-1460
Hours: 11AM–10PM Tuesday–Saturday; noon–5PM Sunday; closed Monday

What every neighborhood needs is a small, intimate spot where you can meet your friends for a glass of wine, have a little snack, and if you really like what you've tasted, buy a bottle to take home. Ballard might be underserved in a lot of other areas, but at least it has got that.

Dianna Wyatt is young, but she worked for a few fancy restaurants in town long enough to figure out her game plan: Open up that aforementioned neighborhood wine and cheese bar, and sell tastes of high-quality wines at really low prices. People will like what they've tasted, and you'll have a steady turnover of wines off your shelves. So simple, yet so perfect.

Her shop has been warmly welcomed, and she's happy to be where she is, in the heart of Ballard's shopping district. She has a small, personally hand-picked inventory. Since she loves Italian wines, there is a great collection to choose from, along with adequate selections of French, California, and Northwest wines. The cheese case is small, specializing in "boutique" producers. I saw Neal's Yard from England and a few other artisan products, but Dianna admits that she doesn't sell a lot of cheese and mostly uses it in the wine bar.

McCarthy & Schiering

6500 Ravenna Ave. NE, Seattle
Phone: 206/524-9500
E–mail: msrav@sprynet.com
Hours: 11AM–7PM Tuesday–Friday; 10AM–6PM Saturday; closed Sunday and Monday

2401 B Queen Anne Ave. N, Seattle
Phone: 206/282-8500
E-mail: msqa@sprynet.com
Hours: 11AM–7PM Tuesday–Friday; 10AM–6PM Saturday; closed Sunday and Monday

Dan McCarthy and Jay Schiering have created an unbeatable combination of selection, price, and service in their two wine shops. They have a reputation for being expensive and a little intimidating, but I'm happy to report quite the opposite. Along with the big-name bottles, I was pleasantly surprised to find a really large selection of "value priced" wines. When I asked them to select a couple of bottles under $10, the treatment I received was as solicitous and helpful as if I had been after the 1982 Mouton Rothschild.

To further sweeten the pot, they have a Vintage Select Club that, for a $100 initiation fee, gives you 15 percent off each bottle, access to allocated wines, and all sorts of extra goodies. Dan feels that given the complex marketing picture today, his shop stands out from supermarkets and big-box retailers just because he can offer such specialized service. While McCarthy & Schiering have an impressive selection from every major wine region of the world, they have built their reputation on Northwest wines. A lot of wine makers in Washington owe a debt to Dan McCarthy. He's been a tireless ambassador, and has worked with many fine wineries from their inception to help them market their products.

SOUTH

Salumeria on Hudson. . . . . see Mediterranean

EASTSIDE

The Grape Choice
220 Kirkland Ave., Suite 6, Kirkland
Phone: 425/827-7551
Hours: 10AM–7PM Monday and Tuesday; 10AM–9PM Wednesday–Saturday; noon–5PM Sunday
Internet: www.thegrapechoice.com

Larry Springer likes to think of his shop as a community gathering place, sort of like the old corner barber shop. He's the mayor of Kirkland too, so everyone knows where to find him if they've got a beef. The shop has been in one location or another in downtown Kirkland for about sixteen years. Larry attributes their staying power to the fact that they have continually reinvented themselves. About seven years ago they installed a wine bar, which has opened up a whole new relationship between the store and their customers.

In a previous life Larry was a schoolteacher, so he's especially articulate about what the future holds for small businesses such as his own, particularly when competing against big-box retailers like the nearby Costco. The key to differentiating themselves, of course, is service. As he puts it, "How warm and fuzzy are you going to feel buying your wine along with your toilet paper and laundry detergent?" At the Grape Choice, they know their products and so can cut through the hype and target their customers directly. They are uniformly strong in all the major wine regions, but Larry's particularly proud of his hefty selection of magnums and Jeroboams.

La Cantina

10218 NE 8th St., Bellevue
Phone: 425/455-4363
E–mail: lcantina@accessone.com
Hours: 10AM–6PM Tuesday–Saturday; closed Sunday and Monday

All wine shops sell their bottles with the right food in mind. But Brian Clark of La Cantina seems to relish the interplay between food and the ultimate liquid food—wine—more than most. When I asked him what the perfect food-and-wine pairing was, a dreamy smile crossed his face and you could almost see his lips smack. "Salmon with a roasted red pepper/ancho chile sauce paired with Châteauneuf-du-Pape. Rosé champagne with raw tuna and caviar. Wine for me is food."

I like his unpretentious attitude. Relax and drink whatever makes you happy, and don't worry about the details. La Cantina is small, so they get to know their customers and their tastes pretty well. Brian said that he has personally tasted about 85 percent of his inventory at any one time, so he knows his products. The shop seems strongest in French and Northwest wines.

Note: There is no relationship between this shop and La Cantina on Sand Point Way in Seattle.

WEST

West Seattle Cellars

6026 California Ave. SW, Seattle
Phone: 206/937-2868
Hours: 11AM–7PM Tuesday–Saturday; closed Sunday and Monday

Spending time in West Seattle Cellars is like being in your friend's basement *rattskellar*. He's a good guy, but he's got this crazy obsession with wines. Inhale as you walk in. The carpet and walls seem to have absorbed the fermented grapiness of countless bottles. A lot of tasting has been done in this little neighborhood joint. It's so tiny and crammed with wine, in fact, that a competitor once said, "It's too small to have anything bad."

The aptly named Bear Silverstein took over day-to-day operations from Matt Mabus two years ago, and he hasn't changed the store much. He's totally unpretentious and friendly and doesn't make you feel like a boob no matter how clueless you are. A very knowledgeable wine friend told me that he likes shopping here because "Bear is always sure to surprise me with some fabulous find that I've never heard of." This is the shop to go to if you want high-end German wines, a niche that isn't being served well anywhere else. Bear loves Reislings, which he characterizes as very affordable, razor-sharp wines with delicate, fruity essences, especially perfect for sipping alone or enjoying with Asian food. Other strengths here are premium Australian and Northwest wines as well as champagnes.

superstores

central market

chefshop.com

larry's markets

pcc natural markets

thriftway

whole foods market

superstores
Somewhere there must be a template for creating supermarket managers. How else to explain their apparently nearly universal belief that opening a can of soup is the limit of our culinary desires or know-how? Aisle after dreary aisle of macaroni out of a box, gravy out of a bottle, and brownies from a mix: no wonder most people consider food shopping on a par with getting their oil changed. There are a few supermarkets, though, that are willing to tweak the mold.

What's the common thread uniting the stores in this chapter? Yes, one-stop shopping, extensive hours, and ample parking define them as supermarkets. But there's a different mentality at work here. Whether they're on the forefront of the movement to explain the risks of genetically engineered foods, are committed to supporting local farmers, or simply have figured out an exciting and appetizing way to present food, these are supermarkets with attitude. I call them superstores.

The five superstores in this chapter are, for the most part, an independent lot. Except for Whole Foods, all are small, regional chains where fresh food occupies center stage. These are stores where the peripheral aisles—the fresh produce, meat, fish, cheese, and bakery departments—dominate. I also include one very different model, ChefShop.com, a specialty food superstore that takes to heart its task of educating its customers.

I like browsing in these markets. I can always find something new and delicious: some fresh, tangy artisanal cheese that I've never tasted before, or a fantastic display of local peaches and cherries, alongside olives and olive oils from the world over. Given that it's necessary to shop for the mundanities of life, at least let me have fun doing it.

At the same time, these superstores are, by their nature, generalists as well. They're in the business of selling laundry detergent and, yes, that can of soup for those people who are "assembling" their dinner. And everything on their shelves has to earn its keep. A big challenge is finding, training, and keeping a sales staff that's knowledgable about what the store is selling. As a result, you might not encounter the kind of solicitous attention and know-how at a superstore that you would at a small store, where the owner or staff often knows everything there is to know about the particular food there.

While none of these stores need much introduction here in Seattle, they all have strengths and particular niches reflecting their owners' visions. Browse through this chapter, and you'll get a feel for what each does best. Whether it's an amazing cheese department or a bakery that is head and shoulders above the rest, every one of these superstores stands out in its own way.

Central Market

15505 Westminster Way N, Shoreline
Phone: 206/363-9226
Hours: 7AM–9PM every day

By all appearances, Central Market packs a double whammy. One area is a traditional supermarket, where Mom and Dad and their four kids can stock up on quantity and value. But step into another, separate area and you'll be amazed by a selection that would put to shame a wholesale produce terminal from a midsized city. Row after row of eye-boggling, impeccably fresh produce, seafood, meat, and Asian comestibles make this market leagues away from anything seen in any other supermarket hereabouts. If bigger is better, then Central Market is the Super Bowl of area supermarkets.

Doing the Central crawl revolves around making choices. Virtually every department offers a plethora of possibilities. Organic, natural, conventional, locally grown, factory-made, or produced on the spot: the choices make for more fun than shopping for cheap pearls.

Another thing about Central: they've limited the aisles of packaged products. That means there's more room for fresh food. For example, the produce terminal is a whopping 10,000 square feet of prime seasonal bounty (as much of it local as possible). The seafood market has enough selection and fin-flapping freshness to rival that of the best stand-alone seafood or International District markets in town. And the meat case—well, let's just say that even Hannibal Lecter might be satisfied.

Fresh is definitely where the store owners, the Nakatas, want to be. Their family grocery business had its roots on Bainbridge Island at the venerable Town & Country Thriftway in Winslow, and later grew to include a string of others (Central Market Poulsbo, Ballard Market, Greenwood Market, and Poulsbo Market Thriftway). In planning their new market, they were determined to evolve from a conventional supermarket to one that genuinely nourishes their customers with food that can be touched and felt and smelled.

When Central Market first opened in January 2000, people were known to travel the aisles with cell phone in hand, breathlessly gushing to their friends and relatives. Clearly they were not drawn by the look of the place, which is strictly "no-frills warehouse." Instead, it's the sheer size, energy, and devotion to quality that impresses.

Produce: The shiny silver silo at the front entrance is a not-so-subtle hint that they take produce very seriously here. The cool temperature in the produce terminal is another. As you might expect given the Japanese American ownership of this market, Asian produce is abundant. Look for things such as galangal and fresh turmeric root, lime leaves and ginger, daikon, cabbage the size of hubcaps, several Asian eggplants, burdock root, taro, dozens of chile peppers, and even spiky, watermelon-sized durian root hanging in a row in the freezer. There's an aisle of New World vegetables and fruits such as *nopales* (cactus paddles), tomatillos, yucca, and cassava, aloe vera leaves, and at least a half-dozen kinds of bananas and plantains. Choose from about a hundred different kinds of organically grown produce. Or baskets and baskets of assorted mushrooms and herbs. The produce people like to go where the market and season leads them, so they don't advertise (because that would mean presetting what they'll be selling weeks in advance, even if it's not the best product around). Instead, customers have to show up in person to find out what treasures have been unearthed.

Meat and Poultry: Central is rightfully proud of their fifty-two feet of lavishly filled meat cases. They carry Painted Hills Natural Beef, free-range chicken, bulk factory-grown Southern chicken, kosher meat, pork, and high-quality, range-fed lamb from New Zealand, as well as duck, game hens, goose, and more. They also offer Cas-Cioppo Brothers sausages and Bavarian Meat wieners and franks. And here's a bonus: Central makes at least fifteen potently flavored seasoning rubs that they'll apply to your meat at no charge, while you wait. The employees are friendly, but their lack of knowledge is sometimes obvious. I was a little pained when I eavesdropped on a conversation between two staffers and a customer who had asked them about the differences between the Rosie organic and the Rocky free-range chickens in the case. Both made halfhearted and incorrect stabs at an answer, which left their customer scratching his head and randomly choosing.

Fish: Walk into Central early in the morning and prepare to inhale a wonderfully briny sea smell that immediately instills confidence. The aroma might be mixed with powerful whiffs of spice and cooking crab that will further stimulate the gastronomic brain synapses. "You know what you're having for dinner tonight," whispers a little voice in your head. Indeed, Central has put the fish department front and center, right by the main entrance, which tells you what their priorities are. Tilapia and sometimes catfish, silver carp or trout, Dungeness crab, and lobster are ready to be plucked and dispatched from the live seafood tanks just moments before you head for the checkout. There's also an incredible assortment of bulk frozen seafood—over forty varieties to choose from, all value-priced. Much of the frozen fish carries the Bruce Gore tag, synonymous with superior harvesting and processing, and a guarantee that all the fish here is wild-caught. Central believes that no farmed salmon can compare to wild salmon in quality, value, and flavor.

Asian Market: Given the demographics of the area immediately around the store (15 percent Asian), Central expected their Asian section to be successful. What they didn't realize was just how successful it would be. This section keeps nibbling away at the prepared food aisles, adding just one more row of rice crackers and snacks, or expanding into one more line of curry pastes or whatnot. There's a tremendous assortment of authentic foods, from the familiar tofus and noodles to the obscure stuff such as young tamarind pickles and lotus leaves from Cambodia and Laos. In the fall, look for Koda rice (from Koda Farms in California), which is distributed only once a year, so supplies are limited. It's a special grade of short-grain rice that makes incredibly delicious sushi.

Prepared Foods and Deli: For a supermarket of this caliber, the prepared foods and deli department is surprisingly basic. There's a pretty standard selection of deli meats from Hormel and better ones from Molinari and Columbus. The Meal Creation Center, also known as the salad bar, is first-rate, though, with enough variety and selection that you won't get quickly bored. Try the slightly sweet and flavorful tossed greens with blackberry dressing or the lemony *taboulleh* (a simple dish that has been badly mangled by way too many cooks). The bacon that Central adds to their broccoli salad both tastes good and was enough to entice the anti-broccolites in my family to at least take one bite. Central also makes some terrific, hearty sandwiches on good, crusty baguettes. Standards such as classic Italian and newer variants like imported French ham and Brie, lamb gyro (using tasty leg of lamb), and portobello mushroom and roasted pepper are carefully put together with faultlessly fresh ingredients and just the right enhancements.

Breads and Baked Goods: If your idea of dessert includes generous helpings of high-fructose corn syrup, modified food starch, partially hydrogenated vegetable oil, lecithin, BHA, artificial flavors, food dyes, and other unpronounceable fine-print ingredients, then you'll be happy here. Otherwise, run, don't walk from this department. Or seek out the few excellent outsourced desserts and breads, such as cookies from Alki Bakery, breads from Essential Baking Co. and Grand Central Bakery, and the locally produced Pan Amoré line of Japanese baked goods.

Cheese: Central's cheese department is adequately stocked, but, to my mind, it's a bit of a disappointment. The bulk of the selection is industrially produced and garden-variety ho-hum: consistent and tasty enough, but definitely not up to the level of some of the fine cheese shops in town (or even some other superstores' selections). Where are the artisan cheeses or the local gems such as Sally Jackson and Quillisascut?

Bulk Foods and Staples: The bulk food bins have a nifty feature: they pull out and down on hinges, making it easy to fill your bag without spilling the contents all over your shoes. It's a little thing, but it's indicative of how carefully this space has been designed. There are also areas where you can grind your own flour and peanut butter, cut your own soap, weigh your own spices and teas, and browse through online resources for up-to-the-minute information. Look for real value with more than a hundred varieties of Town & Country vitamins. The staff here is very knowledgeable; they say they can help just about anybody, except perhaps those used to going to International District herbal shops for the answers to their woes.

Wine and Beer: Steve Shoeberg, Central's wine department manager, used to work for University Village QFC (by all accounts, the largest-grossing wine store in the state), so he's used to a busy and sometimes frenetic atmosphere. But he's not exactly sitting back and taking it easy now. With more than 2,800 different wines and beers scattered throughout the store, there's plenty to keep him busy. He's scattered notes through the store alerting customers to "Steve's Picks": wines ranging in price from $5 to $50 that he's personally tasted and that he considers to be particularly good values. Steve is very friendly, helpful, and genuinely interested in finding the perfect bottle of wine for his customers. The store is particularly strong in California wines, although you'll also find just about everything else as well.

ChefShop.com

1435 Elliott Ave. W, Seattle
Phone: 206/286-9988
Hours: 9:30AM–5:30PM Monday-Friday; 10AM-5PM Saturday; closed Sunday

When you walk into ChefShop.com's brick-and-mortar shop on Elliott Avenue, the first thing you notice is that it looks and feels just like a regular gourmet grocery store. It is that—with a difference. ChefShop.com is primarily a Seattle-based online purveyor of fine groceries, cookbooks, and food information. But it also operates this retail outlet where local customers can partake in an eclectic brew of gourmet foods, classes, cookbook signings, professional workshops, tasting demonstrations, and other food-oriented events. Curiously, what was originally envisioned as a "will call" loading dock for local customers wanting to save on shipping charges has now evolved into a flesh-and-blood food destination for hungry wanderers.

Jeff Bergman is one of the passionate voices of ChefShop.com (along with Mauny Kaseburg, local gourmet diva). For him, good food is about simple meals with great ingredients. If you're the kind of customer who doesn't blink at spending $30 for a bottle of great olive oil, and want to be seduced by the facts supporting your good taste, then he's your man. Jeff, whose food acumen is equaled only by his volubility, is convinced that Seattle and the world are ready for a new (and more expensive) level of food experience. So ChefShop offers a dizzying number of choices for the seriously food obsessed. For you befuddled souls who thought sugar was sugar, think again. Here you can buy about twenty kinds—and learn in detail how they differ in manufacturing, taste, cooking qualities, and appearance. Or you can choose between a $4 bottle of raspberry red wine vinegar and a $230 bottle of *tradizionale balsamico*. Past events at the shop have featured Lynne Rossetto Kasper (cooking food from her newest book, *The Italian Country Table*); Jerry Traunfeld of the renowned Herbfarm restaurant; and Susan Herrmann Loomis, author of *The Italian Farmhouse Cookbook*. Other events have included professional and home chef educational workshops and tastings of vinegars, sugars, olive oils, and more. Making fabulous food isn't complicated; it just takes great ingredients.

Larry's Markets

699 120th Ave. NE, Bellevue
Phone: 425/453-0600
Hours: 6AM–midnight every day

12321 120th Pl. NE, Kirkland
Phone: 425/820-2300
Hours: 6AM–midnight every day

7320 170th Ave. NE (in Redmond Town Center), Redmond
Phone: 425/869-2362
Hours: 6AM–midnight every day

10008 Aurora Ave. N (in Oak Tree Plaza), Seattle
Phone: 206/527-5333
Hours: 6AM–midnight every day

100 Mercer St. (in Queen Anne Marketplace), Seattle
Phone: 206/213-0778
Hours: 6AM–midnight every day

3725 S 144th St., Tukwila
Phone: 206/242-5290
Hours: 6AM–midnight every day

Since president and CEO Mark McKinney assumed the reins of the family business, Larry's seems to have changed its focus to a two-tiered strategy: give the customer the fancy stuff—the high-end specialty foods and gourmet goodies—but, along with that, make sure people can get basic everyday foods at very competitive prices.

Larry's Markets has deep roots in Seattle. They once were known as the epicurean supermarket, the place you went to shop when you were willing to pay for the good life. But that's all changed; you could call it the democratization of gluttony. Sure, you'll still find plenty of pricey, chichi foods here. But Larry's will also fill your belly with the everyday, at prices that can be downright cheap.

Old-timers might remember the McKinney family's first store, Surefine, which opened in 1945 in the Green Lake neighborhood; later it changed its name to McKinney's Thriftway. In 1965 Mark's dad, Larry, opened the original Larry's Market at Oak Tree Plaza. The business has since expanded, department by department and store by store, to its present six locations, but it remains independent and firmly in the hands of the family. Mark himself grew up working in the business and says he's done everything from sweeping the grocery aisles to stocking the cereal shelves.

Larry's doesn't consider itself a "natural foods market." But all things being equal, they try to buy organic and local products as much as possible. If they have access to organic broccoli at a price that's close to that of nonorganic, they'll carry only the organic. Other times they'll give customers a choice. At the newest store, in Redmond, they've shelved their natural foods in with the regular groceries so customers can find them without extra effort, and they're hoping to eventually do the same in all their stores. In the near future, they plan to begin offering only natural beef with no added hormones or antibiotics at their meat counter.

The last time I was at Larry's, it hit me again. More than any other superstore in this chapter, this market offers a winning combination of convenience, fair prices, and fine specialty foods.

Produce: I love the way Larry's displays their local produce by using hand-lettered brown-bag signs stuck into the bins. It gives a down-home feel, and it graphically emphasizes their commitment to local farmers. You'll get some good buys on the most bountiful seasonal produce. The fruits and vegetables here might not be as cheap as other supermarkets' invariably mealy and uniformly flavorless specimens, but they'll taste good—and that makes them a good value.

Meat, Poultry, and Fish: With a fully stocked case taking up a good chunk of floor space, and the beautifully trimmed and displayed beef, pork, veal, poultry, and lamb, you know that Larry's takes its meats seriously. They used to make their own lamb, pork, and chicken sausages in-house; now they're put together by Fischer Meats of Issaquah. Choose from about fifteen different types, with lots of seasonal varieties such as cranberry-walnut and orange-cashew during the holidays, or the ever-popular bratwurst or sun-dried tomato and basil. Since they're all made with no preservatives, water, bread, or other fillers, the taste is big, meaty, and dripping with flavor. There's a gorgeous selection of prime cuts of steak and roasts, along with luxury items such as squab, Muscovy duck, poussin, and rabbit. A big part of the display is devoted to mouthwatering prepared, marinated, and stuffed entrees ready to pop in the oven. All in all, this department is a standout. The fish are equal to the meats in quality and selection.

Prepared Foods and Deli: In keeping with their strategy of offering both high- and low-end selections, Larry's gives you a choice of picnic potato salad at $3 per pound or red-skinned potato salad with blue cheese dressing at $5 a pound. Both are satisfactory, if a little gloppy, and that pretty much sums up the prepared foods here. Everything is convenient, certainly, and reasonably priced, though neither highly seasoned nor terribly imaginative. But then again, this is a supermarket, so maybe it's enough to just fill up without breaking any new ground.

Larry's carries two lines of sliced meats: Freybe from Canada, and Columbus from San Francisco for Italian-style sausages. Both are generally very good quality. And try some of the satiny-smooth Trois Petits Cochons truffled mousse pâté for a cholesterol-clogging, sinful treat.

Breads and Baked Goods: Larry's breads and baked goods are okay, nothing more. They bake their own line of breads, called

Euro and Larry's Own, that are supposed to be artisan and authentic (whatever that means). They're big, I'll give them that, and make acceptable, albeit sweet, sandwich loaves. But if these are artisan breads, then I'm a candidate for chef of the year. Stick to the real artisan breads made by Essential Baking Co., La Panzanella, Macrina Bakery, and the like, all sold here. The pastries come in two varieties: cheap and crowd-filling or high-end fancy. Both suffer from the everything-looks-beautiful-but-tastes-mediocre syndrome. Unfortunately, that's a problem with many bakeries hereabouts.

Cheese: With cheese shops opening all over town, it's easy to forget that Larry's was one of the first markets in Seattle to offer fine cheeses to yearning customers. They obviously care enough to do it right. The staff is knowledgeable and dedicated; one employee told me she learns as much from her European customers as from anywhere else. On her urging, I took home some *bleu des Causses*, an unpasteurized, rarely seen French blue cheese, and smeared it on some perfectly ripe pears for my dinner party. Naturally, I took full credit from my almost speechless guests. Cheeses are usually cut fresh to order here, selection is wide, and they often run promotions and sales on categories of cheeses.

Bulk Foods and Staples: The main aisles are the aspect of Larry's that looks most like an ordinary supermarket. Pallets of discounted goods are stacked on the ends of the aisles. Basic, everyday foods are priced competitively with other supermarkets. Here and there you'll find fine specialty foods, but the big problem at Larry's (as at most supermarkets) is that the education factor is lacking. What's the difference between all those olive oils? Why pay top dollar for something if you don't know enough about it? And who can you find in a supermarket to explain the whys and wherefores?

Wine and Beer: Another exemplary department run by the good people of Larry's. Maybe because they once owned a distributing house, De Gustibus, they make a huge effort to find interesting, off-the-beaten-track wines. The Bellevue store has a wall of chardonnays from France, California, and the Northwest ("ho-hum," says the clerk, who would much rather steer his customers to more exciting varietals). They're also strong in Italian wines and have a surprisingly decent selection of ports, sherries, and champagnes. Happily, every time I've walked into the wine and beer section, I've been approached by the staff within minutes asking if I'd like some help.

Non-Grocery Items: Larry's has an excellent program called the Epicurean Club. For a $15 annual fee, you're entitled to a 15 percent discount on wine, including single bottles, and you pay only 10 percent over cost when buying a case. You'll get that 15 percent discount on some cheeses and other fine foods too.

Larry's cooking school offers classes in everything from holiday baking to Japanese cooking, as well as lifestyle classes and other seminars to help you be at your best.

PCC Natural Markets

Fremont
716 N 34th St., Seattle
Phone: 206/632-6811
Hours: 7AM–11PM every day

Green Lake
7504 Aurora Ave. N, Seattle
Phone: 206/525-3586
Hours: 7AM–11PM every day

Issaquah
1810 12th Ave. NW (in Pickering Place), Issaquah
Phone: 425/369-1222
Hours: 7AM–10PM every day

Kirkland
10718 NE 68th St., Kirkland
Phone: 425/828-4622
Hours: 7AM–10PM every day

Seward Park
5041 Wilson Ave. S, Seattle
Phone: 206/723-2720
Hours: 7AM–10PM every day

View Ridge
6514 40th Ave. NE, Seattle
Phone: 206/526-7661
Hours: 7AM–10PM every day

West Seattle
2749 California Ave. SW, Seattle
Phone: 206/526-7661
Hours: 7AM–10PM every day

If life were fair, then all the well-meaning brown-rice, weeds-and-seeds hippie co-ops of yore would be as prolific as drive-through espresso stands are today. But in this case, peace-and-love-and-bring-your-own-shopping-bag has mostly gone out the door. Except for the biggest and best: PCC Natural Markets, better known by the bright yellow and green "PCC" that appears on all their signs and communications.

To be sure, PCC (Puget Consumer Co-op) has changed with the times. There's a much sexier selection of artisan cheeses, imported Tuscan olive oils, and even organic balsamic vinegars on the shelves than there ever used to be. The one constant through the forty years of PCC's existence, though, is their mission of connecting people to the food they eat.

PCC's seven stores are a part of their neighborhoods, often small, and literally snuggled into their surroundings. Typically, customers come from close by, often on foot and carrying canvas shopping bags. Because PCC is a cooperative, the customers are also the owners. Thirty-five thousand members have paid $60 each to belong to PCC for life, making it the largest retail food cooperative in the nation. You don't have to be a member to shop here, although you can get some price breaks (on sale items) if you are one.

PCC donates time and money to community projects such as the FareStart job program, P-Patch gardens, local schools, and environmental restoration programs. PCC is also at the forefront of the movement to preserve prime organic farmland in parts of the Skagit Valley and the Dungeness Delta near Sequim, and to better manage fisheries resources in the Pacific Northwest.

To make me a regular customer, though, any store has to offer the stuff of good eating first and foremost. In my view, PCC moved in the right direction when they hired a specialty merchandising manager (since departed) to be responsible for the beer and wine, specialty groceries, and perishables. Before that, each store was responsible for its own purchasing, which predictably resulted in a reliance on top-selling products and a certain sameness to the merchandise. The big question is whether PCC will continue to find food that is exciting, tastes good, *and* meets their exacting criteria for natural foods.

It's no secret that since a Whole Foods Market opened in the Roosevelt neighborhood, PCC's stores (particularly the four locations within a two-mile radius of the new store) have felt an impact. Still, Seattle is fiercely loyal to its homegrown business, and PCC showed that it was prepared to enter the new millennium with a splash when it opened its showcase Issaquah store.

Note: The observations below are based on the Issaquah store. Other PCCs don't all have the same breadth or eye-catching layout, although they're likely to carry most of the same items mentioned.

Produce: A panoply of sparkling fresh fruits and vegetables, with an emphasis on seasonally grown produce that's not always available, draws you in initially. Look for local produce, much of it coming from farms supported by the Farmland Fund, which is spearheaded by PCC. Prices are fair, considering that the vast majority of the food is organic, and quality is very high. The de rigueur juice bar featuring smoothies and fresh juices, with and without protein and other supplemental boosts, is a complement to the produce.

Meat, Poultry, and Fish: PCC has been a leader in bringing naturally raised beef to market. They were one of the first supporters of Oregon Country Beef, a cooperative that practices sound animal husbandry; it started with nine ranches and, given the growing demand, has expanded to twenty-one. PCC was also the first to introduce beautiful golden-skinned Rocky free-range chickens, along with Rock Island eggs from cage-free chickens, to this area. In addition, they've begun a process of overhauling their entire fish-buying program to take advantage of nonendangered stock. I picked up a beautifully fresh, tail-end halibut roast there, laid it on a bed of vegetables, and popped it in the oven. Couldn't be easier (and can be eaten with a clear conscience too)!

Prepared Foods and Deli: The store has an extensive fresh deli with a soup and salad bar. It also serves credible entrees, such as a nicely spiced jerk-seasoned chicken and a nice-and-cheesy macaroni and cheese, and not-so-credible sushi (definitely not fresh). You'll do best by sticking to the simpler preparations such as rotisserie chicken, meatloaf, or the many varieties of grilled tofu (although a purist might groan, I was pleased with the tandoori tofu). Or try the very popular Emerald City salad, a mixture of greens and wild rice, artichokes, and Gruyère cheese tossed in a lemony vinaigrette.

A personal plea to PCC: Please, give us plain old soy sauce or tamari instead of nasty Bragg's amino acid liquid at the soup and salad bar!

Cheese: The cheese department at the Issaquah store (although not at all other PCCs) is a cheese lover's paradise. The cheese counter folks seem genuinely knowledgeable and forthcoming with both samples and any information they have. They told me that cheese sales are the fastest-growing segment in food retailing and that the variety of farmstead cheeses (especially American artisan cheeses) available in the last five years has exploded. My only complaint is that too many of the cheeses are precut and wrapped in plastic (cheese hates plastic).

Bulk Foods and Staples: This could arguably be called the heart of PCC. Look for liquid bulk staples such as olive oil, safflower and canola oils, clover honey, tamari, and soy sauce of very good quality, along with an excellent selection of beans, grains, flours, cereals, nuts, dried fruits, and other staples. Prices generally seem lower than those at Whole Foods, and the selection is excellent. PCC's shelves have benefited from the increased availability of natural and organic processed foods; virtually any food sold by a "conventional" company is now also available in a purer, cleaner form. It's good to see that quality is also improving. To my mind, when there wasn't nearly as much competition, a lot of organic processed foods just weren't very tasty.

Wine: PCC's wine departments have had their ups and downs. Some stores are definitely better than others, and the Issaquah store is the best. Great selections of wines from the Northwest, California, France, and Italy abound, as well as interesting, lesser-known wines from Spain, for example. The staff here is particularly knowledgeable, so you'll get all your questions answered.

Non-Grocery Items: PCC wouldn't be PCC without soothing your body and soul as well as your stomach. Aromatherapy products line the shelves, as do rows of homeopathic medicines, tonics, and elixirs for treating everything from sore muscles to jangled nerves. There's also space for natural-fiber clothing, chemical-free makeup, buckwheat neck pillows, and all manner of other earth-friendly products.

PCC has a well-known and popular program of cooking classes, most of which, naturally, have a holistic, vegetarian, natural foods, or multiethnic orientation.

Admiral Thriftway

2320 42nd Ave. SW, Seattle
Phone: 206/937–0551
Hours: Open 24 hours a day, 7 days a week

Queen Anne Thriftway

1908 Queen Anne Ave. N, Seattle
Phone: 206/284–2530
Hours: Open 24 hours a day, 7 days a week

While you may think that presentation and high prices are the most notable characteristics of these Thriftways, you're dead wrong. True, the food does look gorgeous, spilling out the doors, inviting you— no, pulling you—in. But make no mistake, the very first element in these stores' product selection is flavor. It's got to taste great before they'll lay it out in the case or stack it on the floor at these Euro-influenced food stores.

Dick Rhodes opened the Queen Anne store in the early 1970s (he was a founding member of Associated Grocers, the nation's fourteenth-largest wholesale food-buying cooperative) with the idea of introducing a global food store to an ever more appreciative and sophisticated Seattle. His daughter, Melinda Wilker, and her partner, Terry Halverson, now run the business. In the early '80s they added a newly remodeled Admiral Thriftway in West Seattle to their mini-empire.

Like PCC, these two Thriftways (and a third in Tacoma) believe that small is beautiful. The stores are about half the size of a typical supermarket and are entrenched in their neighborhoods (Queen Anne and West Seattle, respectively). That small scalemeans that you're not likely to find pallets of cereals on the end of an aisle. They take things out of the cardboard boxes and *hand-merchandise* them here, if you please.

Jacques Boiroux and Mark Takagi head research and development, along with product selection of perishables and nonperishable specialty groceries, for Thriftway. It's clear that they're completely crazy about good food and are indefatigable about retailing to their particular niche of customers. Both quickly acknowledge a central fact about Thriftway customers: a willingness to pony up more money for their food—*if* Thriftway can demonstrate the superior quality of their food, that is. "That means plenty of sampling and product demos," says Jacques. The enormously successful kiosk demonstration kitchen in every store is the place where Thriftway dispenses recipe cards (only simple and realistic recipes—less than eight ingredients, no more than three steps), offers samples, and meets and greets their customers. To stay ahead in the fickle world of food retailing, Jacques and Mark travel constantly, ferreting out new food sources. "More than anything else, that means keeping an eye out for what Martha Stewart is doing," half-joked Mark.

Thriftway has a reputation for nurturing high-quality small growers and producers, helping them take the many steps necessary to get to market. Mark pointed proudly to Stonewall Kitchens, a now highly successful condiment manufacturer that he first discovered and ordered from at the annual Fancy Food Show. Nettles Farm, a small artisan producer of pasture chicken and pastas (see page 180), is another example. Farmers and producers in turn reciprocate by coming to the stores, explaining themselves and their businesses, and putting a human face on the food.

Note: I find the Queen Anne store more haphazardly laid out than the Admiral Thriftway, with individual departments not giving the same level of service. The comments below apply to the Admiral store only, unless otherwise noted.

Produce: The response to Queen Anne Thriftway's annual Peach-o-Rama has been nothing short of rapturous. During the short-lived peach season, Thriftway features an array of local tree-ripened fruit that have a taste and quality and perfume beyond description. Credit them with introducing us to the concept of using Brix levels as a way of measuring a fruit's degree of ripeness based on its sugar content. Other seasons might bring imported *charentais* melons from France: dense little orbs of pleasure that hover somewhere between excellent and extraordinary. Since Thriftway samples so liberally, it's hard not to get carried away with their superior fruits and veggies. What Thriftway does well is to give a star turn to produce: to feature a given fruit or vegetable as if it were a living national treasure. Obviously, this is a market that takes pains to ferret out produce that doesn't just look good but actually tastes better than the rest. So what if you have to pay two or three times the prices of other markets, when you get the privilege of eating produce that's so delicious?

Meat, Poultry, and Fish: Because of these Thriftways' space limitations, their full-service case selection is a tad small. What is there is generally excellent, though, such as Hempler's smoked meats, made by a small family-run operation out of Bellingham. Grandma, dad, and now son are still making old-fashioned smoked ham hocks, lean thick-cut bacon, and wieners that burst with flavor. Bison meat, Oregon Country Beef, and some prime steaks and roasts round out the selection. As any good butcher should, the staff will cheerfully and time-consumingly cut your chicken into parts and fillet your fish or wrap and tie anything else you need. The self-serve meat case is well stocked and covers all the basics.

Look for excellent fresh fish and shellfish. I splurged on some very fresh, never-been-frozen king crab legs that had been flown in from Alaska, after I was (very cleverly) offered a generous sample. What heaven! And you'll occasionally find other delicacies in the live seafood tanks, such as live scallops and oysters in the shell, as well as a good selection of salmon and other fish common in the Pacific Northwest.

Prepared Foods and Deli: With its recent upgrades, Admiral Thriftway's prepared food department has turned into a first class operation. Oh what happy progress! Like the best New York fancy food purveyors, there is enough repertoire here to keep easily jaded appetites satisfied. Roast leg of lamb, poached and kippered salmon, two or three kinds of stuffed chicken breast, myriad quiches, pot pies, sausage rolls, and pizzas are all on a very high standard. Most of the food preparation is subcontracted to Thriftway's own specifications, but they do use an in-store rotisserie for the roasted meats. The chicken and pork loin are particularly well executed. For store-bought roast chicken, these babies have supremely crisp skins and tender, tasty flesh. Be sure and try the lasagna, especially the meat and cheese version. Baked until the top is crusty, with a delicate ricotta center, they're perfectly cooked and surprisingly light. Salads are fresh and happy looking, holding up splendidly without the dreary, metallic taste that too many pre-prepared salads can have. Deli meats are very high quality, with Marcel & Henri pâtés and terrines, imported French ham, four different kinds of proscuitto, Spanish *jamon Serrano*, Boar's Head meats, and, of course, good old-fashioned baloney and the like.

Breads and Baked Goods: Thriftway boasts an amazing breadth of breads and baked goods, making its bakery department among the best in Seattle. Just about every quality bread baker in town is featured, and then some; it's nice to see the wares of some bakers who aren't normally able to get their products into supermarkets. The Crusty Loaf, Alki Bakery, and Frombach's are neighbors of one or the other of the Thriftways, but it's convenient to be able to buy their products in one stop. Desserts are also the ultimate culinary free-for-all, with representation from 60th St. Desserts, Paris Gourmet, and Seattle Baking Co., among many others.

Cheese: This department is a real strength of the Admiral Thriftway, with a fabulous selection, great signage describing the cheeses in depth, and, as always, liberal sampling. The Queen Anne store's department is self-serve, and to my mind it isn't nearly as likable. I do appreciate that they highlight individual farms and make a great effort to find small, artisan producers. While those fine cheeses might appeal only to small numbers of customers, efforts like these are what set Thriftway apart. The selection is especially strong in French, Italian and British cheeses. For those fans, the olive and condiment bar is well stocked, although I grumbled when they stopped carrying my favorite Mama Lil's Peppers in bulk (and couldn't give me a straight answer about when I'd see them back).

Bulk Foods and Staples: This is a supermarket, so they'll stock laundry detergent and even motor oil along with the imported French preserves and the dozen or so types of sea salt. Because of space limitations, they don't have as great a variety of bulk foods and staples as other places, but rest assured, they carry the essentials. Just know that if you're used to getting your cereal in a choice of sizes ranging from the industrial vat to the single-serving box, it won't happen here. They focus instead on lots of eye candy for grown-ups, strategically placed for maximum impulse appeal. No mere Snickers bars next to the checkout line here; this one places pricey Fran's GoldBars and Frog Hollow organic peach preserves there.

Wine and Beer: An extra-long case running the length of the store, full of chilled beer and wine (with a great assortment of micro-brews), tells you that Thriftway takes their responsibilities seriously here. Ask them questions, tell them what you want, and they'll try hard to satisfy you. I find the selection to be somewhat haphazardly stacked, so it's sometimes hard to find what you want. On the other hand, it's a small space, so you won't have to go far. As in most supermarkets, you won't get the same solicitous attention that you would in a shop specializing only in wines, but for routine purchases, Thriftway is more than adequate.

Non-Grocery Items: Look for a generously sized kitchen shop with every conceivable utensil, gadgets galore, an excellent cook-book section, and beautiful tableware. Thriftway is a great source for Mauviel copper pots and pans, which they import directly from France (so prices are very competitive). These are wonder-ful extra-thick copper utensils lined with stainless steel: real workhorses in the kitchen that will outlive you and your children. And should you have a need for it, check out the beauteous $1,200 all-copper duck press.

Nettles Farm: A Small Farm that Rescues Flavor

Who couldn't fall in love with a farm where the chickens are allowed to roam and peck through last year's tangled old vegetable patch and where they can eye next year's dinner in fields planted with a riot of the tenderest, most flavorful vegetables? I visited Riley Starks and Judy Olsen, agricultural artisans who are raising true free-range, organically grown chickens and creating delicious fresh pasta on Lummi Island, just northwest of Bellingham, after I bought one of their magnificent birds at Admiral Thriftway.

I have been eating free-range chicken for years, but when I first bit into one of Nettles Farm's birds, I realized that this indeed was a different critter. Riley explained that his birds are raised in portable shelters that are moved daily through grass pasture and spent vegetable fields. Each bird is given about four times more space than most free-range chickens to scratch to its heart's con-tent. Of course, the chicks are fed only organic, vegetarian feed and get no antibiotics, hormones, or genetically modified grains in their diet. The birds grow slowly, taking about twelve weeks to get to market size (most free-range birds take only about forty-nine days), and have a discernibly firmer texture and intense flavor. Riley attributes that flavor to the warm microclimate and mineralized soil on the farm. Sauté these chickens and you'll be overwhelmed by the flavor of the burnished gold crust of skin that slides from the meat as the meat slides from the bone. Make a soup out of the leftovers, and realize that you won't need any flavor boosters such as bouillon cubes—or any other crutches, for that matter.

Riley and Judy also make pasta—fettucine, ravioli, lasagna noodles, and more—from their own organic eggs, fresh herbs, and produce. The fillings change according to their whim but always include a bounty of vegetables, all raised just steps from the commercial kitchen attached to their farmhouse. Two favorites of mine are the caramelized Walla Walla onion and cheese and the leek and walnut with fried sage.

Marketing has always been the biggest challenge for small-scale farmers. Riley and Judy realized they would have to leave home if they wanted to survive. They were fortunate to connect with Jacques Boiroux of Queen Anne Thriftway, who offered them a chance to sell their products in Seattle. Since 2000, Riley has been delivering his superb birds and pastas to the store every week. Make no mistake, the birds are expensive; expect to spend about $20 to $25 for a four- or five-pounder. Before you raise your eyebrows, though, think about how much you might spend on a Copper River salmon or, for that matter, on your daily latte.

Ravioli with Chicken and Tomato Broth
Nettles Farm

Judy Olson gave me this simple recipe and noted that since all her ravioli fillings are so flavorful, they don't need a lot of extra fussing.

Serves 4 as a first course, 2 to 3 as a main dish

> *4 cups good-quality chicken broth, preferably homemade with stock from bones and leftovers from Nettles Farm birds*
>
> *1 14-ounce can crushed tomatoes*
>
> *1 cup water*
>
> *1 package Nettles Farm ravioli, any variety*
>
> *Parmesan to taste*

Combine broth, tomatoes, and water. Bring to a boil.

Drop ravioli into simmering stock and cook for 3 to 4 minutes.

Serve ravioli in deep bowls along with the stock and perhaps a little grated Parmesan.

Whole Foods Market

6400 Roosevelt Way NE, Seattle
Phone: 206/985-1500
Hours: 8AM–10PM every day

When the 1,000-pound Goliath known as Whole Foods Market came to town in 1999, it created a buzz among committed food lovers and made some competitors very nervous. "Oh yeah," they say, "Competition is good for all of us." Yes, it's true. But in a crowded field, where just because you say you provide quality by no means guarantees it, it's refreshing to see a supermarket that consistently delivers the goods.

Whole Foods is the nation's largest retailer of natural and organic foods, with more than a hundred stores in twenty states and the District of Columbia. The Roosevelt Way store is the first (but not, I suspect, the last) of their locations in the Pacific Northwest.

Store director Ron Megahan moved here two years ago from the East Coast to open the market. He beamed when I asked him what his impressions were of his Seattle customers. "They're very educated and aware of food issues. They're not afraid to try anything. They're culturally diverse. And they're really committed to supporting local agriculture. I love it here," he said.

Whole Foods has a reputation among the vendors who stock their shelves as being a great company to work with. They give demo time and space; they're flexible with product placement; heck, they even pay their bills on time. "It's all about people," says Ron. That would have sounded hokey had I not known that it's genuine, having spoken to a number of small businesses that sell their products at Whole Foods. This market bends over backward to build relationships, both with their customers and with their vendors—and it shows.

Produce: I challenge you to find a larger selection of organic produce, both regular and exotic, anywhere else. When it comes to fruits and vegetables during their high season, Whole Foods goes whole hog. I spent one fall afternoon cruising the aisles to look at apple varieties, and found more than fifteen kinds of organic apples for sale. Besides the usual Golden Delicious and Granny Smith, there were King David, Sausa, Spartan, McIntosh, Spitzenberg, Ida Red, Honey Crisp, Tsugaru, and more. During tomato season, look for dozens of varieties of vine-ripe tomatoes of all hues, sizes, and shapes. At all times, you'll find just about any kind of green imaginable. You'll see tasteless California strawberries here, just as anywhere else, but you'll also find an exquisite local strawberry variety, Totem, that's good for only two days maximum after picking. If you shop here regularly, you'll meet people such as organic farmer Billy Stote, who supplies Whole Foods with some of their most beautiful and fresh produce. In sum, Whole Foods is working hard at building relationships with local growers. They may not be as tight with area farmers as, say, Larry's, but they're working at it.

Meat, Poultry, and Fish: Here's another meat department that raises the visual bar for meat counters and butcher shops across the city. Full haunches of beef are displayed in the aging case like expensive museum pieces (and sell at those prices, too). The beef comes from Oregon Country Beef, the pork is naturally raised, and the lamb is from free-range New Zealand–grown sheep. In addition, Whole Foods has what must be the city's largest selection of antibiotic- and hormone-free chicken and turkey sausages (over twenty flavors by my last count). Flavors range from the versatile Italian to a Greek feta and lamb sausage. The chicken- and turkey-based ones that I sampled were well seasoned and tasty but suffered from a common fate: too dry. Those who swear by them should note that Diestel free-range turkeys from California are available here, along with Rocky and Rosie chickens, Cornish game hens, and capons.

Prepared Foods and Deli: Whole Foods likes to say that they prepare food the same way you would in your own kitchen. Well, maybe *your* kitchen can live up to that slogan, but only in my fantasies do I have the services of four Culinary Institute of America graduates. On any given day, Whole Foods offers more than 160 different dishes in their prepared foods department. Like an overachieving eldest child, it's not enough for them to offer a salad bar with a couple of greens and a handful of toppings. Here they'll give you about forty toppings to choose from, ranging from the standard to four or five kinds of sprouts, seaweed, and nuts (sliced, whole, or pieces; soy, almond, or sunflower). Many of the foods, reflecting this region's tastes, have a distinctly (though not exclusively) Asian accent. Dishes are clearly labeled as vegan, organic, or whatnot. Meat eaters, have no fear; you'll be well taken care of with roasted prime rib, peppered Spencer steak, and even a delicious chopped liver that would make a Jewish *bubba* proud. The rotisserie uses Rocky free-range chickens, which makes for a memorably juicy, albeit expensive bird.

Breads and Baked Goods: After some customers complained that the croissants were not very good, Whole Foods went out and found the best croissant maker in Seattle, Nicolas Paré of Le Fournil, and now carries his matchless product. Store director Ron Megahan was tickled that his customers cared enough to tell him; I think it's great that he listens. The baked goods at Whole Foods come from many different bakeries, and some are baked on-site. For example, La Brea breads from the famous bakery in Los Angeles are featured prominently. They're wonderful, crisp-crusted breads with a superb wheaty flavor. They are, however, par-baked and frozen far from here and then finished off in Whole Foods' kitchen. You'll find rustic loaves from Grand Central Bakery, La Panzanella, and Essential Baking Co.; sliced breads from Touchstone and Islands Bakeries; and bagels from Seattle Deli Co.

Cheese: Whole Foods certainly knows how to put on a good show. The cheese department looks like the stuff of dreams, with a variety of British, French, Italian, Dutch, and American farmstead cheeses that would rival Dean & DeLuca's legendary counter in New York. They even have an aging room behind plate-glass windows with humidistats and thermostats to help ensure that the cheese ripens to the best that nature can make it. Despite this, it pains me to say, I've bought cheese here that was either overripe or cut before it had reached its point of perfection. Once cheese has been cut, it won't ripen further, which would be a tragedy for some of these expensive little gems. And again, I repeat: too many of the cheeses are precut and wrapped in plastic. I know it's an issue of convenience, but when you're spending $10 to $20 a pound, are you so obsessed with convenience that you won't take an extra two or three minutes to cut a fresh piece?

Bulk Foods and Staples: If you want really great bread, it helps to have very freshly milled wheat. Whole Foods sells Wheat Montana hard red or white spring wheat, and they have an in-store grinder where you can mill your own flour. As you'd expect, the bulk foods section is vast and sells virtually any staple you can think of. Turnover is rapid, so products are exceedingly fresh.

Whole Foods carries several lines of its own—365 brand for staples; their own house brand of jams, teas, cookies, and crackers; the Allegro line of specialty coffee; and Whole Kids baby foods—all meant to be natural, reasonably priced alternatives to commercial processed foods. They like to say that they provide food that's familiar and that tastes identical to or better than the overprocessed junk in regular supermarkets. They are serious about their selection of gourmet specialty groceries, too, so you'll find lots of interesting treasures.

Wine and Beer: Wines are well laid out by varietals, making it easy to select your choice, with Northwest regional wines particularly highlighted. The selection seems strongest in French, Italian, and California wines, although there doesn't seem to be great depth in any one area. There is a central floor area given over to less expensive and promotional wines. There's also a "private cellar" for the reserve wines. Thankfully, they don't seem to rely on number ratings here. Instead, they take the time to write friendly little signs explaining their favorite picks. Maybe I was unlucky, but both times I browsed through the wine aisle, I couldn't find any living, breathing sales staff to guide me.

Non-Grocery Items: As befits this market, there are nutrition and body care products galore to balance, energize and soothe your jangled psyche. I admit I haven't a clue what to do with most of the stuff, but browsing through the well-stocked medicinal and culinary herbs section was fascinating. A natural makeup counter, a reference library (with a good cookbook selection), and aisles and aisles of nutritional supplements make this a great resource for those with an interest in such alternatives.

ethnic food markets

- african
- asian
- eastern european
- indian and pakistani
- latino
- mediterranean
- middle eastern
- scandinavian

african Ethiopia was once literally a land of bread and honey—the bread from vast fields of sorghum, millet, and wheat, the honey from the hives of both wild and domesticated bees. That seems a cruel mockery today, after years of drought, liberation wars, and ethnic conflicts.

The growth of the Ethiopian community in Seattle is directly tied to these upheavals. Ethiopian refugees began arriving here in the 1980s, particularly from 1989 to 1993, along with Eritreans, Somalis, and clusters of other Africans. When Ethiopians and Eritreans lost their refugee status in 1991 and 1993, respectively, the large-scale immigration stopped. Currently an estimated 6,000 to 7,000 Ethiopians live in Seattle. Many have settled in central and south Seattle (Rainier Valley, Yesler Terrace, and Holly Park) and in High Point in West Seattle. A number of families live in north Seattle, Ballard, Redmond, Bellevue, and Kent. The term "Ethiopian" is a catchall phrase used to describe a variety of ethnic groups with nearly 80 languages and approximately 200 dialects among them. The major groups in Seattle include the Amhara, Oromo, and Tigre. Most Ethiopians belong to either the Ethiopian Orthodox Church (Christian) or the Islamic faith.

The Eritreans, who have a proud history dating back to the pharaohs of Egypt, saw their country annexed to Ethiopia after World War II. In 1991, after an armed revolt, Eritrea was able to gain its freedom. Many Eritreans dislike being equated with Ethiopians, even though they speak the same language, since in their home countries the two groups continue to be at war. Here in Seattle, however, since their foods are similar, they shop in the same markets. There are 2,000 to 3,000 Eritreans living in the area, mostly in north Seattle (around 145th Street), south Seattle/Rainier Valley, and West Seattle. Most Eritreans in Seattle are Coptic Christian Orthodox, although some are Catholic and Muslim.

The population of Somalia, unlike that of many African nations, is composed of a single, homogeneous ethnic group. The country's recent, sad history is marked by brutal violence, famine, and inter-clan disputes. In 1991 people began leaving the country to escape sickening hunger, rape, and death. Many settled here in Seattle after stops in large refugee camps that were established to house them. Because they tend to have a strong religious and cultural heritage, Somalis have found it easy to continue traditional dress and cultural practices. Almost all Somalis are Sunni Muslims and follow those dietary laws. During Ramadan, their most important religious holiday, people pray, fast, and refrain from drinking during the day and eat only at night. Immediately following Ramadan is the holiday of Id al-Fitr, which marks the end of the fast. This celebration involves big family gatherings and gifts for children. Religious holidays such as these involve the ritual killing of a lamb or goat. In Seattle, families travel to a farm in Sumner, Washington, where they purchase the needed animal and perform the ritual slaughter.

These, then, are the largest African ethnic groups in Seattle (although there are small pockets of West and East Africans too). In Seattle, people are now especially familiar with Ethiopian food through the many restaurants scattered about the city. For those intrepid adventurers who are interested in delving further, here are a few markets to explore.

Glossary

berbere: a fiery mix of peppers and other seasonings, used in a wide range of Ethiopian dishes.

breadfruit: a soccer ball–sized fruit with thick, green, pimply skin and creamy flesh, used both as a starchy vegetable and in pies and puddings.

callaloo: the green leaves of the dasheen plant, used to make a famous soup.

cassava (manioc, yuca): a cigar-shaped root crop with a brown, often pinkish rind, which is usually hairy, and ivory-white flesh. Eaten as a vegetable (leaves) or processed into a wide range of other products.

chayote (christophene): a pear-sized member of the squash family, with a wrinkled skin ranging in color from white to green, and watery, white flesh.

coffee, green: a favorite drink of Ethiopians, who prefer to buy their coffee unroasted and drink it in leisurely afternoon social gatherings. Beans are roasted, then served unsweetened after being spiced, boiled, and reboiled into a concentrated richness.

crayfish, dried: actually a type of shrimp, used whole or ground as flavoring.

dasheen: a potato-sized fibrous tuber with white starchy flesh. Some varieties of dasheen have a pronounced bitter taste.

fufu: boiled, peeled, and pounded yams or plantains, served as a starchy side dish.

gari: coarsely ground, slightly fermented cassava, a West African staple.

injera: the sour, pancakelike bread, usually made from teff, that is used to scoop up food in place of utensils; a staple food of Ethiopia.

kenke: a West African dumpling, made from fermented corn flour wrapped in corn husks or banana leaves and cooked.

niter kebbeh: clarified butter, flavored with spices.

piri-piri: an African term for both a type of chile and a dish of broiled shrimp basted with a hot chili sauce, and a Portuguese hot sauce.

teff: a cereal grain that is the most important food crop of Ethiopia.

wat: a spicy Ethiopian stew that can be made from chicken *(doro wat)* as well as meat, vegetables, or even fish.

Amy's Merkato

2922 E Cherry St., Seattle
Phone: 206/324-2527
Hours: 9AM–9PM Tuesday–Sunday; closed Monday

Amy's pleasant owners sell their homemade injera in packages of a half dozen; delicious *sambusak*, stuffed with a spicy lentil mixture and an intriguing selection of spices and roots, many completely unfamiliar; and staples such as pulses, dals, teff, and millet. Look also for green coffee and beautiful urns for brewing, in both Ethiopian (with two spouts) and single-spouted Eritrean style.

Kilimanjaro Market

12519 Lake City Way NE, Seattle
Phone: 206/440-1440
Hours: 10AM–7PM Monday–Friday; 10AM–6PM Saturday; closed Sunday

This West African market is a good source for starchy flours and tubers, plantains, frozen grated cassava, palm oils, some meats, and coconuts. There's also a large selection of dried fish—including stockfish, cod, and shrimp (West Africans have a particular flair for using dried fish in spicy stews and fritters).

The Souk

11730 Pinehurst Way NE, Seattle
Phone: 206/367-8387
Hours: 10AM–9PM Monday–Saturday; 11AM–7PM Sunday

This formerly Pakistani-owned shop was sold two years ago to the Ethiopian owner of the restaurant next door. Look for a good selection of esoteric spices, flours, halal meats, and, of course, green coffee. The next-door shack offers some spicy Ethiopian food to whet your appetite.

Note: At one time, this shop was related to the Pike Place Market shop of the same name. That relationship no longer exists.

The Souk . . . . see Middle Eastern

asian The Asian community in Seattle, bustling, dynamic, and highly visible, has transformed the food and restaurant scene beyond imagination. From the Vietnamese pho shops that have seemingly sprung up overnight in every neighborhood to the pungent kimchi available in virtually every supermarket, Asian food has become an integral part of our larder.

Of course, Asian food is an infinitely complex culinary mosaic. There are foods that embrace the commonplace, such as the daily rice and noodles. There are vibrant tastes—the warm tingle of chiles and spices, the exotic perfume of lemongrass, the tang of lime, the fresh, cool tastes of aromatic herbs. Once considered exotic and unusual, these are becoming daily staples in Seattleites' home kitchens.

Historically comprising three major Asian groups—Chinese, Japanese, and Filipino—Seattle's Asian community today also encompasses Southeast Asians, including Cambodians, Laotians, and Vietnamese; Koreans; and Pacific Islanders, including Hawaiians, Samoans, Tongans, and Fijians, all commingling and increasingly swayed by contemporary American influences. Just as the Asian community includes a breadth and diversity of cultures, all Asian markets are not alike. While they may tend to carry similar products, there are differences, some subtle and some more obvious, depending on their base clientele.

Korean markets, for example, are easily identifiable by their selection of chili powders, dried fish, and seaweed, often available in what may seem to the uninitiated like preposterously oversized bags. There are mountains of snow white napa cabbages and gallon-sized tubs of pickles—not just the familiar kimchi, but various other combinations of sour chile-spiked cabbage, daikon radish, cucumber, and assorted herbs—somewhat like the half or full sours in Jewish delis.

Southeast Asian markets tend to carry a tremendous assortment of fresh herbs, such as dazzling bunches of basil, mint, cilantro, and lemongrass, and healthful greens in profusion. Often they also include fresh and live fish markets and in-house butcher shops.

Japanese markets, with their finely sliced meats and aesthetic arrangements of fish and shellfish, tempt the eye as well as the palate. Many of the food products they carry are imported from Japan and demand premium prices (which even the Japanese customers grumble at). Beautifully packaged and wrapped, from intricately laid out seaweed and rice balls to gaudy, wacky packets of sweets shaped like robots or action figures, Japanese foods amuse and delight.

One reminder: The selection of markets I have chosen to include here is idiosyncratic, based on personal taste and my feeling that they offer some product or service that is unique. Particularly in areas with large concentrations of Asians, such as the International District or White Center, there are any number of other markets that are fine, comprehensive places to do your shopping. Park your car, follow your nose, and explore. Take whatever shortcuts and make whatever improvisations are necessary; just make these delicious, health-giving cuisines a part of your diet today.

The New Face of the International District

"If there's one date to remember when talking about the Asian community today in Seattle, it's 1965." Ron Chew, the executive director of the Wing Luke Asian Museum in the International District, is a man who has his finger on the pulse of the community. "That is when Congress reformed the immigration laws and opened the door for the flow of Southeast Asians to this city." After I toured his fascinating museum chronicling the history of Asian Americans in Seattle, Ron patiently sat down with me and explained the intricate threads woven through his community.

During the mid-1970s and the 1980s almost 40,000 Vietnamese, Cambodian, Thai, and Laotian refugees settled in Washington state, almost 60 percent of them in Seattle. Prior to this, what we

Yick Fung is one of the oldest retail establishments in the International District.

now call the International District was a dying, static community, a "small town" shrinking yearly. Its upwardly mobile had fled to the suburbs. Lack of parking, exacerbated by projects such as the Kingdome, had dried up the customer base. The old Chinatown corridor of mom-and-pop shops stretching the length of King Street was in danger of losing whatever life was still left in it.

"Today the stores reflect the changing demographics. Before the Southeast Asians came, you couldn't get things like fresh lychees, durian, and the variety and scope of herbal medicines that you can today. And the action has shifted to Jackson Street and south along Rainier Avenue."

Major new commercial and residential developments have recently been completed or are currently under way in the International District. The Union Station makeover, along with the Village Square development, Safeco Field, and the newly expanded Uwajimaya will undoubtedly reshape and the area in the twenty-first century.

Wing Luke Asian Museum
407 Seventh Ave. S, Seattle
Phone: 206/623-5124
Hours: Tuesday–Friday 11AM–4:30PM; Saturday and Sunday noon–4PM; closed Mondays
Admission: $2.50

Glossary

agar agar: a vegetarian jelling agent obtained from seaweed, which does not require refrigeration to set. Available either as a powder or in translucent strands.

amaranth leaf (Chinese spinach): a dark green leaf tinged with red, with a fuzzy texture. Can be used interchangeably with spinach and requires less cooking time.

azuki bean: a small red bean, used primarily in cakes and desserts, available both whole and in a sweetened paste.

bird's nest: the tasteless, gelatinous regurgitated spittle of the swift. Top grades are nearly complete white cups. "Black nests," which are cheaper, have moss, feathers, and grass mixed with the saliva.

black beans, fermented: partly decomposed, dried, and salted soybeans used as a seasoning. Considered a wonderful complement to seafood.

bonito: used in a dried flake form, together with kombu seaweed, to make dashi soup stock and also as a garnish.

burdock *(gobo)*: a slender, hairy taproot eaten in Japan as a vegetable. Chinese use it only medicinally.

candlenut *(kemiri)*: a large, waxy nut used to thicken curry pastes. Raw macadamia nuts are the closest substitute.

chili oil: a fiery red chile pepper–infused cooking oil. Store-bought chili oil tends to go rancid quickly, but the Kadoya brand is pretty good.

Chinese broccoli *(gai lan)*: a dull green plant with clusters of white flowers resembling broccoli; a little more bitter, but quite delicious.

Chinese cabbage (bok choy): a green resembling Swiss chard, with snow white stalks, a bulbous base, and dark green leaves. There are over twenty kinds of bok choy, with four or five kinds regularly available here.

Chinese chives: a plant with long, dark green flat leaves, with a stronger flavor than Western chives. Also sold blanched and complete with buds.

coconut milk: the liquid wrung from the grated and soaked meat of the coconut, not the cloudy water found inside. Fundamental to soups, stews, roasts, beverages, puddings, candies, and cakes in Asia. A recommended brand is Chaokoh from Thailand. Leftovers freeze well.

dashi-no-moto: an instant granular form of soup stock containing bonito, kombu seaweed, and, unfortunately, lots of MSG and additives.

durian: a large, notoriously stinky, spiky, green-skinned fruit prized in Southeast Asia. Its pungent smell has been described as a cross between Camembert and turpentine.

fish sauce *(nam pla, nuoc mam, patis)*: a thin, brown, salty liquid, rich in protein, produced from fermented shrimp and small fish, and used similarly to soy sauce, as a salty flavoring. Look for the Viet Huong Three Crabs brand from Thailand.

five-spice powder: a fragrant, golden brown powder; not always exactly five spices, but commonly includes star anise, cinnamon, cloves, fennel seed, licorice root, Szechuan peppercorns, ginger, and cardamom.

galangal: a fresh rhizome, similar to ginger but larger and pale yellow, with zebralike markings and pink shoots. Used extensively in Thai cooking.

gingko nut *(ginnan)*: a yellowish green fruit from the gingko tree. Must be shelled before steaming or grilling. The Chinese use it in stuffings and puddings.

glutinous rice: rounded, short-grain rice that acquires a sticky texture when cooked. Used in broth and sweet and savory dishes.

golden needle (lily bud): a dried, unopened flower of the yellow or orange day lily, popular in vegetarian cooking.

kaffir lime: a large lime with bumpy, dark green skin. Glossy lime leaves and shredded dried rind are both used in Thai cooking and add a distinct citrus flavor.

kampyo: dried gourd strips used as a filling for some sushi, or for tying food.

konnyaku: a bland, gelatinous paste made from the root of the devil's tongue plant, formed into either bricks or strings. Konnyaku noodles, called shirataki (meaning white waterfall), are sold packaged in water.

kudzu: a high-quality thickening starch made from the kudzu vine.

lemongrass: a fibrous, gray-green grass with a white bulbus base and a subtle lemony perfume. Widely available fresh and dried. Fresh is far superior.

longan: a small, brown-skinned fruit related to the lychee, with translucent flesh and a large glossy black seed. Available fresh in bunches or canned.

lotus root: a rhizome shaped like a large sausage link; when sliced, it is beautifully porous. The flesh reminds some people of artichokes. Used pickled, simmered, stir-fried, and in tempura. Lotus seeds are sold dried, and lotus leaves are used as food wrappers.

mirin: a sweet, liquid flavoring made from glutinous rice and distilled spirits. Used exclusively in cooking for its sweetness, not for its alcohol flavor.

miso: a fermented paste of grains and soybeans, available in a variety of colors and flavors. A highly nutritious basic foodstuff, but very high in sodium.

mochi: cooked glutinous rice, pounded to a paste and shaped into a cake. Eaten particularly at the time of the Chinese New Year.

mustard greens (gai choi): a green large-leafed plant, sold fresh, dried, or pickled.

natto: fermented soybeans with a pungent smell and a thready stickiness. Can be found in the freezer case.

noodles:

cellophane (mung, bean thread): a fine, threadlike noodle made from mung beans, usually soaked before cooking.

rice, dried and fresh: sold in a variety of thicknesses. Dried rice noodles need to be soaked before cooking. Fresh ones should not be refrigerated, or they'll be impossible to separate.

soba: made from wheat flour and buckwheat; sometimes flavored with tea.

sweet potato: made from sweet potato starch; used in Korean and Japanese cooking.

udon: a wheat flour noodle sold fresh along with a powdered soup base to make the dish of the same name.

pandan leaf (screwpine leaf): a long, thin, dark green screwpine leaf, sold fresh in bunches. They add a unique floral, somewhat grassy flavor and a green coloring to desserts and rice dishes.

pea eggplant: a tiny pea-sized eggplant with a sharp, bitter taste, used especially in Thai cooking.

rambutan: a fruit resembling a hairy red egg. The name comes from *rambut*, Malay for hair. Inside is a translucent, juicy egg-shaped fruit, prized for its refreshing qualities.

rice vinegars: an array of mild vinegars, ranging from delicate white rice vinegar to sweet red rice vinegar and rich black rice vinegar (similar to balsamic).

rice wine (Shaoxing wine): a wine made from glutinous rice, rice millet, and yeast; has a high alcohol content (about 18 percent). Used for both cooking and drinking.

sansho: the seed of the Japanese prickly ash; closely related to Szechuan peppercorns. Highly aromatic, with a slight numbing effect on the tongue.

sauces:

> **bean sauce:** a paste made from fermented soybeans, which comes whole or ground and is vital to Szechuan and Hunan cooking.
>
> **chili pastes:** pastes used in cooking by the Chinese, but as condiments by Southeast Asians. Ingredients vary but usually include chile peppers, salt, oil, and often garlic. They may also include black beans, preserved radish, ginger, and soybeans. Southeast Asian brands are usually preserved with potassium sorbate and can vary in quality. Sriracha is a sweet table condiment, on the order of ketchup, and can be used very creatively in non-Asian as well as Thai cooking.
>
> **hoisin:** a fine, brownish red paste; almost always sweet, garlicky, and spicy, with five-spice powder and a hint of chile. Texture is very jammy.
>
> **oyster:** a Cantonese staple made from oysters, water, salt, cornstarch, and usually caramel coloring.

sea slug (sea cucumber, *bèche de mer*): a sea-dwelling gastropod whose name in Chinese means "ginseng of the sea." Usually sold dried. Sea slugs must be boiled in several changes of water and then cleaned, leaving them with a tasteless crunchiness.

seaweed:

> **hijiki:** a particularly nutritious rich black seaweed, often simmered and lightly pickled.
>
> **kombu:** a dark, large-leafed seaweed used in making dashi stock.
>
> **nori:** thin green sheets of dried seaweed, often toasted, used for sushi and crumbled over soba noodles.
>
> **wakame:** a type of seaweed mainly used in miso soup.

sesame oil: a nutty, toasted, golden-colored oil made from sesame seed. Not to be used interchangeably with raw sesame oil from the health food store.

shark's fin: the dried fin of a warm-water Asian shark; a luxury item. It is soaked repeatedly in successive changes of water and served as amber-colored gelatinous strands suspended in an exquisitely rich stock.

shiso: the leaf of the perilla, or beefsteak, plant; available in two forms. Red is used mostly to give color to pickles, especially umeboshi; green has many uses at the table.

shrimp, dried: small, shelled, dried pink shrimp, with a strong, salty flavor. The larger the shrimp, the more expensive they are.

shrimp paste *(blachan, terasi)*: a stinky paste made from fermented shrimps, dried and available in many forms, from solid brown blocks to a bottled pink-gray liquid.

star anise: a dark brown, star-shaped pod from a small evergreen tree, with a distinctive licorice flavor and scent.

Szechuan peppercorn: a reddish brown berry, not related to peppercorns, with a strangely numbing effect and a clean spicy-woodsy fragrance.

tempeh: a pressed fermented soybean product, with a nutty taste and a very high protein content.

thousand-year-old egg: a duck egg, blue-black in color from salting and preserving, with a pungent flavor. They are in fact usually only about a hundred days old.

tree ear (cloud ear): a dried cultivated tree fungus, with little flavor but a pleasing crunch. The smallest tiny gnarled black flakes are the best, and the least fibrous.

trefoil *(mitsuba)*: a Japanese wild chervil used in soups and salads and with vinegared and fried food. Its name literally means "three-leaf" in Japanese.

umeboshi: dried, salt-pickled Japanese apricots, usually colored red with red shiso leaf. Check brands carefully to make sure they are not adulterated with food coloring.

wasabi: a powder or premade paste of horseradish powder and green food coloring (see page 216).

water chestnut: the edible tuber of a water plant. When fresh, it has a wonderful sweet crispness similar to jicama and is very refreshing. Choose firm ones with as few blemishes as possible.

yuzu: a Japanese citron used mostly for zest. The juice is also mixed with soy sauce and vinegar to make ponzu sauce.

CENTRAL SEATTLE (INTERNATIONAL DISTRICT)

Shopping in the International District requires you to take the approach you would if you were going abroad: Be self-sufficient, and be aware of the rough lay of the land. Unlike Chinatowns such as San Francisco's or New York's, our International District is more spread out, without much produce or action spilling out into the streets. Meander through those streets, though, and you'll find bargains galore, with enough quality and variety to put any mainstream supermarket to shame.

Asian Connection

625 S Jackson St., Seattle
Phone: 206/587-6010
Hours: 9AM–8PM every day

In most traditional Chinatowns, a large percentage of the business is done out on the sidewalks. This isn't the case in Seattle, though, so our shopping district looks drabber. Asian Connection is one of the few grocery markets that *has* spilled out into the street. All of the produce turns over quickly here, so expect freshness and quality. At first you might be taken aback by the unfamiliar and unusual array of produce, but look closer and you will see more familiar items—such as cabbage, potatoes, and beans—among the pea shoots, water spinach, and lotus roots. The produce I've picked up here has generally been excellent, but that doesn't mean you won't occasionally get a bad apple. I'm not as impressed with the fish: most come cellophane wrapped and don't look very appealing, although there is a refrigerated case of shrimp, both heads on and headless, in various sizes at very reasonable prices. As in many Asian markets, the meat available here is mostly inexpensive stewing cuts, perfect for a slow-cooked, savory stew.

Canton Noodle House

506 12th St. S, Seattle
Phone: 206/329-5650
Hours: 10AM–6PM Tuesday–Sunday; closed Monday

My Chinese brother-in-law says the true test of a Chinese restaurant is in their basic won ton noodle soup. Canton Noodle House, on the southern outskirts of the International District, passes this test with flying colors. A steady stream of customers shows up here looking for the ultimate Chinese comfort food. The won tons are available in two varieties: standard pork and shrimp, and the *sau kiu*, which are similar but also include crunchy cloud-ear fungi. Both are ethereal, light as clouds, and bursting with meat and flavor. They are available frozen along with a selection of chow mein, won ton noodles, and Shanghai noodles, all made on the premises. My fusion-minded son asked me to include his favorite quick snack recipe here—open a can of Campbell's chicken noodle soup, add a few slices of fresh ginger, bring to a boil, and drop in a half-dozen frozen Canton Noodle won tons. Cook till they float to the top, sprinkle with a few drops of sesame oil, and serve.

King's Barbecue House

518 Sixth Ave. S, Seattle
Phone: 206/622-2828
Hours: 10AM–6:30PM every day

Hanging barbecued duck at King's Barbecue House.

2710 Beacon Ave. S, Seattle
Phone: 206/720-4715
Hours: 10:30AM–6:30PM every day

You can always expect a line out the door of this small, spartan shop. Customers are drawn by the succulent hanging meats in the window, which are made on the premises. Barbecued pork here is tender and juicy with a caramelized, almost burnt crust. Buy it by the pound or have them hack it into greasy, finger-licking slices served on a mountain of rice. You can also buy soy sauce chicken, salt-roasted chicken, and crispy roast duck and pork, all excellent and convenient for midweek meals with a little stir-fried veggie accompaniment.

Long Khanh

309 12th Ave. S, Seattle
Phone: 206/568-0636
Hours: 9AM–7:30PM every day

Although this market doesn't present an inviting entrance (it looks more like a wholesale warehouse), it is worth checking out for a good selection of cooking utensils and an excellent assortment of produce. If you love Vietnamese-style coffee, this is the place to buy inexpensive little brewers, Vietnamese coffee (which is similar to espresso, but with a little added chicory), and sweetened condensed milk.

Saigon Deli

1200 S Jackson St., Seattle
Phone: 206/322-3700
Hours: 7:30AM–7:30PM every day

Saigon Deli is one of those busy little storefronts on 12th Avenue, with cars double- and triple-parked in front. Their specialty is *banh mi*, my son's favorite lunch-box sandwich, featuring a legacy of French colonial occupation of Vietnam, the baguette. Here it is stuffed with a combination of pâté, sliced pork, a bit of pickled carrot and onion, cilantro, and chile. All for just $1.50 each (buy five, get the sixth free). They'll also sell you fresh rice paper rolls stuffed with shrimp and noodles, an assortment of rice dumplings, some hot entrees to go, and those luridly colored corn- and bean-based desserts and drinks so popular in Asia.

Thanh Son Tofu

118 12th Ave. (½ mile N of Jackson St.), Seattle
Phone: 206/320-1316
Hours: 8AM–7PM Wednesday–Monday; closed Tuesday

In the great American tradition of entrepreneurship, Hung Do arrived in Seattle three years ago to open the first Vietnamese tofu-making shop. He describes the difference between Vietnamese and other styles of tofu as being more soybean flavor, but I would say that the key to his incredibly voluptuous and silky tofu is freshness: the difference between canned and fresh peas, or anemic winter tomatoes and gorgeous sun-ripened summer ones. The store even has an area where day-old tofu is sold for half price. That's taking the art of tofu making seriously.

Hung Do is full of ideas for expanding his product line. He plans to introduce lemongrass-flavored tofu, tofu with onion and mushroom flavors, organic tofu, and more. Till then, try the onion-flavored fried tofu cakes, which are surprisingly meaty tasting and pretty yummy. Look for soy milk, tofu pudding, and a selection of Vietnamese desserts (each of which is painstakingly assembled to order, layer by layer).

The biggest drawback of this place is that no one seems to speak English. Never mind, just persist, and "Grandma" at the register will eventually figure out what you want. It's worth it.

Viet Wah Supermarket

1032 S Jackson St., Seattle
Phone: 206/329-1399
Hours: 9AM–8PM every day

This store is a credible alternative to Uwajimaya. It doesn't have the long local history, but it is big and comprehensive, and its prices are a bargain. The store is owned by ethnic Chinese who cater to a large Southeast Asian community. Check out the in-house herbalist, mimicking the Western supermarket trend toward one-stop shopping. Look for unusual cuts of meat and offal such as fresh goat meat, frog's legs, and an assortment of cow and pig innards. The produce selection is large and gives good value; the fresh fish selection is extensive and leans toward lesser-known, inexpensive "trash" fish.

Wong Tung Seafood

210 S 12th Ave., Seattle
Phone: 206/323-9222
Hours: 9AM–6PM every day

Here's one of my favorite places to buy seafood, especially shellfish
and live spot prawns in season. The selection isn't huge, but what is
there is fabulously fresh fish, particularly shellfish, at rock-bottom
prices. Owner Mui Truong and her husband work hard every day and
have done so since 1988. Spot prawns from Hood Canal are half the
price you'd see at Pike Place Market. Choose your fish as Asians prefer to: live, thrashing, and gloriously fresh. But as a sign sternly notes,
you must not take any fish off the premises live. You'll have to be content with having Mui take it behind the counter, give it a sharp rap to
the head, and then gut, clean, and wrap it for you to take home.

Yick Fung & Co.

705 King St. S, Seattle
Phone: 206/623-5966
Hours: 8:30AM–5PM Monday–Saturday; closed Sunday

Exotic Chinese snacks at Yick Fung & Co.

Poke your head into Yick Fung & Co, housed in a designated land-mark building. This old-fashioned purveyor of Chinese dried fruits and nuts offers a tantalizing glimpse of what the International District must have looked like in years gone by. Rows of glass jars lined up on wood shelves contain all manner of dried fruits and seeds. Chinese people have traditionally preferred to snack on these in lieu of candy (although youthful tastes today are becoming more Americanized). I saw everything from sweet Malay dried lemon to preserved Thai and lemon ginger in bulk. Although I don't normally associate them with Chinese food, I tasted spiced fire-red olives—an intriguing blend of spicy, sweet, and salty, all in one mouthful. James Malcolm Mar is the elderly owner of this business that has been going for over eighty years, and he won't hesitate to chat and offer you samples.

Uwajimaya

519 Sixth Ave. S, Seattle
Phone: 206/624-6248
Hours: 9 AM–8 PM every day

NE 24th St. and Bel-Red Rd., Bellevue
Phone: 425/747-9012
Hours: 9 AM–8 PM every day

In the almost seven decades of its existence, Uwajimaya has become synonomous with "Asian market" here in Seattle. Its success is in no small part due to its ability to change, reinvent itself, and appeal to its legions of non-Asian customers.

From its beginnings in 1928 when founder Fujimatsu Moriguchi started selling fishcakes to Japanese laborers in Tacoma out of the back of his truck—until today, Uwajimaya has stayed true to its mission: to be known as *the* information specialist on all things Asian. As the still family-owned business prepares to enter the new millennium, what this translates into is a well-stocked emporium devoted to offering a breadth of pan-Asian gifts, groceries, kitchenware, produce, seafood, meat and poultry, and deli items.

Uwajimaya Village, the newest transformation of this venerable Asian institution, encompasses a 60,000-square-foot market, and several restaurants, along with condominiums, at the corner of 6th and King. Surprisingly, given the no-expenses-spared mindset, the layout seems somewhat chaotic and poorly designed. From the parking lot to the checkout counters, it doesn't take a lot of people to create gridlock here. Shop there anyway, but do yourself a favor: if you can help it, avoid peak weekend hours.

Fish and Shellfish: The new Uwajimaya takes its fresh fish and shellfish section seriously. The department has been considerably expanded and doesn't rely as much as the old location did on pre-cut and wrapped items. Live fish tanks usually offer six or seven types of oysters, clams, mussels, spot prawns in season, and farmed fish like tilapia and sea bass. Those who are lazy like me and find picking through Dungeness crab somewhat of a chore will be pleased with giant live king and spider crab. The store offers an excellent selection of sashimi cuts already sliced and trayed as well as plenty of sashimi-grade fillets of fish. Reflecting on its roots, there's an assortment or imported frozen fish, many from Japan. Prices are very reasonable and staff willingly answer questions and seem to know what they are talking about.

Produce: Produce has always played a substantial role in Uwajimaya's business and the selection at the new location is even bigger and better. Displays are abundant. Prices are resonable and quality is top of the line. You can always find great bunches of *gai lan*, *choi sum*, baby bok choy, amaranth, fresh water chestnuts, taro root, long beans, shiso and chrysanthemum leaves, and much more. I have been elbowed and pushed aside by little old Japanese ladies when creamy white, unblemished lotus root has been brought in. Fresh *matsutake* mushrooms, for those who can afford them, are available in the fall and are one of life's great experiences. Uwajimaya doesn't skimp on everyday fruits and vegetables either, and there is now a small but welcome organic section.

Meat and Poultry: Uwajimaya specializes in cutting paper-thin slices of meat ready for sukiyaki and grilling. Beef and pork with various gradations of marbling are sliced, neatly packaged, and displayed alongside more traditional steaks and humble stewing cuts. Poultry tends to be factory-produced industrial grade, but in a bow to their Asian clientele who appreciate such luxuries, squab, duck, and Cornish hens are readily available. This place also stocks spicy Filipino *longaniza* sausage, made of lean and fat pork well flavored with pepper, garlic, and other ingredients and briefly cured, as well as various Hawaiian imported meat products.

Prepared Foods and Deli: Uwajimaya's deli is a popular spot that now has an expanded seating area. If the program includes lunch, a hot food counter sells pan-Asian fast food, none extraordinary, but all speedily delivered and filling. As of this writing, several planned outside eateries have not yet opened. A central counter has packages of sushi and other prepared foods. Should you get homesick for the islands, pick up that great Hawaiian delicacy—Spam sushi. I love the *onigiri* rolls, not least because of their clever packaging. These are rice balls stuffed with everything from umeboshi (pickled plum) to shiso leaf to salted salmon. Since they are so portable, they make a great meal on the go. Japanese confections, made locally of sugar and various beans and root vegetables, are wrapped and ready to go.

Frozen Foods, Noodles, and Groceries: Row upon row of Asian groceries, neatly separated by country, make it much easier to find the exotic ingredient you need. The store is strongest in its Japanese sections, but you'll find a broad selection from the entire Asian spectrum. If you don't see what you're looking for, just ask; Uwajimaya employees are uncommonly helpful. The refrigerated aisle carries most every Asian perishable, including a good selection of fish cakes for *oden,* a hearty, peasant-style stew of fish dumplings with flavor absorbers such as radish, bean curd, or potato. As you might expect in a Japanese market, there are a variety of miso pastes, made from rice, barley, or soybeans. In the freezer case you'll find big packages of dumplings (Chinese, Japanese, or Korean style) and natto (fermented soybeans, thready and sticky, with a strong aroma and flavor—definitely an acquired taste). I always take home a package of edamame, delicious fresh soybeans, sold frozen in one-pound bags. Boil and lightly salt them, then set them out as pre-dinner munchies.

Gifts and Non-Grocery Items: Kinokuniya is a chain of bookstores carrying a huge range of Japanese-language books including phone-book-thick comics and magazines with titles like *Not Fashion, Fruits,* and *Gong Women's Pro-Wrestling,* that occupies a corner of Uwajimaya Village. They also stock a great assortment of English-language cookbooks specializing in Asian cuisine, as well as lavish books on Japanese and other Asian decorative arts. Calligraphy pens and paintbrushes, lacquerware, china, bonsai, makeup, fabric, you name it—this store stocks it all.

NORTH

Aurora Oriental Market

15202 Aurora Ave. N, Seattle
Phone: 206/362-5575
Hours: 9AM–9PM Monday–Saturday; 9AM–8PM Sunday

This large Korean supermarket caters to the Korean community located in North Seattle and Shoreline. They are a great source for large tubs of chile-tinted kimchi (both cabbage and other veggies) as well as fermented fish, squid, and oysters, strong foods meant to be counterbalanced with vast quantities of steamed white rice. Thinly sliced, trimmed, and packaged meats are ready for sukiyaki, kalbi, and bulgogi in the butcher shop. A large selection of noodles, tofu, teas, soy and other sauces, and chili pastes rounds out the grocery section.

Thai Curry Barbecue Shrimp in the Shell

This marinade is very simple and is fabulous on chicken and flank steak as well. Serve the shrimp with cucumber salad, spiked with chile and fresh mint and dressed with rice vinegar, and lots of white rice.

Serves 3 to 4

   1 heaping tablespoon Thai red curry paste

   1 tablespoon brown sugar

   2 tablespoons soy sauce

   1 teaspoon oyster sauce

   Juice of ½ lime

   1 or 2 cloves of garlic, minced

   2 tablespoons olive oil

   1 pound medium shrimp (about 45 to 60), left in the shell but slit down the back

Preheat grill to high heat.

Mix all ingredients but shrimp. Pour over shrimp and marinate for about 1 hour.

Thread shrimp through two parallel bamboo skewers for support and ease of turning. Grill over hot fire for about 2 to 3 minutes per side. Serve.

Note: You can buy red and green Thai curry pastes in most Asian markets. The flavor varies from brand to brand. Green is the more incendiary, having a base of green chiles, cilantro, and spices; red has dried red chiles as its base. I find the Mae Ploy brand to be very good, and it keeps forever in the fridge. You can use these pastes as seasonings in home-fried potatoes, noodle soups, fried rice, and sautéed meat and fish.

SOUTH

Great Wall Shopping Mall

18230 East Valley Hwy (just off Hwy 167), Kent
Internet: www.greatwallmall.com

This is the first mall of its kind in this area, patterned after similar enterprises in southern California and Vancouver. Incongruously situated in a no-man's-land of business parks and industrial estates near IKEA, the giant Swedish home store, the upscale Great Wall Shopping Mall is devoted to Asian food, restaurants, gift items, and sundry services. Even with an occupancy that currently hovers around 50 percent, this mall is definitely worth the drive if you have an interest in Asian food and culture.

Champion Gourmet Co.

Suite 122
Phone: 425/251-1604
Hours: 9AM–9PM every day
Internet: www.champion.jumpbusiness.com

With the speakers cranked up full volume, Jacky Chiu and his hardworking staff irrepressibly demonstrate just how delicious Taiwanese-style sausages and jerky are. "Here, try a taste of this—it's my favorite," he says. "Taiwan-style is better, juicier and sweeter. You like spicy?" And boy, did I. This company smokes and cures, on the premises, all sorts of beef and pork and even bean curd jerky (available in flavors such as satay, teriyaki style, and black pepper). I took some home and my always ravenous son, a confirmed meatatarian, wolfed down the honey-sweet beef jerky and the five-spice bean curd jerky with equal zest.

The Chinese love what they call crispy pork floss, which is pork cooked and dried with soy sauce and sugar till it is the consistency of candy floss. It's used as a flavoring sprinkled on rice or noodles. In this shop it is available in several styles, all curiously "morish" (as in "keep eating more"). Handsome squid steaks are also smoked on the premises. There is truly something for everyone here.

Asian Eggplant Caviar

I prefer to use round globe eggplant for this dish; the long, narrow Asian style is not meaty enough. Use this dish as a starter, or as a side dish with grilled tuna or chicken. The leftovers make great sandwiches.

1 large eggplant

1 tablespoon neutral vegetable oil, such as canola

2 to 3 cloves garlic

2 to 3 thin slices ginger, minced

3 to 4 scallions, diced

1 tablespoon fermented black beans

1 tablespoon brown sugar

1 tablespoon rice vinegar

1 to 2 tablespoons soy sauce

Cilantro leaves

Preheat oven to 475 degrees F.

Prick eggplant all over and bake till soft and collapsed, about 15 to 20 minutes. Remove from oven, split in half, and scrape flesh away from skin. Chop flesh roughly. Discard skin.

Preheat wok on high heat on stovetop. Have rest of ingredients ready. Add oil to pan, then garlic, ginger, and scallions. Stir for a minute, then add eggplant puree, followed by black beans, sugar, rice vinegar, and soy sauce.

Cook for about 5 minutes or till any moisture has evaporated and mixture has the consistency of thick peanut butter.

Turn onto serving dish and garnish with cilantro leaves. Can be served hot or at room temperature.

Note: Chinese fermented black beans are an ancient condiment made of soybeans that have been partially fermented, then dried and sometimes salted. They add a sharp, winelike flavor and a pleasing saltiness to many foods, and are especially good with seafood. Some recipes suggest rinsing the salted variety, but I don't find that necessary; simply chop them and add to your recipe. The fermented variety is usually sold in glass jars and may be flavored with ginger, sugar, chile, and sometimes orange peel.

Imperial Tea Court

Suite 135
Phone: 425/251-8191
Hours: 9AM–9PM every day
Internet: www.imperialtea.com

Lu Yu, the "sage of tea" who lived in the 8th century A.D. and wrote the earliest book on the subject of tea, the *Cha Jing* or *The Treatise on Tea*, advised tea enthusiasts to copy his treatise on four to six scrolls and then hang them up for quick and ready reference at all times—thus revealing his own sense of self-importance.

Imperial Tea Court has followed his injunction. This serene and utterly beautiful tearoom is devoted to presenting and educating the public in all the nuances of top-grade Chinese tea. And yes, Lu Yu's scrolls hang on the walls and are immortalized in the Lu Yu Room, available for private use and decorated with hand-laid split bamboo flooring from Taiwan, mahogany seating, and an exquisite split bamboo tray for use in a full-blown tea ceremony.

This store, an offshoot of the San Francisco location, has been open since 1999. As he graciously sat with me, manager James Burke described and prepared with loving attention to detail a pot of Monkey-Picked Tie Guan Yin. (The name is intriguing, but rest assured that Tie Guan Yin is no longer monkey picked but rather denotes the best of the house.) About fifty varieties of tea are for sale, as well as a beautiful assortment of teapots and paraphernalia. As you might expect, none of this stuff comes cheap, but the price per cup is no more than you would pay for a drink in a bar.

99 Ranch Market

Phone: 425/251-9099
Hours: 9AM–9PM every day

The anchor store of the mall is quite a place. Picture a vast full-service supermarket, spanking new and sparkling clean, entirely devoted to Asian food. Aisle after aisle reveals everything from freezers of rice balls and buns to expensive delicacies such as sea cucumbers, bird's nests, and shark's fin. The deli is a carnivore's delight, with both Hong Kong– and Taiwan-style barbecue. The produce section is huge and well labeled. In the seafood section, fish buried in ice front tanks containing live tilapia, catfish, striped bass, and clams, all sustained by steady streams of running water.

When I visited during the height of the Moon Festival, held during the September full moon to mark the end of the harvest, I saw stacks of bright red boxes of moon cakes: dense, sweet, golden brown pastries filled with red bean paste or lotus seed. Embedded in each was a preserved duck egg yolk, symbolizing the moon itself. (Avoid the bakery, though; the egg custard tarts, a favorite of my family, here are rubbery and totally tasteless.)

Maruta Shoten

1024 S Bailey St. (just north of Boeing Field, off exit 162 from I–5 south), Seattle
Phone: 206/767-5002
Hours: 9:30AM–6:30PM Monday–Saturday; 10AM–6PM Sunday

This large market caters to a sprawling Japanese community with an in-depth assortment of basics, from miso paste to soba noodles. Prices are reasonable and generally cheaper than Uwajimaya. Especially popular is the selection of ready-made dishes such as sushi, bento boxes, and sukiyaki. During the fall, baskets of prime-grade *matsutake* or pine needle mushrooms, with their tightly closed caps and slight pine fragrance, are an expensive seasonal delicacy. I was told that many customers buy them to ship to Japan because, as expensive as they are here, they are still far cheaper than in Japan. Fresh *mochi* (pounded rice cakes) and other traditional foods are available at the time of the Asian New Year. Mochi are an essential celebration dish, and many people try to eat a lot of them when they are fresh and still soft. Later, when they become hard, they are toasted till they puff up and develop an enticing golden color, and are then dipped in soy sauce or sugar and eaten.

Mrs. Nasatka shows off her famous sushi at Lee's Produce.

WEST

Lee's Produce

9435 Delridge Way SW, Seattle
Phone: 206/762-5220
Hours: 9AM–9PM every day

Mrs. Nasatka makes the best kimchi in town, and everybody knows it. Or at least all the readers of *Seattle Weekly* know it, because they have voted hers the best. She says it's so good because it is home-made: no shortcuts, no premade sauces, everything from scratch. She says Americans like kimchi before it has had a chance to fully fer-ment, when it is still fresh and crunchy, whereas Koreans like it pun-gent and nose-wrinklingly sour. It's all a matter of personal preference. What I tasted was pretty darn fine.

Big fat rolls of Korean-style sushi, made with pickled daikon, fish cake, spinach, and sesame (no raw fish), are made daily at this mar-ket and are usually sold out by morning. Customers have been known to call after tasting it once and ask for some to be put on hold regularly. In addition, this rabbit warren of a market is crammed with a great selection of Korean groceries and very fresh-looking and inexpensive produce stacked in boxes in the front.

New Angkor Market

9660 16th Ave. SW, Seattle
Phone: 206/763-9269
Hours: 8AM–9PM every day

The largest concentration of Cambodians in Seattle is here in White Center, and they like to shop at Angkor Market. Cambodian food is similar to Thai or Vietnamese, with a little more Chinese influence. Full of flavor and delicate nuances, with a huge variety of herbs (many completely unfamiliar to Westerners), it is a cuisine based on the prod-ucts of fresh water and fertile land. Sauces are tropical, with extensive use of coconut milk, lemongrass, galangal, lime leaves, and fish sauce.

I saw an impressive selection of exceptionally fresh herbs at Angkor Market. These are typically eaten as salad accompaniments to soups and stews. The market has an in-house butcher, a fish market, and a big jewelry market with a resident gemologist. Also available is the usual hit parade of groceries, rice, and noodles, as well as kitchenware, including the absolute best mortar-and-pestle set you will ever use.

A Tale of Wasabi

Sushi lovers know wasabi as the ubiquitous green paste that can violently bite if applied too enthusiastically. That paste is not the real thing, however, but merely a cheap substitute-horseradish powder dyed green and mixed with mustard. Fresh wasabi (*Wasabia japonica*) is an entirely different creature. This rather ugly rhizome, knobby and pale green, is delicate and mildly vegetal tasting, surprisingly refined. It's got a kick, but that fades fast and is followed by a little sweetness. People who have tasted it are wildly enthusiastic. It is to the reconstituted preground stuff what Chateau Lafite-Rothschild is to Andres Cold Duck.

Fresh wasabi is scarcely available in the United States and is considered rather difficult to grow—except here in the Pacific Northwest. Catherine Chadwick is an agronomist with a mission: to educate the public and win them over to this captivating aromatic; she discovered the perfect habitat for growing wasabi on Pat and Doc Johnson's farm in the mountains around Shelton, Washington, and persuaded them to plant it. The wasabi is grown in ice-cold shallow streams, conditions that duplicate closely the habitat of wild wasabi. The water in the Johnsons' stream is exceptionally pure, with very little temperature fluctuation year-round.

"When I took the fresh wasabi to local sushi restaurants, they all gasped, then hustled me out the back door," Catherine recalls. "I was told, 'We can't serve that stuff. It's too expensive, and the customers wouldn't want the other stuff if we let them taste this.'"

Fresh wasabi *is* quite expensive, but a little goes a very long way. It should be grated very fine and then allowed time to breathe so that the flavor can build and develop. Mixed with sesame oil, mayonnaise, salt, and pepper, it makes an excellent sauce for grilled salmon. Or, best of all and simplest, serve it with sashimi-grade raw tuna dipped in a bit of soy sauce, the perfect union of ocean and stream.

Catherine, who has advised the Johnsons through the stages of farming and marketing their wasabi, has now moved on to other projects. The Johnsons' wasabi, known as Olympic Mountain Wasabi, is available by mail order. Call 360/426-0353. Uwajimaya also sometimes carries fresh wasabi, though theirs comes from a farm in Oregon.

eastern european Eastern Europeans
are serious carnivores. In fact, you might call them geniuses who
regard cured meats as a genuine art form. Whereas American delis
might be content with a few pale, water-injected examples of the art
of charcuterie, any self-respecting Slavic deli will have nothing less
than dozens of variations, many based on serious pig.

This is not food for the faint of appetite. The typical bitter winters
mean that the essential ingredients are those that can be smoked,
salted, preserved, or otherwise put down. While the foods might
make your cardiologist weep, the glories of smoked pork chops, delicate fat-encased hams, sausages laced with garlic and paprika, blood
puddings, unctuous liver pâtés, and all manner of preserved fish and
fowl can't be underestimated.

Every Friday night between 7 and 10 PM, the Polish Home Association on the periphery of Capitol Hill hosts a delicious Polish dinner, open to the public, of traditional soups, pierogi, cabbage rolls,
sausage, pastries, and tortes. At this point some definitions may be in
order, because the various cuisines of Eastern Europe use similar
words to mean very different things. Pierogi, which are Polish, are
small half-moons that are boiled or fried and served with broth, a little melted butter, onions, and sour cream. Their Russian cousins,
piroshky (as made at tiny Piroshky Piroshky in Pike Place Market),
are oversized turnovers made of warm ground meat and cheese (or
cabbage or potatoes or mushrooms) swaddled in soft flaky pastry. All

delicious really, and who wants to split gastronomical hairs when stuffed to bursting with such delectable morsels.

Eastern European food isn't all as heavy and fattening as it sounds, though. There are also flavorful, warming stews and soups based on millet, barley, and buckwheat. Grains and cereals have always been important crops in Eastern Europe, and rye bread is a staple throughout. In parts of the Caucasus, a healthful diet based on fermented milk products such as yogurt and kefir might be responsible for producing more spry hundred-year-olds than anywhere else on Earth. Food as heartwarming and homey as this will always find legions of fans.

And find it I did. Throughout the Eastside, in pockets of Kent and Renton, in nondescript shopping centers off Aurora Avenue—in fact, in far more places than I ever imagined—are a plethora of markets catering to Eastern Europeans, particularly to the burgeoning Russian population. With numbers estimated at 25,000, the Russian population in Seattle has built up in layers. Waves of immigration have generally tended to precede or follow unrest and political upheaval in the former Soviet Union. The Bolshevik revolution, World War II, glasnost, and the Jewish "refusenik" movement uprooted thousands of Russians seeking to better their lives.

The Russian community today continues to grow, crossing the lines of both ethnicity and age. Far from charging into the American melting pot with abandon, Russian emigrés here seem conscious of their heritage and determined to maintain strong cultural ties. For many, the hub remains the church, particularly St. Spiridon Cathedral on Yale Avenue, with its distinctive blue onion spires. Russian Jews have also settled here in large numbers, many on the Eastside around Crossroads Mall.

The Eastern European communities here don't come close to competing in numbers with those of Brooklyn's Brighton Beach, Detroit's Polish Hamtramck, or Chicago's Croatian South Side. Even so, they open a window for anyone who remembers a beloved grandmother's *galompki* (Polish cabbage roll) and *baba* (sweet cake) or hankers to sink their teeth into the finest kielbasa this side of Ukraine.

Seattle is a city of many cuisines.

Glossary

buckwheat: a triangular brown-green grain. Buckwheat flour is used in blini (yeasted pancakes).

cheeses:

    brynza: an aged sheep's-milk cheese originating in Ukraine.

    kaymak: a rich Armenian concentrated cream.

    Quark: a yogurt cheese. Can be full fat or nonfat.

kasha: a Russian dry porridge made with grain, usually buckwheat.

kefir: a cultured-milk product. Made by inoculating kefir grains (coagulates of active microbial cultures) and fermenting.

kvass: a lightly fermented sour-sweet beverage commonly made of black bread or grain with yeast. Has a taste somewhere between beer and tea.

pelmeni: Siberian meat-filled dumplings.

pierogi: filled pasta pouches of meat, mushrooms, fish, potatoes, cabbage, or cheese.

sausages:

> **basturma:** Armenian dried, salted beef.
>
> **Bundnerfleisch:** air-cured beef.
>
> **cervelat:** a mild German sausage; can be soft spreading like braunschweiger, or a firm mixture of smoked beef, pork, and seasonings.
>
> **head cheese:** pressed chopped meat, vinegar, and spices.
>
> **Kassler:** smoked pork loin.
>
> **kielbasa:** a Polish word for many kinds of sausage; in Seattle, almost always a highly spiced mixture of beef and pork.
>
> **kolzsvari:** all-pork Hungarian smoked sausage.
>
> **krakauer:** chopped ham and garlic bologna.
>
> **landjäger:** chewy, heavily smoked beef jerky.

uszka: little packets of dough filled with meat or mushrooms and added to soups.

varenyki: Ukrainian dumplings filled with meat, cheese, or sauerkraut.

vodkas:

> **Goldwasser:** a liqueur flavored with anise and caraway seed, with flecks of gold suspended in it.
>
> **Krupnikas:** a honey-based liqueur very popular in Lithuania.
>
> **Zubrówka:** a Polish vodka lightly flavored with buffalo grass.

CENTRAL

Bavarian Meat

1920 Pike Pl. (in Pike Place Market), Seattle
Phone: 206/441-0942
Hours: 9AM–6PM Monday–Saturday; closed Sunday

When I asked Lyla Hofstatter why the family business located in the Market had been so successful all these years, she pointed to Siegrid and Agnes, her two longtime employees. Siegrid herself says, "They come because they love the market. We sing in German with them at Christmas. We're crazy and nobody minds. They've known us forever."

Even Siegrid has lost track of how many years she's worked for the Hofstatters. Max Hofstatter started the business in 1961 in a garage over on Western Avenue. He sold hot dogs at the 1962 World's Fair, and till this day, his Bavarian wieners remain the most popular item the company makes. Some years back Max's sons Gerry and Bob took over, and now Gerry's daughters Lynn and Lyla are running the show.

The products themselves are all based on old Max's recipes: Munich-style wieners, bratwurst, bockwurst, braunschweiger, veal loaf, real German-style bologna (which, quite honestly, didn't taste that much different to me than real Safeway-style bologna), and an unforgettably described (alas, untasted) blood and tongue sausage featuring chunks of beef tongue suspended in a beef blood mix. Lyla tells me they sell some 300 pounds of it a week.

Bavarian Meat products are widely available in this area, but the Market store has the full line (over forty-two items) as well as, of course, Siegrid and Agnes. Look for Larsen's and Morning Star bread, as well as a selection of German groceries.

George's Sausage & Delicatessen

907 Madison St., Seattle
Phone: 206/622-1491
Hours: 9AM–5PM Monday–Friday; 9AM–3PM Saturday; closed Sunday

I'd driven by George's hundreds of times without noticing. Its location isn't conducive to stopping, parking is a chore, and besides, who would have guessed at the glories within? Then some in-the-know folks at the Polish Home Association clued me in to a very big hole in my culinary map of Seattle.

Polish pigs can have the comfort of knowing they've given their lives for a good cause. Redemption comes in the almost limitless variety of hams, bacon, and sausage produced here by a gifted Polish butcher named George, who makes no fewer than four kinds of kielbasa. The long, thin *kabonys* are a mini-snack easily eaten before you've gotten back in your front door. The kielbasas are so good and smoky and garlicky that it's difficult not to turn around immediately and drive back for more. The Canadian bacon is the real thing, big and meaty and slow-smoked for honest flavor.

Everything is made in the back kitchen and won't keep for more than a few days (not that you'd need it to), because George's knows that their kielbasa credentials depend on meeting their Polish customers' high standards. For some reason, I have a sudden hankering for a couple of fried eggs plopped down on some of George's sliced and fried kielbasa, along with good buttered black bread fingers (a definitive feel-good fast-food meal that just about anyone, no matter how ham-handed in the kitchen, can throw together).

NORTH

Continental Store

5014 Roosevelt Way NE, Seattle
Phone: 206/523-0606
Hours: 10AM–6PM Monday–Friday; 9AM–5PM Saturday; closed Sunday

If you're wondering what's with the Friday crowd in front of Continental a half hour before the store opens, they're there for the rye bread. People who've grown up on a diet of rye swear that they have to have it daily for their digestion. They're ruined if they don't.

Continental brings in bread from several sources through the week, but the best selection is on Fridays and Saturdays. Here you'll find breads from Larsen's Original Danish Bakery in Ballard; Morning Star, which used to have a retail shop but is now wholesale only; Hess Bakery of Tacoma, which makes the sweetest, crunchiest, most authentic German pretzels you're likely to taste (apologies to Morning Star); and a bakery out of Canada. It's worth lining up just for Morning Star's pumpernickel bread. Till I tasted theirs, pumpernickel seemed merely a dark brown, slightly sour, inevitably stale vehicle for holding meat, not the glorious, perfectly crackle-crusted, almost blackened loaf that is Morning Star's pride and joy.

And there's more: Just about every German comestible, including the largest selection of European chocolate bars and marzipan in Seattle, an all-German meat case, cheeses, German beer, groceries, magazines, videos, and personal toiletries provide an atmosphere of *gemütlichkeit* for homesick expats.

Continental, one of a handful of longtime specialty food businesses in Seattle, has been around since 1964. Owner Barbara Shea bought the business over twenty years ago from the original German family who founded it. She says it's been able to prosper all these years because of her staff, some of whom have been here longer than she has, and her customers, at least half of whom she knows by name and face.

European Foods

13520 Aurora Ave. N, Seattle
Phone: 206/634-1524
Hours: 10AM–6:30PM Monday–Friday; 10AM–4:30PM Saturday; 10AM–3:30PM Sunday

European Foods' décor doesn't give a hint of its ethnicity. It's a large bland space taken up by walls of refrigerators holding mostly Cryovac packs. Open those refrigerator doors, though, and you'll find an intriguing selection of typical Russian cold cuts, most neatly presliced and wrapped in Cryovac packaging. Dense-looking barley sausage, pressed veal, cervelat, rolled chicken, pork sausage—Russians seem to make sausage out of everything. That doesn't even take into account the smoked fish, which are a national obsession. The salads are unusual and delicious, many based on copious amounts of garlic and oil. I tried a marinated eggplant containing loads of dill and garlic and enough oil to give OPEC pause.

They don't speak English very well here, but when I expressed an interest, the forthcoming cook insisted that I try a bite of everything.

In the back is a little room where you can sit down to a larger plate of any of the delicacies.

SOUTH

Green Mart

21012 108th Ave. SE, Kent
Phone: (253)852-7737
Hours: 10AM–8PM Monday–Saturday; 10AM–6PM Sunday

In the same plaza as India Bazaar and the Chandri Fashion shop is a grocery store that will make you feel as if you've taken a right turn into Odessa rather than suburban Kent (or Bombay, for that matter). A Ukrainian couple, Igor and Lubika, own this store, where they sell a typical Eastern European mélange of Russian, German, Polish, and Ukrainian staples. Walk in and the first thing you'll be greeted with is a case displaying rows of sausages and smoked fish and caviar. Ask for the smoked sablefish (black cod), arguably better than lox (at half the price). Then again, if you really love the pungent aroma of smoked fish, go for the smoked mackerel, or sprats, or whitefish, or salmon bellies.

Since virtually nothing in the meat case costs more than $5 a pound, I figure this place is worth a visit if you're in the area. The other striking feature of Green Mart is the astounding assortment of chocolates and bonbons, with baskets and boxes displayed everywhere you look. You'll find standard Belgian chocolate here, but also chocolates from Poland, Latvia, Moldavia, and Ukraine. As in most Russian grocery stores, the dessert cakes and Napoleons are from that epicenter of contemporary Russian exiledom—Little Odessa, aka Brighton Beach, Brooklyn.

Hans' German Sausage & Delicatessen

717 SW 148th St., Burien
Phone: 206/244-4978
Hours: 10AM–6PM Monday–Friday; 9:30AM–5PM Saturday; closed Sunday

As a graduate student, my husband says, his idea of a pretty decent week's worth of lunches was a loaf of bread, a jar of pickles, and a five-pound loaf of braunschweiger sausage (which cost him the then princely sum of 89¢ per pound). The day I showed up with four different kinds of braunschweiger, all made by Hans Stewin in his long-time Burien market, my now oh-so-sophisticated gourmet licked his chops and threw years of nagging on my part, and dietary p.c. on his, to the wind. As my husband knew in his penny-pinching days, braunschweiger is the poor man's pâté. But whether you call it pâté or plain old liver sausage, Hans has a magic touch with the stuff. Granted, not too many people are going to make a journey to Burien just to pick up a pound of it.

But plenty of people make the trek from all around Puget Sound to pick up any of the other dozens of German sausages here, all made in the one-hundred-pound-capacity sausage stuffer in the back. They come for the wonderful bratwurst, blutwurst, knackwurst, liverwurst, and a few other wursts, plus the alder-smoked wieners that Hans first learned to make while growing up in Berlin and working as a butcher. I liked the Westphalian ham, a heavily smoked cured ham sliced paper thin à la proscuitto, that's not as salty as some other versions. Game hunters regularly bring Hans their catch for processing into sausage. And while there, everyone picks up Hess's bread from Tacoma and all sorts of imported German groceries, beer, and wine.

Kassler Rippchen mitt Sauerkraut
(Smoked Pork Ribs with Sauerkraut)

Ursula McCaughan (known as Uschi to her friends) has been working for Hans for over twenty years. She's bicultural: married to an American, yet as German as can be. She offered this recipe and told me her little secret is putting a dollop of applesauce in because her husband likes the sweetness that apples give, but not the taste.

Serves 4
   4 thick slices bacon
   1 onion, sliced
   1 pound sauerkraut, rinsed and drained
   1 heaping tablespoon applesauce, or 1 Golden Delicious apple, chopped
   1 beef bouillon cube

4 thick-cut smoked Kassler ribs
About ½ cup of water

Preheat oven to 375 degrees F.

Dice bacon and sauté till brown. Add onion and continue cooking for an additional 3 to 4 minutes. Add sauerkraut, applesauce, and bouillon cube and continue cooking till warmed through.

Empty mixture into ovenproof container. Place smoked Kassler ribs on top.

Deglaze frying pan with water and add to ribs. Bake for 20 to 25 minutes.

EASTSIDE

Alpenland

2707 78th Ave. SE, Mercer Island
Phone: 206/232-4780
Hours: 9AM–3PM Monday; 9AM–6PM Tuesday–Friday; 9AM–5PM Saturday; closed Sunday

According to Linda Gadola, some customers have been eating daily at Alpenland, her and her husband Toni's little café within their retail market, for almost twenty-six years. That kind of food had better taste great—and it does.

Customers especially rave about the soups. All are simply made by Swiss-born Toni, and all are unquestionably fresh. For example, the afternoon I visited, Toni was preparing the next day's red cabbage borscht. Just as with any good homemade soup, the powerful smells of onions sautéing and broth bubbling wafted through the market and restaurant, making it difficult for me to concentrate on anything except my dinner plans. The potato and leek with little shreds of ham is another favorite of Toni's fans, and mushroom in port wine is a big seller too. Regulars know the schedule and show up for their favorites.

The market itself offers some sausages, mostly from Bavarian Meat; a few cheeses; the usual bonbons, chocolates and biscuits; soaps and lotions; and German cards, as well as Hess's pretzels on Thursdays. This little neighborhood market/café keeps packing them in because they understand a simple concept: treat all your customers as if they're your best friends who've come for dinner.

Delicatessen of Europe

129 106th Ave. NE, Bellevue
Phone: 425/455-9590
Hours: 9AM–8PM Monday–Saturday; 10AM–6PM Sunday

While I was talking to owner Anna Babajan, at least three customers, one dreadlocked, another in exercise tights, and the third speaking Russian, dashed in for an order of borscht. While Anna smiled modestly, they all made a point of telling me that the borscht here is exceptional, the best in town. "You should also taste the pickled mushrooms, especially the giant oyster 'shrooms," the exercise lady exclaimed, "and the wonderfully smoky tomato and pepper salad is out of this world." As she chattered, Anna offered up samples, and we both nodded in agreement: delicious. I bought some of each, as well as chopped liver masquerading as chicken liver pâté and some rolled stuffed veal sausage. The chopped liver was livery and the veal roll was, what can I say, a little funky, but the borscht was superb—a heartfelt elixir that could fight off the cold of any bone-chilling Seattle day. Look for a full line of smoked fish, sausages, sweets, and chocolates (Russian delis seem to delight in eye-catching baskets of hundreds of different bonbons).

From Russia with Love

1424 156th Ave. NE, Bellevue
Phone: 425/603-0701
Hours: 9:30AM–9PM Monday–Saturday; 11AM–8PM Sunday

It's imperative that you try *pelmeni*, Siberian meat-filled dumplings. If you are a true dumpling devotee, then these little walnut-sized morsels, filled to bursting with seasoned beef or chicken, will make you sing for joy. From Russia with Love sells their version frozen and ready to go in one-pound bags.

To me, a good dumpling has to fulfill several criteria. First, the filling has to have flavor and enough fat to keep things juicy. Then, the wrap should be thin enough to feel silky. Finally, the whole should add up to more than the sum of its parts. You should feel a delicious sense of satiety without feeling as if you've swallowed a plate of dough-balls that are proceeding to an unpleasant expansion in your gut.

The queen of borscht in Bellevue—Anna Babajan of Delicatessen of Europe.

I'm happy to report that the pelmeni at From Russia with Love meet these criteria. Boil a dozen and serve them in beef or chicken broth, with a dollop of sour cream and perhaps a sprinkle of dill or fried onions. Afterward you may have scant room in your stomach for anything else, but it will feel good, I promise.

Liebchen Delicatessen

523 156th Ave. SE (in Lake Hills Shopping Center), Bellevue
Phone: 425/746-7810
Hours: 10AM–6PM Monday–Saturday; closed Sunday

On the wall at Liebchen is a wonderful map of the world that today contains a vast web of lines, all drawn between the points showing where customers have come from to shop at this longtime German deli. They've been connecting the lines since 1971, when Lynne Rosenthal opened the business.

She and her assistants have settled on a simple (and surprisingly difficult to execute) formula to satisfy their customers. Make a few basic homemade salads: good old-fashioned potato salad—plain, German, or French; regular old albacore tuna salad; a few chicken salads and pasta salads and the like. And here's the revolutionary part: Don't try to be too fancy—no arugula or mango salsa to jazz things up—just really fresh salads, like the kind your mom would make if she still had time.

Look for sausages from Schaller & Weber of New York, Freyve Meats from Vancouver, and a good selection of products from Seattle's own Bavarian Meat. There's also an excellent assortment of chocolates from Switzerland, Holland, and Norway. Funnily enough, Lynne has never been to Europe, yet she's nailed the German deli concept.

indian and pakistani To the uninitiated, Indian cooking seems like a jigsaw puzzle incapable of solution. We know we love it, but how to take a cuisine so superbly varied and delicious, with so many unfamiliar ingredients and foreign cooking techniques, and make it work for ourselves in our own kitchens?

Seattle has a number of good Indian restaurants, but as those who've been to Britain know, Indian restaurants haven't penetrated the fabric of our city the way they have in that country. Walk into any supermarket in Britain these days, and a good variety of Indian and Pakistani foods is readily available to you. So, how to make this relatively mysterious yet seductive cuisine as familiar to us as it is to the average Briton? As always, the answer to that conundrum is to muster a sense of adventure; an interest in health, history, pleasure, and convenience; and, not least, a willingness to poke around some of the food markets listed in this chapter.

The term "Indian cuisine" is a catchall phrase covering the diverse cuisines of India, Pakistan, Bangladesh, Myanmar (formerly Burma), and Sri Lanka and, consequently, a huge spectrum of regional, religious, and cultural differences. In fact, it's been pointed out that India today is larger than the whole of Europe (except Russia) and that it embraces at least five major faiths, fifteen major languages, and over 1,500 minor languages and dialects. The cuisines of the seventeen states that were created after independence differ from each other as much as do the cuisines of the various countries of Europe.

As far as Seattle is concerned, however, most of the Indian chefs who cook and operate restaurants here are from the Punjab (on the northwestern border of India) or Bangladesh (not even India!). They are the ones who've introduced us to the joys of tandoor cooking, with its grilled meats and wheat-based naan bread, and the refined cooking of north India, which is basically Moghul food. The Moghuls came down to India through Persia and brought the dishes that we now consider typically Indian. The Persian influence is apparent in the subtle use of spices and nuts, and of course in dishes such as *pullao*, a descendant of the pilaf. From this luxurious court cuisine come kormas (rich, braised meat in nut or poppy seed–based sauces), *koftas* (ground meatballs, simmered in spices), and kebabs.

More recently, some restaurants specializing in the food of southern India have opened. Whereas flat wheat breads such as paratha and chapati are staples in the north, southern food is heavily vegetarian and based on rice, dals, and coconut. Coconut milk is used in many dishes. Because of the hot climate, fermentation is a well-used culinary technique. In addition to being eaten as a grain, rice is ground and mixed with lentils and allowed to lightly ferment before cooking. A few southern Indian restaurants have introduced us to *dosas*, enormous rice-and-lentil-flour crepes, golden brown and crispy and stuffed with curried vegetables; and *idlis*, fat little spongy rice-and-lentil cakes that are slightly soured, steamed, and served with chutney.

What is it, then, that gives Indian food its unifying, characteristic flavor? Above all, it is the variety, the combinations, and the uses of spices, judiciously mixed and subtly introduced, that distinguish Indian cooking from any other cuisine in the world. Acquire a working knowledge of the specific properties of each Indian spice, herb, and root and how they behave with other ingredients, and you will soon be cooking and improvising like an Indian master.

Glossary

asafetida (*heeng*): an extremely stinky spice made from dried gum resin of the giant fennel plant. Used in place of onions and garlic by some Indian vegetarians. Look for the Vandevi brand.

bitter gourd (*karela*): a knobbly skinned, cucumber-shaped green gourd with a distinctive bitter flavor and digestive properties.

black salt: brownish black salt in lump or powdered form with a pleasant tangy taste and smoky aroma. An important ingredient in appetizers *(chat)* and some chutneys.

bottle gourd *(hula)*: a large, smooth, bottle-shaped, green-skinned gourd. Tastes like a cross between baby zucchini and chayote. Used to relieve indigestion.

cardamom: a spice with a green or white pod; sold whole, hulled, or ground. The small green pods are preferred over the white, being more aromatic, and are used in sweets, puddings, and pilafs. Black cardamom is used exclusively in savory dishes, and gives a warm, aromatic flavor with eucalyptus overtones.

carom *(ajwain)*: a celery-sized spice seed closely related to caraway and cumin, with a sharp, medicinal, thymelike flavor.

chapati flour *(atta)*: a low-gluten, soft-textured whole wheat milled to a very fine powder. Particularly suited to flat breads because dough made with it offers little resistance during rolling.

chenna: an unripened fresh cheese similar to ricotta, used in Bengali sweets.

chickpea flour *(gram or besam)*: a finely milled, pale yellow flour made from roasted chickpeas and used extensively in batters for vegetable fritters and savories.

chutney: a spicy relish eaten as a side dish, often freshly prepared for each meal. Ingredients vary according to region and tastes.

cluster beans *(guar)*: fine, straight, green beans.

coriander: a plant whose seeds and fresh leaves (commonly known as cilantro) are both used extensively in Indian cooking.

cumin: a small, oval, greenish, finely ridged seed that is a relative of caraway; almost always toasted before use and then ground. Black cumin, which is rarer, has a more pronounced herbal flavor.

curry leaf: a powerfully fragrant leaf that resembles a minature lemon leaf. Fresh leaves keep well in the freezer and lend curry powder its characteristic flavor.

dal: any dried legumes, such as lentils, beans, or peas, and the dishes made from them. Sold either whole or split, and hulled (shelled) or unhulled. Don't substitute whole dals for split ones; it will affect the end result.

channa dal: a yellow chickpea also known as Bengal gram bean; perhaps the most popular legume in India. Looks more like a yellow split pea than a chickpea.

moong dal: a yellow, split mung bean used both hulled and unhulled. Considered the easiest to digest of the legumes.

urad dal: a black lentil closely related to mung beans. Available whole with black skins; split, with skins; and split, without skins and thus ivory in color.

fenugreek *(methi)***:** a plant whose small, hard, yellow seeds and bitter-tasting leaves are both used in Indian cooking. The seeds have a strong, bitter flavor as well and are used in pickles; the dark green leaves, which look similar to clover, are combined with potatoes or spinach and used in wheat-based flat breads.

garam masala: an aromatic spice blend of several dry-roasted and ground "warm" spices. Available in many versions and conducive to experimentation.

ghee: clarified butter with a nutty flavor. Because of the clarification, ghee can be used at high temperatures and has a very long shelf life.

jaggery and gur: unrefined, pale brown sugars made from the sap of sugar cane stalks and various palm trees, such as date, coconut, or palmyra.

lemon crystals: light-colored crystals used as a souring agent.

mango powder *(amchoor)***:** a tan powder made from sun-dried, unripe mango slices. Used to add a tart flavor.

mustard oil: a pungent yellow oil, used extensively in Bengali and Punjabi cuisine. In its raw state, used externally as a massage oil to ease arthritis pain and promote hair growth.

mustard seed: a tiny, round, black seed widely used in southern cuisine. Warning: Eating too many mustard seeds can cause flatulence.

panch phoran: a blend of five whole spices, often associated with Bengali cuisine, containing equal amounts of cumin, black mustard, fennel, nigella, and fenugreek seeds.

paneer: a firm, white cheese with the consistency of tofu. A valuable source of protein for Indian vegetarians.

pappadam *(papad)***:** a sun-dried, parchment-thin wafer made from split peas and flavored with garlic or spices. Can be fried in oil or flame-toasted till it puffs up and becomes crispy.

phalooda: transparent, threadlike noodles made from wheatberry starch and flavored with pine or rose essence. Used in desserts, to garnish *kulfi*, and in a drink of the same name.

pomegranate seed *(anardana)*: a dried wild seed with a distinctive sour taste, used primarily in northern dishes.

poppy seed, white *(khas khas)*: an off-white whole seed used primarily in northern cooking. Often roasted and then ground as a thickener for kormas and stews.

rice: India's most important food grain. The most famous and expensive of all varieties is basmati, an especially nutty and milky strain, whose distinctive feature is that, upon cooking, each grain doubles in length rather than just plumping. The best grade of basmati is the well-aged Dehradun basmati from the state of Uttar Pradesh.

rose essence *(gulab jal)*: a delicate, diluted form of pure rose oil made from highly scented rose petals, most often from the intensely perfumed damask rose.

saffron (*kesar***)**: the dried stigmas of a crocus variety, sold in thread and powdered form. Don't bother with the powdered variety, as saffron is expensive and very easily adulterated.

sapodilla *(chikoo)*: a fruit similar in appearance to kiwifruit, with a fine, brown, furry skin, pink-brown grainy flesh, a few glossy pips, and a honey-maple flavor.

seviya noodles *(sevian)*: very fine, threadlike vermicelli made from durum wheat, primarily used in a creamy, raisin-nut milk pudding called *seviya kheer*. Look for the Elephant brand in one-pound boxes.

snake gourd: as the name suggests, a long, narrow, twisted green gourd with bland, squashlike flesh.

spiny bitter gourd *(kantola)*: a small, spiky, egg-shaped relation of the bitter gourd.

tamarind: a fleshy, cinnamon-brown pod of the tamarind tree with a sour-sweet flavor, used as a souring agent. Available as fresh pods, or dried in two forms: pressed one-pound bricks of pulp, and a jellylike tamarind concentrate sold in one-pound jars. Used as a dipping sauce or chutney for drizzling over savories and pastries.

taro: a fibrous tuber with brown, hairy skin and flesh that may be white, pink, or purple. Taste is light without being insipid, and sometimes sweet and mealy.

turmeric: an underground rhizome with orange flesh, similar to ginger in appearance, rarely available fresh outside Indian grocery stores. The dried form is used extensively in all regional cuisines.

varak: an opulent, edible, fine foil of pure silver or gold that is tasteless, odorless, and visually stunning as a garnish for special occasions.

CENTRAL SEATTLE

The Souk

1916 Pike Pl. (in Pike Place Market), Seattle
Phone: 206/441-1666
Hours: 10AM–6PM every day

Most Seattleites, when needing to buy Indian or Middle Eastern groceries, automatically think of this longtime Market shop. Manzoor Junejo is the jovial owner of what he calls the most exotic and oldest Indian grocery store in Washington. He told me that he started out with four or five partners almost twenty years ago. Little by little they learned on the job, and little by little they dropped out, till only he was left. He manages just fine, catering to local Muslims for their religious needs, filling mail orders from customers up and down the West Coast, and greeting walk-in trade like long-lost relatives.

Note: Manzoor is very happy to share the nuggets of wisdom he has collected over the years. For instance, he pointed out that he sells asafetida, which, in addition to its uses in cooking, can be rubbed around children's necks as an antibiotic. The smell is reputed to scare colds away.

Seattle's Indian-Pakistani Community

Seattle's Indian and Pakistani population is reckoned to be about 15,000 to 20,000 strong and generally very well educated. The community is spread out; many live in Kent and Everett, with pockets on the Eastside. A few trickled into the Pacific Northwest

Come in and say hi to Manzoor Junejo, owner of The Souk.

as early as 1955, but the vast majority came in the late 1970s and '80s, lured by high-tech jobs. Well-organized cultural and professional groups address their needs, the most prominent being the Indian Association of Western Washington. An interesting Web site, www.seattleguru.com, lists cultural events, news of the community, and shops and groceries.

The biggest cultural and religious event of the year is Duwali, the Hindu New Year festival, which is generally celebrated in the fall. This festival marks the darkest night of the year, when dead souls return to Earth and must be shown the way by the lights in the houses. Families get together for parties, to light their houses, and to exchange sweets with neighbors, friends, relatives, business associates, and colleagues. Another joyous and colorful Hindu festival Is Holi, celebrated in early spring. A variety of legends are associated with this festival, most of them relating to the activities of Lord Krishna. On Holi day, men, women, and children gather together and douse each other with colored water in trick-or-treat fashion, play games, and of course eat and snack all day long.

NORTH

Continental Spices & Halal Meat

7819 Aurora Ave. N, Seattle
Phone: 206/706-0326
Hours: 10AM–8PM every day

Halal meat is meat that has been slaughtered according to Islamic rituals. Muslim teachings emphasize the importance of humane care of animals and specify that the animals must be conscious when their throats are slit. Supposedly, the use of a razor-sharp knife ensures that the animal feels no pain, thereby making the process more humane.

Continental sells fresh halal and "kosher style" (which in this case means the animal has been slaughtered using kosher methods, but not under rabbinical supervision) meats to both Muslims and others looking for high quality. The manager, Sheikh Shehzad, told me that Muslims come for the meat, then try the spices he sells. Westerners, on the other hand, come for the spices, then try his meat, and are sold. They always come back for more.

India Sweets & Spices

18002–D 15th Ave. NE, Shoreline
Phone: 206/367-4568
Hours: 11AM–8PM every day

The piles of food crammed into every nook and cranny of this market make navigating somewhat challenging. Look closely, though, and you'll find a good selection of groceries. Bins of beans, tea from Calcutta, rows and rows of spices (including masala mixes), and some ready-made curry pastes are all haphazardly scattered. Juices of guava and mango mingle with leftover relics of India's colonial past such as Horlicks powder and Lucozade. In a cooler sit paneer and naan. Videos, cheap little doodads, and kitchen tools are stuffed between all remaining spaces.

SOUTH

India Bazaar
20936 108th Ave. SE, Kent
Phone: (253)850-8906
Hours: 10AM–9PM every day

One-stop shopping: People want to park their car just once when they go out. That is the beauty of the American shopping center, reinterpreted Indian style. Buy a sari, choose the latest Bollywood potboiler, or pick up a sack of basmati rice, all within sight of a single parking space. India Bazaar is nestled between a Punjabi jeweler and the Chandri Fashion Shop (with the most up-to-date sari styles), so you can do all the above—and, to finish off, stop at the House of India restaurant for a *thali* dinner combo.

India Bazaar is an Indiaphile's dream: Technicolor trays of sweets; bins of *boonji* (spicy forerunners of Western trail mix); fresh Asian vegetables such as fresh curry leaf and spiny bitter melon; shelves of pickles; and aisles of spices, chutneys, rice, and flours such as besan and chapati (the latter in enormous bags)—all with fast turnover and reasonable prices.

K.K. Foods and Video
23805 104th Ave. SE, Kent
Phone: (253)854-5236
Hours: 10AM–9PM Monday–Saturday; 10AM–8PM Sunday

This shop bustles with customers browsing through an excellent selection of fresh fruits and veggies, focusing particularly on the less familiar Indian and Pakistani ones. Indians, like other Asians, tend to be very fussy about their produce. They like to pick through the mounds of green beans or okra, searching for the most tender specimens. Their cooking techniques generally require generous quantities of fresh vegetables. As a result, a shop like this one, which caters to the Indian community, will generally have very fresh and flavorful produce at extremely reasonable prices. There is also a good selection of basic Asian foodstuffs here, from pappadams to paneer.

Mathai—Indian Sweets and Savory Snacks

The *mathai*, meaning sweet, is an object of affection in the Indian diet, eaten as a snack and given as an offering of hospitality. It is based on a different tradition from that of European confections. For years, many aficionados could only wax nostalgic about spectacular sweetmeats, puddings, and elaborate "dry snacks" that were fond memories from the old country. Lately, however, *halvais-wallahs* (sweet makers) have set up shop here and there in Seattle. On many an Indian grocery counter, you may find a dizzying array of sweets and snacks representing every region of the subcontinent, from the northern Punjab and Bengal to the deep, tropical south.

Sweetmeats have a special significance in the Hindu religion. They are considered as highly suitable offerings for the gods, and desirable spiritual states are described in terms of sweetness and nectar. Sweets are an important part of the festival of Duwali, which is celebrated in the fall and marks the start of the Hindu New Year. Sugar is an important ingredient of mathai, but substantial quantities of cereals, pulses, and milk products are also used, in a manner completely alien to European desserts.

Tastewise, Indian sweets run the gamut from straightforward honey-sweet to fudgelike complex flavor explosions of cinnamon, cardamom, pistachio, and pepper. A distinguishing feature is the use of milk products, often reduced by boiling to a creamy substance that acts as a base and binder. Unrefined brown sugars called *jaggery* and *gur* add their own distinctive flavor to *barfi* and toffee sweets. Nuts, particularly almonds, cashews, and pistachios, add flavor and texture. Together with edible gold or silver leaf, they are much used for decoration. A final distinguishing feature of Indian confectionery is the frequent use of deep frying; *jalebi, gulab jamun,* and many other kinds of dumplings are all deep-fried before being soaked in a sugar syrup.

Aesthetically, Indian sweets alternate between representational fantasies and outrageous abstractions. A favorite from the first category are juicy *chenna* cheese sweets, made with two basic ingredients, milk and sugar. Puffy, soft white or colored globes looking for all the world like bloomy plums, speckled with seeds, nuts, or citrus zests, nestle in paper pillows in the halvais' case.

The second category includes specialties that would make a postmodern abstract sculptor proud: polychromatic rectangular and trapezoidal shapes studded with nuts and edible foils. Prime examples are the vegetable halvah—carrot, winter melon, yam, or summer squash—cooked in cream and reduced to pastelike fudges of brilliant hue.

Indian sweets are generally intended to be eaten within a few days of manufacture. The milk-based ones can be stored for the short term and are highly nutritious. Specific sweets are given to invalids and to new mothers. Often a savory snack is eaten simultaneously to balance flavors. Snacking in this yin-yang way—a balance of sweet with savory plus a beverage—is a favorite Indian pastime.

Pabla Indian Sweets & Spices

364 Renton Center SW, Suite C60, Renton
Phone: 425/228-4625
Hours: 10AM–10PM every day

Walk into Pabla Indian Sweets in Renton's Fred Meyer Plaza on any given day, and the first thing you'll notice is the array of sweets lined up, fifteen to twenty deep, running the length of the shop. The second thing you'll notice is the imposing photo of the old gentleman glaring down, with the label "Phagwara, Old Sabzi, Mandi Barga Road, New Delhi." It turns out that this is a photo of Pabla Sr., who has been a sweet maker since 1947. He taught his sons the trade and they somehow found themselves in Renton three years ago, recognized a niche market, and opened this shop, which has a restaurant attached. A Sikh temple is nearby, and the Pabla brothers draw big crowds at all its festive occasions with their purely vegetarian (no eggs or gelatin) homemade confections. The sweets are sold by the pound, as are Indian dry snacks, highly nutritious and marvelously complex compositions of nuts, puffed rice, lentils, spices, and slender dried noodles called *seve*. They're highly addictive and the perfect accompaniment for pre-dinner drinks.

EASTSIDE

Asian Foods and Video

15920 NE 8th St., Bellevue
Hours: 10AM–8PM every day

Every Friday, Asian Foods brings in fresh vegetable samosas that are out of this world. Flaky pastry encloses a plump chile-flecked pea and potato dumpling that is greaseless and really tasty. A couple of these make a great walking lunch or reheated quickie afternoon tea snack. The rest of this store carries everything an inventive Indian cook would need, including a wide variety of pickles, basmati rice, paneer, and chapati flour for making your own Indian bread.

Regal Foods

2245 148th Ave. NE, Bellevue
Phone: 425/562-8112
Hours: 10AM–9PM every day

South King County has a large Indian and Pakistani community, with shops, restaurants, and temples; the Eastside also has a burgeoning Asian population, many of whom are professionals with enough disposable income to insist on choice and American-style shopping. The spacious Regal Foods caters to every need of these folks, with hundreds of spices, herbs, dals, savory snacks, flours, teas, and herbs laid out in neat aisles. In the back of the store is a refrigerated walk-in area with stacks of Asian fruits and vegetables. A wall of refrigerators is stuffed with a truly impressive selection of frozen Indian meals, paratha and roti breads, and fresh paneer. In the tea section is a terrific sign that reads, "Havan Samagri Tea. Fragrant and sacred. For comfort, peace, and prosperity of marriages and other festive occasions." And oh yes, should you require it, Regal will make you a *paan* (betel leaf rolled with spices and herbs) to chew on. This is the Indian substitute for an after-dinner digestive. All in all, enough to satisfy both Asians and Western Indiaphiles.

latino Driving down Delridge Way into White Center in West Seattle, one can see evidence of the new blood infusing our city. Cambodian grocery stores stand next to Vietnamese pho houses, which abut Mexican taquerias and Salvadoran bakeries. All these new immigrants, as waves of ones before them have, are adding to the energy of a Seattle present and future.

Spanish-speaking Americans have settled throughout the greater Seattle area, creating their own enclaves in areas such as Rainier Valley, White Center, Georgetown, and Burien. Although many of the businesses there are decidedly not fancy, you can assure yourself of some fine eating and happy shopping should you visit.

Latin American food encompasses an enormous range. It is a kaleidoscope of cuisines coming from an area nearly three times that of the United States, stretching nearly 7,000 miles from the southern tip of Argentina to the northwestern corner of Mexico. It includes Spanish, Portuguese, and African influences, the latter brought by slaves from West Africa. Most of all, it is Indian—that is, inherited from the Indian civilizations of the New World: the Aztecs, the Incas, and others.

The vast majority of Latinos in King County are from Mexico, with others coming from Puerto Rico, Cuba, the Dominican Republic, Guatemala, Honduras, Nicaragua, Panama, El Salvador, Colombia, Ecuador, and Peru. Historically, many came as migrants to work in the farm fields of eastern Washington and, as educational and economic opportunities opened up, moved into more urban areas. Today many Latinos have invested in and operate their own businesses.

Seattle is also home to a major manufacturer of Mexican foods, La Mexicana, which specializes in tortillas, both corn and flour. Their products are widely available both locally and nationally.

Latino foods have become far easier to find in supermarkets. Not too many years ago, you'd have been hard pressed to find anything more adventurous than bottled taco sauce and canned jalapeño peppers. But today, especially in better markets, the range of products is excellent. This progress, though, has come with a price—the North Americanization of Latino food—with the result that what is a vast, piquant brew of products gets condensed to a shelf or two of homogenized pan-Latino foodstuffs.

The small markets profiled in this chapter offer a more authentic, assertive, and unambiguous experience, as well as a range of food far more varied than anything you'd find in a supermarket. Several will also stoke your appetite with adjacent taquerias serving spicy, inexpensive, hearty food that everyone loves. I'm talking about real food, like the carnitas tacos at La Guadalupana on Lake City Way, filled with seemingly grease-free, slightly dry, smoky shreds of pork—wickedly good! Or menudo, the beautiful and hearty tripe soup that's a one-bowl meal, offered on the weekends at Del Rio. I hope you have as much fun exploring these markets as I did!

Glossary

achiote (annatto seed): the small, dark red seed of the annatto tree *(Bixa orellana)*, used as a food coloring in everything from cheese to lard. The whole seed is ground and used as a spice or mixed with spices, garlic, and citrus juice in a paste.

avocado leaf: an anise-flavored leaf used as an herb or a mild spice when toasted and ground.

beans (frijoles): one of the chief sources of protein for Latinos. There are dozens of popular varieties, many of which are named for their color (red, white, black, pinto) or for their supposed place of origin.

cheeses: Mexican-style cheeses made in the United States are widely available and of reasonable quality. Here are some of the most important:

queso anejo *(cotija)*: literally "aged cheese"; a cheese that is dry and salty enough to be ground.

queso asadero: a mild melting cheese, somewhat like cheddar.

queso fresco *(ranchero)*: literally "fresh cheese"; a moist, cream-colored cheese with a mild flavor and a crumbly texture. Not a very good melting cheese.

chiles, dried: Many varieties are routinely available. Look for these:

ancho: broad, heart-shaped, fairly mild to hot.

arbol: about one inch long, skinny, pointed, and extremely hot.

cascabel: literally "jingle bells," because its seeds rattle in the pod; fairly hot.

cayenne: the general name for a group of small, very hot varieties mostly grown today in Africa, India, and Louisiana. The powdered form can include a mixture of cayenne and other, differently flavored chiles.

chilhuacle: smooth-skinned and about the size of a small bell pepper. Robust and very hot.

chiltecpin: literally "flea-chile," because it's very small and bites sharply.

chipotle: a variety of jalapeño that is dried in the smoke of a fragrant wood fire on bamboo screens. Smoky and fairly hot. Also widely sold in cans, in a thick, pungent, adobo-like sauce.

guajillo: long, thin, dark red to maroon. Semi-hot to hot.

morita: a small variety of jalapeño that is smoke-dried. Can be extremely hot.

New Mexico: the dried version of the Anaheim chile. Ranges from mild to hot.

pasilla: refers to several different dried chiles. In most places it is the semi-hot version of the chilaca chile.

chiles, fresh: Many varieties are available, with the greatest selection in the fall. Look for these:

Anaheim: large and fleshy green; developed for a new cannery in Anaheim, California, around 1900. Mild to hot.

Fresno: developed in the early 1950s. Wide stubby pods, used for seasoning sauces and pickling.

habanero: short, wide, lantern-shaped orange pods, with an aroma of tropical fruit. Very, very hot.

jalapeño: the most popular chile in the United States. Small and fat; available in dark green or bright red when ripe. Available canned in several different forms, especially pickled (*en escabeche*).

mirasol: the fresh, yellow version of guajillo chiles; called *mirasol* because the peppers grow pointing up at the sun.

poblano: the fresh version of ancho chiles. Fairly mild.

serrano: small tubular pods shaped like little torpedoes. Sometimes very hot.

corn husk: a papery husk from corn, used to wrap food when cooking it, lending a distinct flavor. Can be used dried or fresh.

epazote: a very pungent-smelling herb/weed used in Mexican, Central American, and Caribbean cooking. Also known as pigweed.

Hoja Santa (holy leaf): an anise-flavored herb used as a food wrapper, tamale-style, and to flavor stews.

huitlacoche: the corn smut fungus, *Ustilago maydis,* which grows on corn and is considered a delicacy to be used in quesadillas or soups. Very rarely available fresh.

jicama: an underground tuber with deliciously juicy ivory flesh and the texture of water chestnuts. Can be eaten raw or cooked.

maguey: a term for various large succulents of the *Agave* genus. Used as a source of pulque, mescal, and tequila.

masa: corn dough used to make tortillas and tamales. Check whether the masa you have purchased has had lard and flavorings added to it, before proceeding with your recipe.

masa harina: a powdery meal made from fresh corn masa that has been force-dried and then powdered. Used for making tortillas and tamales. Will keep for a year or more in the pantry.

nopal: the general term for several kinds of paddle-shaped stems of the prickly pear cactus. Usually cut in strips and simmered before use.

oregano: Mexican oregano, which is distinct from the more familiar Mediterranean variety. It is more closely related to the verbena family.

piloncillo *(panela)*: a hard, tawny brown cone of unrefined sugar, which tastes like very molasses-y brown sugar. Difficult to crush; you might try grating.

plantain: a starchy, large, thick-skinned cooking banana with a yellow flesh. Used in various stages of ripeness.

pumpkin seed (pepitas): a key ingredient in many Mexican dishes, either toasted or fried, then ground, where it acts as a thickener.

tomatillo: not actually a tomato but a small green fruit with a papery husk, related to the cape gooseberry and ground cherry. Most commonly used in green salsas. Usually simmered or dry-roasted before use.

vanilla: one of Mexico's greatest contributions to the world. Unfortunately, most Mexican vanilla is in liquid form and little of it is pure extract. Most often it is adulterated with coumarin, which is toxic in high doses. Look for pure vanilla extract.

CENTRAL SEATTLE

El Mercado Latino
1514 Pike Pl. (in Pike Place Market), Seattle
Phone: 206/623-3240
Hours: 9AM–5:30PM Monday–Saturday; closed Sunday in winter

El Mercado Latino specializes in all manner of foods from the Caribbean, South and Central America, and Africa. It stocks the usual Mexican and Latino products as well as African and Caribbean staples like *gari* (a kind of flour made of yucca root), cassava, taro, palm oils, dried shrimp, and chiles both fresh and dried.

I was impressed with the wall of hot sauces, ranging from the volcanic Dave's Insanity (which, in my opinion, you'd indeed have to be insane to like since it has no flavor besides excruciating, almost nauseating heat) to the more gentle and fruity La Guacamaya from Mexico. There must be over a hundred kinds to choose from.

This is also the only store I've seen that occasionally carries fresh avocado leaves. They're used lightly toasted for flavoring, as you would bay leaves (which are botanically related). They give a dish a characteristically anisey, herby aroma and flavor, according to restaurauteur and noted Mexican food authority and writer Rick Bayless.

For a long time, this was the only store in Pike Place Market to carry a year-round selection of fresh chiles, Key limes, plantains, taro, yucca, cilantro, and so on, and they weren't always in prime condition. Now that there is some competition, the quality has improved.

La Bodeguita

2528-A Beacon Ave. S, Seattle
Phone: 206/329-9001
Hours: 10AM–7PM Tuesday–Sunday; closed Monday

"Anything from Central America and South America that you want, I can get," says Tony Gonzalez, the Cuban-born proprietor of this little shop in Beacon Hill. He's an importer, so he can get his hands on a lot of things that aren't readily available in other Latino shops.

The last time I was at La Bodeguita, I talked to a Spanish-speaking couple purchasing *maiz perla* to grind for their *humitas*, which are what tamales are called in Bolivia. The maiz comes in white, yellow, and blue varieties, each of which taste different, they told me. I also spotted typical Andean ingredients such as *papa seca*—boiled potatoes, frozen and dried, which are very common in Peruvian food.

I bought a packet of frozen chicken tamales because Tony told me they were the best frozen tamales on the market, and brought them home to the tamale expert of the family. They were terrific: light and airy and smelling deliciously corny, perfect for an after-school snack.

The Mexican Grocery

1914 Pike Pl. (in Pike Place Market), Seattle
Phone: 206/441-1147
Hours: 9:30AM–5:30PM Monday–Saturday; closed Sunday

Fresh masa, made of dried corn kernels and lime, boiled till soft and then wet-ground, is at the heart of Mexican cooking. Without it, Mexican food would be unrecognizable. When I lived in California, I was able to easily buy fresh soft masa whenever I got the crazy notion to make homemade tortillas or tamales. I had a hard time finding it here till I came upon this shop, which carries it in five-pound sacks on most weekdays. Does it make a difference? Absolutely! While dried masa harina makes a very worthwhile and acceptable product, fresh masa is unsurpassed for taste and texture. Just once, everyone should try to make tortillas from scratch using fresh masa. Comparing the difference between store-bought and these fresh-baked tortillas, and smelling that evocative fragrance of warm corn and lime, returns a body to a sense of elemental nourishment that you will never get from a package of off-the-shelf tortillas.

This market always has a variety of fresh salsas, made in-house, for sampling. They are all excellent, but beware of the extra hot kind. They are not joking with those warning labels!

NORTH

La Guadalupana
8064 Lake City Way NE, Seattle
Phone: 206/517-5660
Hours: 10AM–9:30PM Monday–Saturday; 11AM–8PM Sunday

The TV blares Spanish soap operas. The grocery section is minimal, merely covering the basics of beans, tortillas, and chiles. What this modest little store can boast about, however, are the best tacos you are likely to taste in Seattle. The fillings range from *carne asada* and *lengua* (tongue) to *tripa* (tripe) and *al pastor* (marinated pork). The corn tortillas are quickly warmed on the grill and remain soft; a pair of them, stacked and loaded down with pork carnitas, plus tomato, onion, and cilantro, and the salsa of your choice, are the *über*-taco experience as far as I'm concerned.

Menudo, the tripe soup Mexicans consider the sure panacea for hangovers, plus posole and a mean *caldo de camaron* (shrimp broth) are available on weekends. Try them with some fresh radishes and a squirt of lime juice, plus a dollop of hot sauce to taste.

Mi Tiendita Latina
8558 Greenwood Ave. N, Seattle
Phone: 206/789-3909
Hours: 11AM–10PM Monday–Saturday; 11AM–6PM Sunday

It's fun to browse through all the Latino tchotchkes and admire the satin party dresses, stitched with brightly colored flowers, and lavishly embroidered baptismal pillows at Mi Tiendita Latina. Like any market in Central America, this shop is organized (if that's the right word) into different areas selling various goods. In the front are toys, a wall of painted ceramic piggy banks, piñatas, paper flowers, religious icons, herbs and spices, a selection of cooking implements, and some fruits and veggies. Other sections sell South American groceries, frozen foods (including *lorocos*—squash blossoms used as pupusa fillings), and Salvadoran and Mexican pastries. Two or three times a week, a local vendor brings in fresh apple and pineapple turnovers.

Teresa Salazar and her daughter run this shop on the Phinney Ridge commercial strip. They are from El Salvador and tell me that Salvadoran food is similar to Mexican but not as spicy. Try the Salvadoran tamales: fillingless masa wrapped in corn husks, fried in a little butter, and drizzled with a tangy crème fraîche.

SOUTH

Carniceria Zacatecas

123 SW 152nd St., Burien
Phone: 206/988-1559
Hours: 10AM–9PM Monday–Saturday; 10AM–7PM Sunday

Mexicans are great pork eaters, and Mexican pork is incredibly succulent. Even though they are using U.S.-reared animals, pork is clearly the star at this market. Try the awesome house-made chorizo sausage, sharp and spicy with chiles and succulent with grease. They also prepare Mexican-style marinated meats, ready to take home and throw on the grill. Pork and beef are marinated in an *adobado* sauce pungent with onions, garlic, guajillo and pacillo chiles, and vinegar. When I introduced myself to owner Miguel Garcia, he enthusiastically insisted that I taste some of the house special chicharrón—fried pork skin. Addictively good, especially with a dab of bottled red hot sauce and a squirt of lime. How can something that tastes so good be so bad for you?

Mexi-Mart

8601 14th Ave. S, Seattle
Phone: 206/762-9038
Hours: 9AM–9PM every day

In the barrio of South Park is a community of taquerias, *restaurantes*, video shops, *librerìa*s, the Sea-Mar Medical Center . . . and Mexi-Mart, a combination bakery, grocery, and taqueria. Mexi-Mart is not fancy, to put it kindly, but it offers a grand selection of *pan de dulce*, the often luridly colored and heavily sweetened Mexican pastries, as well as fresh tortillas, *sopes* (nifty little masa boats handy for stuffing with cheese, beans, and such), chiles, cheeses, and a fine selection of Mexican medicinal herbs and liquids.

EASTSIDE

La Española

13433 NE 20th St., Suite A, Bellevue
Phone: 425/641-0249
Hours: 10AM–9PM every day

When I walked into this neat little Eastside shop on a Wednesday morning, owner Sandra Lucia was packaging bags of fresh masa, which naturally made me perk up and take note. Here it comes in fresh on Wednesdays and Fridays and seems to be particularly sweet, with a fresh corn aroma that fills the whole store. The shelves are conveniently laid out and divided by nationality, so if you are looking for Colombian, or Brazilian, or Spanish foods, you can head immediately for the appropriately marked section. There is a huge assortment of yerba maté teas, made from an aromatic herb from Brazil. The tea reputedly has slight narcotic qualities and is being discovered as the next trendy drink.

Mi Mazatlan

16142 NE 87th St., Redmond
Phone: 425/881–3151
Hours: 9AM–10PM Monday–Saturday; 10AM–9PM Sunday

16720 Redmond Way, Suite D, Redmond
Phone: 425/883–3653
Hours: 9AM–10PM every day

103 West Main St., Monroe
Phone: 360/805-9227
Hours: 9AM–10PM every day

Mi Mazatlan carries 10 to 15 different kinds of packaged chiles.

High-tech capital Redmond, and the service industry supporting it, has caused a lot of folks to pull up stakes and relocate. The Latino population has especially boomed, particularly in the last two years. Alfonso Loreto staked out his claim by opening a *tienda* on 87th Street in 1994, selling clothing and footwear. Almost immediately bowing to demand, he expanded into Mexican groceries, videos, and music, and a stupendously large array of mexican candies and bonbons. The next step in this strategy was to open a second Redmond location in 2000; this one a *carniceria* selling all those succulent, stewy cuts that Mexicans love so dearly—innards like tripe and pig's feet for making *menudo*, or thin-cut beef *milanesa* for breading and frying till crisp. He also provides custom grinds of *chorizo* sausage, using whatever cut and fat content the customers dictate. The Monroe store is the latest piece in the Mazatlan empire and the biggest one of all, and includes a *tienda*, *carniceria*, and a bakery selling fresh breads and pastries, Mexican-style.

WEST

Del Rio Food Processing

10230 16th Ave. SW, Seattle
Phone: 206/767-9102
Hours: 9AM–9PM every day

This is a family-owned business that tries to offer the biggest selection of everything Mexican. They make their own tortillas, which are delivered fresh on Mondays, Wednesdays, and Fridays. Masa harina comes in three grades: fine, coarse, and yellow. You can buy blue-corn dried niblets, which you must soak in lime and water before using them for menudo or posole, those earthy one-bowl meals reputed to cure any hangover. Brick-red dried chiles of all descriptions are stacked in bins throughout the store. *Duritos*, a kind of dried, hard snack in a variety of shapes, are meant to be deep-fried and eaten like tortilla chips. *Piloncillos*—real Mexican brown-sugar cones—come in either a golden or a more unrefined black version. And if you're hungry, be sure to try one of Del Rio's soft tacos, tamales, or burritos. They make beef, goat, tongue, and chicken fillings. Wash it down with one of the Jarritos brand Mexican sodas.

Pasteleria del Castillo

10434 16th Ave. SW, Seattle
Phone: 206/242-6247
Hours: 7:30AM–9:30PM every day

This little bakery specializes in fresh-baked Mexican breads, cookies, and cakes. I must confess that most Mexican pastries leave me cold—they're way too sweet for my tastes—but the cinnamon-flavored croissants here were delightful. Airy, shattering into crumbs on your first bite, and lightly dusted with cinnamon and sugar, they are a treat. The shop's cookies are also reputed to be excellent, although I didn't try them. This is the place to order a special cake for a baptism or *quinceañera* celebration (a Latina girl's coming-of-age party, held on her fifteenth birthday).

Salvadorean Bakery

1719 SW Roxbury St., Seattle
Phone: 206/762-4064
Hours: 8AM–9PM every day

This lovely bakery has a lavish selection of cakes, pastries, and all-occasion cakes baked on the premises Salvadoran style, as well as some savory snack foods. Salvadoran pastries are often made with rice flour and come topped with an abundance of tropical fruits, nuts, or custard. The *ilusiones*, filled cookies drizzled with bits of sugar cane; the *lagrimas de mango*, topped with mango and walnuts; and the fat-free sponge cake were all pleasant enough, but what really got me salivating were the savory snacks. A sweet corn tamale topped with homemade crème fraîche had a wonderful flavor with a hint of spice and vanilla. The pupusas were my hands-down favorite, though: thick, handmade cornmeal tortillas patted around a filling of cheese or meat, then cooked on a griddle and served with a side of tangy, spicy cabbage relish. The *queso con loroco*—a delicate pupusa filled with squash flowers and cheese—left me smacking my lips and ordering more to take home.

mediterranean My attachment to the foods

of the Mediterranean goes back to my infancy. My mom says that, as
a baby, the only thing that would pacify me was a giant green olive,
from brine salty enough to float raw eggs in. And that was only the
start. Charcoal-roasted and pickled peppers, *sambusak* (dainty little
cheese-filled turnovers), flat wedges of pita bread, the dish we called
jben ou basal (simple roasted sweet onions with softened cheese)—all
these are foods of my Sephardic Jewish background that to this day
I still relish.

As I grew older, an even more seductive love affair began with Italian food. What a revelation it was the first time I visited Italy and discovered, among other things, spaghetti al carbonara, perfect
Gorgonzola dolce, and the diminutive *calamaretti fritti* served in the
little beach towns up and down the Adriatic coast.

The foods of the Mediterranean have been a lifelong passion not
just for me but for just about everyone else in Seattle too. This is
food that at its best is truly a celebration of simplicity. It's easy to
prepare and oh-so-satisfying to eat. No wonder this has resulted in a
lasting romance with Mediterranean food—and culture.

Truthfully, one doesn't have to seek out specialty food markets to
eat Mediterranean food. A quick trip to the local supermarket will
provide all the ingredients needed to put together a pizza, a risotto,
or a vegetable stew with a little meat or cheese added for flavor. Add
a good loaf of bread, available in almost all supermarkets these days;

wash it all down with a good red wine; and you have the makings of a healthful and delicious Mediterranean meal.

But even though for most of us the convenience found in the supermarket aisle is a necessity, shopping in a specialty food market is so much more fun. Ask Armandino Batali of Salumi a question about his sausages, and you'll get an answer infused with excitement and a real respect for taste and tradition. Talk to one of the older, wiser heads such as Louis DeLaurenti in Pike Place Market, and you'll quickly realize that this guy knows a lot about what he's selling. No ordinary supermarket could hope to make shopping so entertaining.

Armandino's maternal grandfather opened the first Italian grocery store in Seattle in 1903, the Metropolitan Grocery in Pioneer Square. The store imported thousands of traditional products from Italy, Greece, France, and the Middle East to feed the growing Mediterranean community. By the 1940s Polet's Grocery, Castle's, M & M Produce, Borrachini's Bakery, Oberto Sausage, Joe Desimone the greengrocer, and others were scattered throughout Seattle. Seattle also had (and continues to have) a sizable Sephardic Jewish population whose food is predominantly Mediterranean and Middle Eastern. The Italians and Sephardic Jews lived in the same neighborhoods, with a particular concentration in the Rainier Valley and South Park, and shared similar food habits. There were also small scatterings of Greeks, Spaniards, and Portuguese.

Today there is no longer a Little Italy in Seattle. The old neighborhood was irrevocably changed with the coming of Interstate 90, which plowed through the center of it, and since then the Italian community has been largely assimilated and scattered. Sephardic Jews, as they became more affluent, moved on to clusters in Seward Park and Mercer Island. The Greek community's social life revolves around the Greek Orthodox Church, and most members are third-, fourth-, or fifth-generation and well educated. There are probably about 1,500 families of Greek-American descent here in Seattle.

Interestingly, unlike some other groups, Mediterranean people tend to keep eating what they've always eaten, even as they become assimilated. They don't lose their taste for the warm foods of the sun—the olives and olive oils, the rice and pasta and fresh herbs, the eggplant and tomatoes and peppers. What has changed is that the rest of America has joined them, becoming deeply interested and enthusiastic eaters of Italian, French, Greek, Spanish, and Portuguese food virtually every night of the week.

The Italians of Seattle

John Croce, proprietor of Pacific Food Importers on the edge of the International District, says that if you put three Italians in a room, you'll have three opinions. The way he tells it, back in the '60s Seattle's Italian community had the Italian Cultural Club on 17th Avenue and Madison Street. When they sold it to the phone company in 1968, they put the money in the bank till they could agree on what to do with it. It's still sitting in the bank today, the money having grown to about $1.5 million, and they still can't agree on how it should be spent.

John's an old-timer. He started out in the olive oil business in the '40s; today his company, now mostly run by his children, imports thousands of products from the Mediterranean and Middle East. He knows a lot about the old neighborhood—Rainier Valley, bounded by Beacon Hill on one side and Lake Washington Boulevard on the other. Garlic Gulch, it was called, because of all the Italians with their pots of garlic and red spaghetti sauce.

Italian laborers settled in the city in the early 1900s. They came mostly from Calabria and Abruzzi, leaving a life of grinding poverty and drudgery to embrace the customs of their adopted home. They had no loyalty to the old country; after all, few had good memories of what they had left behind. Still, they clung together, since they didn't speak English, and settled mostly in south Seattle, especially Rainier Valley and South Park. They made wine in the fall and struggled to grow their familiar vegetables in our mild but less than ideal climate. And they helped rebuild Seattle after it burned down in 1889; they were the bricklayers, masons, and skilled and unskilled workers who built the infrastructure of the city.

Many Italians had truck farms in south Seattle, the area from Spokane Street to the Kent valley. Greengrocer Joe Desimone of Pike Place Market fame came from this area, and he is rumored to have given some of the first land for what is now Boeing Field. The Italians from Genoa ran the garbage business in the city, and until the Filipinos came along in 1929, the Italians were the major greengrocers at Pike Place Market.

At one time Rainier Valley had thirteen baseball teams and was able to field several all-Italian teams. Italians had their own grocery stores, bakeries, and three macaroni factories. The Italian Cultural Club engaged in friendly rivalry with the Sons of Italy and held competing Columbus Day wine and sausage festivals. The neighborhood revolved around the church, Our Lady of Mount Virgin, still there on Bradner Place. The building of Interstate 90, however, marked the beginning of the end of the community. The freeway split the neighborhood in half, and slowly, as fortunes improved, people moved on to better addresses.

There has also recently been a small influx of native Italians in the Pacific Northwest. They're the cultural opposites of the old immigrant laborers, though: highly educated professionals, coming mostly to take jobs with dot-coms and other high-tech companies.

The curing room at Salumi.

Today there's talk of building a new Italian cultural center. This might might include housing for exchange students, a theater, and a Montessori school. However, to date it's been difficult to find a site.

The Ultimate Olive Oil

Make me poor in wood,
I'll make you rich in oil.
Caress me, don't beat me,
If you want my fruits another time.
Prune me hard, fertilize me well,
If not, leave me for another.
—Moroccan proverb, voiced by the olive tree.
　from *Olives* by Mort Rosenblum

Mustapha Haddouch, the man behind Mustapha's Moroccan Olive Oil, is intense, friendly, and a gusher on his favorite subject, namely Moroccan olives and olive oils. Moroccan olive oil can be the equal of any trendy, estate-grown, artfully packaged Tuscan oil, he told me. And when it comes to olives for eating, Moroccans are the world champions. Yet Moroccans are the Rodney Dangerfields of the olive world—they get no respect.

Much of Morocco is olive country; in fact, the country is second only to Spain in exporting oil. But most Moroccan oil is exported in bulk with no producer's label and ends up in Italian packaging, elegantly labeled and marketed as "packed in Italy." Estate-grown Moroccan olive oil is almost a misnomer; in truth, there is no such thing, at least not yet. Mustapha is almost single-handedly trying to revive an artisanal, haphazard process in his country and to create a market for his superb oil here in the United States.

I met with Mustapha on a typical Seattle day—drizzly and dank, about as far from a Mediterranean state of mind as possible. He came to the United States as a student in the '70s and bumped around for a few years, he told me. He landed in Seattle in 1982 and, after a few years cooking at Mamounia, a now defunct Moroccan restaurant, he went to work as a waiter for Thierry Rautureau at Rover's. That was a good experience, he told me. It gave him a chance to meet some of the players in the local food scene, and to talk to lots of Americans who could explain the vagaries of his adopted country.

Mustapha is passionate about Moroccan olive oil, but he is also a realist. "To sell Moroccan oil, first I have to sell Morocco," he sighed. "No one in America knows about us. My goal is not to make a quick buck. I want to have an influence in how people see food, both here and in Morocco." In his own country, he had to teach farmers who were producing olives in the old ways that dated to the Middle Ages, and he had to build his own press so he could control the processing. The quality of olive oil is directly related to the meticulous steps taken all along the way; any step in the process, if mishandled, can sabotage the finished product. Mustapha found that he had to control every single aspect, from growing to pressing and bottling and on to marketing, and every step has been an exercise in frustration and setbacks.

It has been five years since he began the business, and every year he is more confident that his vision will bear fruit. He started his product line with just olive oil, but has now expanded to about fifteen varieties of spiced olives, Moroccan-grown capers, and preserved lemons, all in the distinctive contemporary Moorish labels that he commissioned. The olives are delectable, plump and firm *picholines*, marinated in an assortment of tradi-tional Moroccan spices and herbs. I loved the Tunisian style, spiked with a jolt of harissa, as well as the intriguing cinnamon and clove version.

As for the olive oil, the bottle is elegant, as fashionable as a first-label Tuscan, and the taste is rich and vegetal, with a sharp, fresh breath of artichoke. It's an oil for real aficionados, with that catch at the back of the palate the Italians call *pizzica*. In fact, it won a silver medal for "best new product" at the 1999 Fancy Food Show, which featured thousands of exhibitors from around the world.

Mustapha's Moroccan Olive Oil is available at many specialty food markets in the area. Their Web site is www.haddouch.com, and you can e-mail them at oliveetc@cs.com.

Glossary

baccala: pungent, salted, dried cod that needs soaking for many hours before cooking and eating.

bottarga: gray mullet roe, removed in their intact membrane, salted, pressed, dried in the sun, and covered with a protective coat of wax.

farro: a whole grain that looks like wheat kernels but cooks faster. Eaten like pasta, with almost as many different sauce possibilities.

gkyko: preserved fresh fruits, such as quinces, cherries, and fresh pistachio nuts in a sweet syrup; eaten by Greeks. Traditionally offered to guests with coffee.

halloumi: a firm, white cheese with a rubbery texture, often flavored with nigella seeds.

kashkeval: the Bulgarian and Romanian name for a hard yellow cheese made from sheep's milk.

kataifa: a vermicelli-like pastry, formed by pouring batter through a fine sieve onto a hot surface; usually packaged frozen. Used similarly to phyllo.

mozzarella, fresh: a bland white cheese famously used in Neapolitan pizza (although I personally find it too wet for that use). The rarer and more expensive buffalo mozzarella is somewhat tangier. Baby mozzarella are called *bocconcini*. Fresh mozzarella is worth the price only if very, very fresh.

pancetta: unsmoked, cured pork belly, similar to bacon.

panettone: a rich Italian yeast cake made of flour, butter, eggs, sugar, and milk, featuring raisins and candied fruit, that is eaten on festive occasions such as Christmas and Easter.

pecorino: an Italian sheep's-milk cheese that can be young and fresh, or aged and suitable for grating. Pecorino Romano is most common; some others are Pecorino Sardo from Sardinia, and Toscana from Tuscany.

phyllo: the paper-thin pastry used in both sweet and savory dishes. It's always available frozen, but occasionally fresh phyllo can be found and is far superior. When using phyllo, be careful not to let it dry out and become brittle.

piri-piri: a hot Portuguese sauce made from chiles, a culinary legacy from Portugal's colonial past.

porcini: wild boletus mushrooms, available fresh in the fall and spring and prohibitively expensive; more commonly available dried. The best are in big pieces and smell of loam, roasting meat, and the forest. Inferior porcini mushrooms smell like weak bouillon cubes. Store them in your freezer and use within a year.

quince paste *(membrillo, marmelo):* a thick, golden, jellylike paste made from quinces and eaten in Spain as a sweet or as a classic accompaniment to cheese.

risotto rices: Arborio is the best known of the short-grain rice varieties, but look for Carnaroli and Vialone Nano, which have a little more body and character. Valencia rice is the Spanish equivalent. When these rices are cooked, the starch is released but a firm core remains, which gives the rice a pleasant combination of textures. Never rinse or boil and drain these rices, or the creamy starch will be wasted.

sausages:

bastourma: a dark, short, spiced and dried sausage eaten by Greeks.

coppa, cappricola, capocollo: different words for the same cuts of Italian cured meat—pork shoulder or neck. Can be sweet or hot, spiced with fennel or hot pepper.

finocchio: an Italian salt-cured and dried sausage flavored with fennel.

loukanika: a thin sausage popularly flavored with allspice, savory, and orange peel or coriander seed, eaten by Greeks.

mortadella: an oversized pink pork sausage studded with large flecks of white fat and flavored with peppercorns, pistachios, or olives. Real Italian mortadella has recently been allowed into this country and should not be confused with the American version.

tarama: smoked gray mullet roe or, more commonly, cod roe, used to make *taramasalata*.

CENTRAL SEATTLE

DeLaurenti

1435 First Ave. (in Pike Place Market), Seattle
Phone: 206/622-0141
Hours: 9:30AM–6PM Monday; 9AM–6PM Tuesday–Saturday; closed Sunday

Since 1947, DeLaurenti has been a terrific source for Italian and other high-quality imported and domestic foodstuffs. In fact, they consider themselves to be a "condiment store." In other words, they sell everything you'd add to complement the basic building block of your meal. Within their crowded confines, you'll find an incredible cheese counter, a salumeria (deli meat counter), a full bakery, a wine shop, and a huge selection of oils and vinegars, pastas, canned goods, and packaged items.

Cheese: The cheese case at DeLaurenti is one of the highlights of shopping here. It boasts a bounteous variety, all seemingly at the peak of ripeness. Look for Neal's Yard cheeses from England prominently displayed on the counter. The definitive, magnificent farmhouse cheddar is worthy of worship. Cheese manager Connie Bennett pointed out a snow white *caprini* (baby goat cheese) that was round and studded with black truffles. "Mix it with a little cream and throw it over some pasta," she suggested. Sounds heavenly.

DeLaurenti sells whole five-pound wheels of Colston Bassett Stilton in the winter. One of these would make the perfect entertainment solution, splendidly arrayed on a board with some fine red wine and vintage port, and served with sweet fruit and nuts. You'll notice they don't sell low-fat cheeses here. As Connie bluntly put it: "Eat less, eat good."

Deli: In the deli case you'll find Boar's Head products as well as first-rate imported proscuitto di Parma and San Daniele from Italy, *jamon Serrano* (mountain ham, recently reintroduced into this country) from Spain, and Westphalian ham from Germany. While I was there, a customer wandered in looking for fresh duck confit, which the store used to carry. They no longer stock it but could offer a canned French version, which they said was superb.

Wines: Wine manager Steve Springston likes to think of his area with a sense of theater. "Give the customers what they want, but always leave something in reserve to spring out with a dramatic flair of surprise," he told me. Perhaps one of Seattle's best-kept secrets, this is one heckuva wine store, emphasizing mostly Italian products although not forgetting Northwest wines. The Spanish wine section, Steve told me, is the most rapidly growing. They don't like to focus on brand names here, but instead on good food-and-wine pairings. Prices are probably not the lowest in town, but on the other hand, you're getting knowledge and passion, and that seems reasonable for the level of service.

Packaged Foods: Everything here is nicely displayed and available in enough varieties to make you feel as if you are constantly discovering treasures you've never seen before. As would be expected in a shop catering to lots of tourists, a good portion of the merchandise is devoted to snack foods—biscuits, crackers, chips, and so on. There's a wonderful selection of olive oils and vinegars, jams, jellies, and the like.

Another reason I love DeLaurenti is because they search for the best products and are often the first, if not the only, shop to carry something that is truly unique. This shop might be your best bet to find a treasure that you tasted while traveling in Italy and would dearly love to have again.

Nonna Maria

530 First Ave. N, Seattle
Phone: 206/378-0273
E–mail: nonnam@nwlink.com
Hours: 7AM–10PM Monday–Friday; 4PM–10PM Saturday; closed Sunday

For two years, I'd rush down to the University District Farmers Market every Saturday for some of Nonna Maria's excellent ravioli, only to be crushed by a "sold out" sign. So I was in heaven when I heard they were opening their own rosticceria and pasta shop in lower Queen Anne. Italian Roberto da Vica and his beautiful Venezuelan-born wife, Oana, first started experimenting with homemade ravioli as newlyweds in Paris. The recipes came from Roberto's *nonna* (grandmother) and from his own experiments with flour and filling.

Nonna Maria makes ravioli stuffed with pumpkin and sage, porcini mushrooms, squid ink, spinach, and ricotta—a dizzying selection of whatever the season and Italian sensibilities dictate. Roberto told me, in his heavily accented English, that the secret to their pasta was the good flour they use (only semolina) and his nonna's recipes. The simple spinach and plain pastas are flavorful and well textured. The porcini mushroom–filled ravioli are loaded with porcini. The pumpkin ravioli are delicate and delightfully sweet and nutty. Only the cheese ravioli disappoints, being a tad skimpy on the filling.

Still, this utterly charming slice of Italy has a lot to offer. The rosticceria, which offers food to go, invariably holds gorgeous trays of roasted vegetables as well as crispy-skinned roast chicken or tomatoey baked chicken, vegetarian lasagne, colorful panini (sandwiches), and desserts from Gelatiamo. Look for a full line of products imported by Ritrovo (see page 265), as well as an all-Italian wine section.

Queen Anne is the new home of Roberto da Vica's Nonna Maria.

Nonna Maria's Pasta with Porcini Mushrooms

Serves 4

½ cup dried porcini mushrooms, about ½ ounce

3 tablespoons finely diced onion

1 clove garlic, minced

½ bunch Italian parsley, minced

⅓ cup olive oil

1 15-ounce can tomatoes (preferably Italian San Marzano type), pureed

1 pound fresh Nonna Maria fettucini (or 1½ pounds if you really like pasta, says Roberto)

Grated Parmesan (optional)

Soak porcini mushrooms in warm water for about 20 minutes. Drain and save soaking liquid, and chop mushrooms into little pieces.

Sauté onion, garlic, and parsley in olive oil. Mix in mushrooms. Continue to sauté for about 5 minutes, then add mushroom-soaking liquid and tomato puree.

Cover pan and cook for 1 hour over low heat.

Cook pasta in lots of boiling salted water for 2 to 3 minutes. Drain loosely and combine with tomato-mushroom sauce. Continue cooking for a minute or two.

Serve with grated Parmesan if desired. Roberto says it is optional but permitted with porcini. Italians have a finely defined sense of whether or not to serve cheese with pasta.

A Love Affair with Slow Food, Italian-Style

Ritrovo is a lovely Italian word that has a double meaning. It can mean to refind something once lost, and it can also refer to a meeting place, one you'd suggest for a rendezvous with good friends. Ritrovo is also the name of an import company based in Seattle that seeks to educate people about the biological, historical, and cultural values of the traditional slow foods of Italy.

Eating is more than a question of taking in nutrients or hedonistically consuming fine food. The very names of dishes, along with their recipes and ingredients and historic antecedents, are part of what we consume if we eat thoughtfully. This is what the owners of Ritrovo believe in, and it is the reason they have chosen to concentrate on importing a carefully screened product mix of high-quality chocolates, vegetable conserves, pastes and creams, honeys, truffles, pastas, olive oils, grains and baked products, and coffees made by small family farms and artisan manufacturers.

The seeds of what would become Ritrovo were planted when owners Ilyse Rathet and Ron Post went to Italy on Fulbright scholarships to teach English. Ardent believers in the value of intercultural interactions, they spent years attempting to set up a program for cultural exchanges between teachers. That was an exercise in frustration. As they put it, the Americans had the money but to find it was difficult, while the Italians were eager but had mounds of paperwork to overcome. In the meantime, Ilyse discovered fine Italian wines through a couple of professional sommelier classes she happened upon.

The Italians don't see wine as a special drink or as an arena for one-upmanship by wine snobs, she found. Rather, wine is profoundly linked to food and to the values of the land and culture it comes from. Realizing this made Ilyse deliriously happy.

Ultimately, the desire to bring to America the authentic products and tastes of a country that is so rapidly changing led the couple to move back to Seattle about a year ago and set up Ritrovo. Among their products is an extraordinary olive oil: Trampetti vintage-dated extra virgin olive oil from Umbria. The olives are hand-picked and transported from the orchards twice a day to minimize bruising and oxidation. All this cosseting means there is so little oxidation of the olives that even five years after pressing the oil has not even a hint of rancidity.

Ritrovo also sells an artichoke and truffle paste, from a small farm in Abruzzo, that is delectable—not least because Italians harvest their artichokes only in the bloom of youth, long before any hint of woodiness has developed. And they carry a line of organic sauces made by Radici Farms of Tuscany, located in the village of Loro Ciuffenna and forever associated with Burton Anderson's idyllic description of his home and farm in *Treasures of the Italian Table*.

Every one of their products has a real story (as opposed to a gauzy, marketing-driven photo-op) that involves real people committed to keeping the best from the past and to making fine products with homegrown, homemade flavors. Perhaps it takes effort to "refind" these products, but the truth, corny as it may sound, is that their loss would make the world we live in far more mediocre. Besides, I don't know if I could live without some of their sensational Domori chocolate.

Look for Ritrovo's products at DeLaurenti, Whole Foods Market, and Nonna Maria, and watch them develop their business.

Ritrovo Italian Regional Foods

Phone: 206/985-1635
E-mail: ritrovo@aol.com

Pacific Food Importers

1001 Sixth Ave. S, Seattle
Phone: 206/682-2022
Hours: 9AM–5:30PM Tuesday–Friday; 10AM–2PM Saturday; closed Sunday and Monday

This well-known warehouse is the retail arm of John Croce's import empire. It specializes in foods of the Mediterranean and Middle East at rock-bottom prices in a decidedly no-frills atmosphere. Plastic pails filled with spices, rice, lentils, and dals hint at the breadth of the selection. Yards of shelves are stocked with everything and anything—from Middle Eastern pomegranate molasses to a full line of Italian De Cecco and Barilla pastas, Yugoslavian plum preserves, *ful medames* (a type of bean and the national dish of Egypt), and anything else eaten in between. I always find something new to try here—they're constantly introducing new product lines.

The other component of PFI's appeal is the cheese and olive counter. There is always a good selection of British, Italian, and Spanish as well as basic block cheese, all at big savings. Expect to pay about 30 to 50 percent below supermarket prices. The drawback is that you have to buy a minimum of one pound of all cheeses, olives, and meats, although they've been known to waive that rule if you ask nicely.

Beware of some of the grocery items, though. I have been burned by paying considerably more for some items than I would have at regular supermarkets.

Salumi

309 Third Ave. S, Seattle
Phone: 206/621-8772
Hours: 11AM–5PM Tuesday–Friday; closed Saturday, Sunday, and Monday

Armandino Batali says he grew up on the family farm in Yakima, where they produced their own proscuitto, *biroldo* (blood sausage), salami, and wine. All that practice explains why his sausages are out of this world. This long and skinny little shop is modeled after a *macelleria* in Italy, where only a few choice goodies would be out on the counter and the best stuff would be brought out to order.

It is a labor of love by Armandino and his family, and you're liable to find one or the other working behind the counter, helping Pop. At lunch, there is usually a good-natured line that snakes out the door, waiting for made-to-order sandwiches the likes of which are not often served in Seattle: braised pork cheeks piled with heaps of fried onions and peppers, *porchetta* (roasted and spiced pork), or lamb sausage as juicy and tender as you're ever likely to taste, all thickly smeared with lusty parsley-flecked pesto and a garlic sauce. I have watched petite women chow down on this food like hungry trenchermen. Armandino has been known to ply the waiting masses with copious samples of salami, proscuitto, and anything else he's got on the counter. My favorites are a toss between the oregano-scented salami and the spicy, chile-flecked soppressata.

On the other hand, I'm also wild about the fresh sausage, which is surprisingly lean and studded with fennel and pepper and garlic, fabulous for pizza night. And the lamb sausage has to be the definitive version of one of my favorite meats. The secret, says Armandino, is a very coarse grind so that the fat and juice don't drain out when it cooks.

Discovering the Secrets Behind Salami

It's not every day that you find your arms entwined with those of a maestro of Italian salami at 6:30 AM, but Claudio Serra and I were linked just so one morning over a fifteen-pound batch of Salumi's salami. My job as the "novice" was to carefully crank the handle of the sausage stuffer, slide my two fists between his to neatly tie off the links, and cut them apart without stabbing him or myself in the process. Owner Armandino Batali joked, "Everybody wants to come and help the first time. Getting them back the second time around is harder."

Armandino had invited me to come and watch him and Claudio, his friend and relative, make *cotto* salami. On the theory that there is no better way to understand the miracle of the salumeria than a trip to the Mecca of Seattle salami—the refrigeration

The maestro himself—Armandino Batali of Salumi.

room of Salumi—I eagerly began my crash course with that early-morning lesson.

Cotto means cooked in Italian, and Salumi makes approximately thirty-pound batches at a time in links as big and sweet as a baby's thigh. Armandino's obsession with quality has led him to use pork cheeks, as in the two one-pound nuggets hanging off a pig's jowls that provide just the right degree of cartilaginous fat to give the meaty richness that is needed for cured sausage. These are eastern Washington–grown pork cheeks, excised from full-grown pigs weighing about 220 pounds. The pigs are slaughtered on a Wednesday and are in Salumi's pro-cessing room by Friday, being mixed with his closely guarded spice blend. The meat has no time to hang, but that doesn't seem to affect its tenderness or its crimson-as-blood color.

The air around Salumi during these early-morning marathons is incomparably rich with intoxicating aromas, vigorous enough to be tasted. Once the meat is stuffed into the collagen or natu-ral skin casings, it is gently lowered into a burbling pot of water to cook through. The meat slowly melds, releasing fat and gela-tin to bind its rich, tender flesh. Armandino offers me a slice of the still-warm meat, and when he tells me that's his favorite way to eat it—straight out of the pot before it's had a chance to cool—I have to agree. This does taste as good as it smells.

As we worked, Armandino talked about the mystique of Italian *salume*, salt-cured meat in the form of hams, sausage, salami, bacon, and less familiar delicacies. Only the air and diet from a peculiarly Italian kind of environment, enhanced by generations of sage craftsmanship, can result in tender perfection—or so claim the local arbiters. Armandino chuckled his disagreement. "Great marketing, but it just ain't so. I don't know too many peo-ple who can taste the chestnuts that the pigs from Parma were raised on." It's an issue of creativity. Respect for tradition and the old ways is important, but it can also work in the opposite direc-tion by stifling creativity.

Certainly, there's no lack of creativity at Salumi. The salamis are all soundly grounded in the traditional Italian idiom. Armandino is no slavish follower, though. For example, he says it took him a year to persuade his Italian teachers to try a proscuitto made from lamb. While admitting the merits of his proposal, they remained suspicious. It's only here in Seattle, where we pay less heed to tradition, that he's entirely free to make his interpretations.

The sausage-stuffing process was over, the cotto all cooked and cooling on the counter. As I made ready to leave, Armandino insisted I take home a hunk of the succulent meat, now glisten-ing with its natural gelatin. In this gesture, I think, lies the expla-nation for Salumi's resounding success. People can distinguish a bona fide original from a slick copy, and they respond with pleas-ure when offered the fruits of their labor.

The Spanish Table

1427 Western Ave., Seattle
Phone: 206/682-2827
E–mail: tablespan@aol.com
Hours: 9:30AM–6PM Monday–Saturday; 11AM–6PM Sunday

Steve Winston visited Spain in 1985 and loved what he saw. He came back home to Seattle and realized that there was a niche to be filled: no one here knew much about Spanish and Portuguese food and products. When he opened his shop four years ago on Western Avenue just below Pike Place Market, his game plan was to appeal to tourists, students, military personnel who had spent time in Spain, and a few expatriates. But instead his store has become wildly popular with everyone, and he is now known as a national resource for Spanish and Portuguese products. He was the first to stock *pimientos del piquillo*, and when *Saveur* magazine did a feature on these incredibly intense, smoky-red peppers, they directed customers his way.

Because the Spanish Table is an importer, they can sometimes get great buys on Spanish and Portuguese olive oils. Nunez de Prado is a Spanish olive oil that turns customers into faithful devotees. In fact, each bottle carries an invitation to visit the mill. The Spanish Table will give you tastes of this and just about every other oil they carry. I think, although I could be wrong, that the store carries wines from just about every region of Spain, as well as an incredible selection of rare ports and Madeiras. The breadth of the Spanish and Portuguese wines goes way beyond Rioja and Portuguese *vinho verde*. I tried a bottle of 1998 Albariño, a white wine that has gotten rave reviews in the press recently. It certainly whet my appetite. Browsing the bins here has turned up some great underpriced buys.

Lately, Steve tells me, his store has also become somewhat of a center for Cuban music. They carry the largest selection of Spanish-language CDs in Seattle. This is where I first heard the Latin jazz of the Buena Vista Social Club, and you can usually find music from Brazil, Cuba, the Basque country of Spain, Chile, Argentina, and the lovely, haunting *fado* music of Portugal.

SOUTH

Salumeria on Hudson

4918 Rainier Ave. S, Seattle
Phone: 206/760-7741
Hours: 10:30AM–8PM Monday–Saturday; closed Sunday
Internet: www.salumeriaonline.com

Lisa Becklund and Sherri Serino made a name for themselves with La Medusa, a Sicilian restaurant just across the street from this store. They recently extended their vision to open Salumeria, a casual, stylish shop pulled together by their love of Italian soul food. The focus is again Sicilian, but more importantly it revolves around a sense of community and an appreciation of good, simple food that serves their charming Columbia City neighborhood. They've started small and are responding to people's needs as time goes on.

I was excited when I saw them making their own pancetta, the unsmoked cured Italian pork belly. Clean, meaty flavor and fat that is pure and sweet-tasting put this pancetta head and shoulders above any better-known commercial brands. Chicken, sausages, and a lightly smoked bacon are all made in-house. Look for unusual pastas such as Sardinian *fregola*, coarse durum wheat pasta that resembles couscous and is excellent in soups, as well as some curiosities like *bottarga* (dried, pressed fish roe) and a smattering of Italian groceries and olive oils.

Salumeria has become known for their high-quality prepared foods, available for eat-in or take-out. The menu isn't exactly *piatti dei paisani*, but they do favor the hearty over the fussy. Roasted meats, sausages, and earthy stews, both meat and vegetarian, present some of the tempting possibilities. There are always lasagne and pizza, two or three antipasto, and a few simple homey desserts, as well as Procopio gelato. I have the sense that this shop will always reflect its owners' enthusiasms and good taste and will, over time, evolve into a showcase market.

EASTSIDE

middle eastern

Just across the street from Bellevue Square is a tiny little outpost of the Middle East. Byblos Market & Deli is another example, right in the heart of clean-cut, all-American Bellevue, of our continuing ethnicization. This offshoot of an Edmonds market opened in the last year and offers a mixed bag of goodies, mostly of Arab and Iranian origin. The Microsofties and other high-techers living on the Eastside come from a rainbow of cultures, and they're supporting businesses where they can shop for the familiar foods of home. In the process, they're slowly changing the face of Bellevue.

"Middle East" is a broad and fluid term that means different things to different people. I have chosen to define the markets of the Middle East as those selling the foods of the following countries: Syria, Lebanon, Egypt, Iran, Turkey, Iraq, Saudi Arabia, Yemen, Sudan, Algeria, Tunisia, Morocco, Jordan, and Israel. Most of the businesses profiled here carry foods that are used interchangeably in Middle Eastern as well as Mediterranean cooking. There are, however, big differences in styles of cooking between the countries (see page 294).

Only a small number of families of Middle Eastern descent are known to have settled in the Pacific Northwest before 1960. Many Arab men came to the Seattle area with the expansion of the aerospace industry. They were later joined by a large number of students attending area colleges and universities. The civil wars in Jordan and Lebanon caused many families to immigrate here to join their sons. Palestinian families and Iraqi political refugees fleeing the Persian

Gulf War have also settled here. The 1990 census estimated the Arab population of Washington state (defined as those who said they spoke Arabic in their homes) at about 4,000, and today the total is closer to 10,000.

Most Iranians in the Pacific Northwest can date their arrival to the Islamic Revolution of 1979. With the fall of the Shah of Iran, many educated middle-class Iranians with American ties relocated to the United States. Most settled on the East Coast or in southern California, but about 10,000 came to the Seattle area. The majority of Iranians live on the Eastside, with smaller numbers in the University District and Queen Anne.

Middle Easterners in the Pacific Northwest tend to be well educated and hold jobs in government or industry, or own their own businesses. Political convulsions in their homelands have brought them here, but unfortunately they sometimes face not-dissimilar conflicts in their adopted land as well. Relations between Americans and people perceived as being followers of Islam sometimes zigzag up and down depending on war and peace, and economic relations between the United States and the Middle Eastern countries. But Middle Eastern food with its tradition of mezze, boasting small dishes of salads, savory pastries, olives, cheeses, and flat breads, along with the smoke of grilled kebabs and roast lamb, will entice and beguile all your senses no matter what your religion or politics.

Middle Eastern Cooking

Claudia Roden, an authoritative and fascinating writer on Middle Eastern cooking, identifies its four main strands as Iranian or Persian, Arab, Ottoman Turkish, and North African.

Iranian food is considered the ancient source of much of the haute cuisine of the Middle East. Long-grain (preferably basmati) rice forms the heart of the cuisine. Iranian rice cookery is prized for its flavor and exquisite garnishes. The combination of meat with fruits or nuts is the hallmark of Persian food, exemplified by dishes such as *koresh-e-fesenjahn*, chicken with walnuts and pomegranate sauce.

Arab cuisine is based on beans and legumes, or pulses as they're also called, and milk products, such as yogurt and cheese.

All of these are flavored with both strong-tasting herbs such as mint and coriander and fragrant spices such as cardamom, cinnamon, cumin, and allspice. Grilled meats are popular, served with flat breads and rice or *burghul*.

During the Ottoman period, Turkish cuisine was exceptionally luxurious. The kitchens of the Topkapi palace were so specialized and sophisticated that by the mid-eighteenth century, each of six varieties of halvah was assigned to a separate master chef, with a hundred apprentices working under him. Ottoman food spread throughout the Mediterranean basin and the Balkans. In all these countries, you'll find the same kebabs and rice and nutty, syrupy pastries based on paper-thin phyllo or shredded wheat dough. Dolmades (stuffed vegetables) are very popular throughout the Middle East, and both the Turks and Greeks claim to have invented them.

North African food, in contrast to the others, introduces a fiery element, produced by hot sauces such as harissa. Moroccan food is especially magnificent. It is based on staples such as couscous, a grain product that can be wheat, barley, millet, or any other grain shaped into tiny balls of dough, steamed, and then served like rice with stew or sauce.

The influence of Islam means that certain dietary laws are followed throughout the Middle East. Lamb is the most prized meat, pork is forbidden, and all meat must be ritually slaughtered and drained of blood. Alcohol is for the most part avoided. Instead, people satisfy their thirst with refreshing yogurt-based drinks.

Glossary

Aleppo pepper: a coarse-ground, dark red, earthy and robust pepper that is unique and famous throughout the Middle East. Similar to paprika but spicier.

apricot paste sheet *(kamradeen)*: a sticky orange sheet made from apricots and eaten out of the hand, or diluted with water and made into puddings or drinks.

barberry *(zerezhk)*: a tart red berry, used dried in Iranian cooking to add color or flavor. Often used as a garnish for cooked rice.

black cumin (*kalonji* **or** **nigella***)*: a small dull black seed, wedge-shaped and pungent, mistakenly called "black onion seed." Sprinkled on bread or used for flavoring vinegar and pickles. In Arabic, its name means "seed of grace."

bulghur *(burghul)*: parboiled, cracked grains of wheat, available in coarse to fine grind. Use fine-ground for kibbehs and coarse-ground for cooked dishes.

couscous: fine yellow nuggets of cereal, usually made from semolina, that have been steamed and then dried. Israeli couscous consists of larger grains of semolina that have been toasted; it's prized for its especially nutty flavor.

dibbis: a thick, dark brown syrup made from dates. Mixed with tahini and used as a dip for bread.

dried lime *(noumi basra, limoo)*: a hard, brown dried fruit used to add a distinctive flavor to Iranian and Iraqi soups and stews. Used in folk medicine to calm an upset stomach.

halvah: a confection usually made of ground sesame seed sweetened with sugar syrup or honey and pressed into a solid cake. Can also be made of sweetened semolina, wheat, or even vegetables.

harissa: a fiery red chili paste used in Tunisia, Morocco, and throughout North Africa.

kadaif: a vermicelli-like soft white dough that looks like shredded wheat in its cooked state. Used to make baklava-like desserts.

kashk: extremely nutritious stony lumps of dried wheat or barley mixed with either buttermilk or yogurt. Can also be made of dried, plain yogurt or buttermilk curds.

labne *(laban)*: a thick, strained whole-milk yogurt that has been concentrated and sometimes flavored with mint.

mahlab: a spice made from the kernels of black cherry seeds. Ground and used to give a sweet and spicy flavor to biscuits, cakes, and breads.

mastic: an aromatic resin of a tree specially cultivated on the Aegean island of Chios and used as chewing gum. Also used to flavor stews in Egypt and Turkish delight in Turkey.

melokhia: a green leafy vegetable, similar in flavor to gumbo filé powder, used in an Egyptian soup to give a mucilaginous, glutinous quality. Usually available dried or canned.

merguez: a beef or lamb sausage of North Africa, heavily spiced with harissa.

orange-flower water: a fragrant flavoring made from orange-flower essence, used in sweets, drinks, and desserts.

phyllo: a paper-thin pastry dough, usually found frozen but occasionally and preferably available fresh.

pomegranate molasses: a thick, tangy, piquant syrup made from the concentrated juice of sour pomegranates and used in Iranian cooking. Not to be confused with grenadine syrup.

quince: a hard, lumpy yellow fruit nearly always used cooked, whereupon its flesh turns pink.

rice, long-grain: a Middle Eastern staple. Middle Easterners like their rice to be relatively dry, with each grain remaining individual. Basmati rice is the most popular.

rose water: an essential fragrant oil made from attar of roses and used in sweets and desserts.

salep: a thickening agent made from dried, crushed orchid roots, used in Iran to thicken ice cream. Reputed to be an aphrodisiac (the name means "fox's testicles").

sumac: a dried, powdered dark red spice made from crushed sumac berries. Used as a lemon substitute or as a spice sprinkled on kebabs and pilaf in Iran, Iraq, and Turkey.

tahini: an oily cream extracted from sesame seed. The light ivory-colored Middle Eastern brands are superior in both taste and texture to the brands found at health food stores in this country.

vine leaf: the large, distinctly shaped leaf of the grapevine, usually sold bottled and used all over the Middle East for making dolmades.

zahtar: a spice blend of sumac, salt, roasted sesame seed, and often thyme, used as a topping for bread or a flavoring for yogurt or fried eggs.

CENTRAL SEATTLE

Pacific Food Importers . . . . see Mediterranean

The Souk . . . . see Indian and Pakistani

NORTH

Mama's Grocery & Deli

1125 N 152nd St., Shoreline
Phone: 206/362-4472
Hours: 9AM–8PM Monday–Friday; 10AM–7PM Saturday; closed Sunday

Walid Joudi gently pokes fun at his father, Lamis. "Look, he comes in every day wearing his suit and tie. He sits down, signs a few checks, while I do all the hard work." Lamis and his family emigrated from Lebanon to Kuwait to Shoreline to join his brother Saleh, who was already here and running his wildly popular restaurant, Saleh al Lago near Green Lake. Generations of cooking and eating have convinced the Joudis that theirs are the best and most authentic versions of dearly loved old recipes. "Hummus and baba ghanoush in supermarkets are too garlicky," they say. "The texture isn't right, and it's full of preservatives."

Saleh al Lago's brand of hummus, created here at the market and production facility, seems to have everything right: creamy, lighter-than-air texture, nutty garbanzo beans, lemon, and just enough salt to meld all the flavors together. The baba ghanoush is also exemplary. It's a rich combination of strong flavors—the smoky taste of eggplant balanced with the sharpness of tahini and lemon. The trade-off for the fresh ingredients is a short shelf life. Whereas most supermarket hummus will keep for up to a month, this one has got to go within a week. Believe me, you'll manage.

Look for the two spreads under the Saleh al Lago label in area supermarkets, but come here to taste the complete range of the Joudis' culinary expertise. The market stocks a good assortment of Middle Eastern groceries, feta cheese, and olives, as well as *shwarma* and gyros sandwiches. Lamis says he is planning to go to Lebanon soon to import directly, instead of via California, so his prices and selection will be the most competitive in the region. At the market, be sure to taste the baklava (made here with more-expensive pistachios instead of the common walnut version).

Medina Grocery & Deli

1421 NE 80th St., Seattle
Phone: 206/528-5526
Hours: 11AM–9PM Tuesday–Sunday; closed Monday

This shop (which is in north Seattle, not Medina) advertises itself as a halal meat market, international grocery, and pizza joint. I was tempted to try the pizza, but the chicken kebab won me over. Served with a side of Greek salad, it made a delicious, if messy, lunch on the run. When the owners told me that their pastries were made in-house, I had to try them. Unfortunately, the baklava and *kataifa* exhibited a common shortcoming, being a little soggy and overly sweet.

The lively owners of this shop are two Tunisian brothers, Mohammed and Slimane Souaiaia, so the foods of North Africa figure heavily in their stock. Middle Eastern groceries line the shelves, with a wonderful selection of jams, teas, biscuits, pita bread, olives, jars of pickled turnips and cucumbers, grape leaves, harissa pastes, and many other things. The deli case has two or three sorts each of fresh feta cheese (Bulgarian, Greek, and French) and olives from Greece, Tunisia, and Morocco.

Pacific Market

12332 Lake City Way NE, Seattle
Phone: 206/363-8639
Hours: 8:30AM–8:30PM Monday–Saturday; 11AM–7:30PM Sunday

You'd never guess it from the name, but this is a Persian market that serves terrific meals, both eat-in and to-go, as well as a good selection of groceries, fresh *barbari* bread, nuts and dried fruits, halal meats, and Iranian pastries. Besides sporting a not very illuminating moniker, this storefront's other small problem is that the chef/waitress/clerk/dishwasher/sole employee doesn't speak a word of English. No matter: when my Farsi-speaking mother came visiting, I dragged her over there to get the lowdown. Owner Mahim Vaziri came from Iran four years ago to join her son. While waiting for the rest of her children to join her, she's opened her contribution to the Middle Eastern scene. She communicates with her customers using a lot of smiling, pointing, and shrugging of shoulders.

Try her *ghormeh sabzi*, a peppery, herbaceous stew of lamb, greens, and a dozen herbs and spices such as fenugreek, dill, mint, parsley, and coriander. *Bademjan kashk* features roasted eggplant, saffron, loads of garlic, and yogurtlike kashk for a creamy Persian take on baba ghanoush. Served warm, with hunks of barbari, it's a robust and distinctive dish. The barbari comes in fresh every Tuesday from California, which is a hub of the Iranian community in this country. Mahim also whispered to my mom that she sells California pistachios over the counter but saves the Iranian nuts, which they both agreed were far superior, for her best customers.

SOUTH

Northwest Halal
15047 Military Rd., Sea–Tac
Phone: 206/431-0941
Hours: 10:30AM–8PM Monday–Friday; 11AM–7PM Saturday; 11AM–6PM Sunday

One of the hazards of this job is all the sampling that has to be done. (Someone's got to do it!) Baklava, the pan–Middle Eastern confection of phyllo dough with nuts and syrup, is a revelation at this nondescript shop just north of the airport. I intended to take one decorous nibble for research's sake. Instead, I demolished a massive slab in three gargantuan bites before I'd even gotten out the door. Chewy and bursting with walnuts, it was sweet and rich without being cloying. After enduring so many bad versions of this quintessential dessert, I'd forgotten that I once adored baklava. (Note that the market also sells factory-produced baklava, which is not so terrific.)

They also sell Afghani yellow rice here, which on closer examination is really basmati rice from Pakistan. Years ago, I tasted basmati rice at a Pakistani graduate student's dinner and was blown away by the nuttiness and length of each individual kernel—almost one inch long. I've never seen anything like that since, till spotting this Afghani yellow rice. The rest of the shop is fairly funky, but that is more than offset by the warmth of the welcome you'll receive from Sayed, the owner.

EASTSIDE

Byblos Market & Deli

102 Bellevue Way NE, Bellevue
Phone: 425/455-4355
Hours: 10:30AM–9PM every day

All those lovers of Middle Eastern food must have cheered when this little market opened its doors across the street from Bellevue Square. Neat little bins of six kinds of olives, fresh-cut feta cheese from Greece or Bulgaria or France, and slabs of halvah and Turkish delight are all attractively displayed on huge trays. The shelves are lined with Iranian and Middle Eastern spice mixes, tahini, pickles, teas, and fruit syrups. Gyros are prepared to order, although the meat is precooked and microwaved as needed.

Old Country Bakery

900 160th Ave. NE, Bellevue
Phone: 425/649-2171
Hours: 8AM–8PM Monday–Saturday; 8AM–4PM Sunday

My mother, who knows something about *naan-e-barbari*, having grown up eating this Persian flat bread, says that Old Country Bakery's is almost as good as the bread she remembers from her childhood. If you knew my mother, you'd know that is high praise indeed. Tucked into a little shopping plaza behind Crossroads Mall is this Armenian/Persian bakery selling beautiful three-foot-long, snow-shoe-sized loaves of *barbari*, as well as several other thicker, softer loaves of naan. When the loaves are hot from the oven and fragrant with a sprinkle of sesame seed, I dare you to refrain from demolishing at least one before you get in your front door.

Pars Market

2331 140th Ave. NE, Bellevue
Phone: 425/641-5265
Hours: 10AM–8PM Monday–Friday; 10AM–7PM Saturday and Sunday

Iranians are convinced that their nuts and dried fruit are the best in the world. I've got to say they have a point. I have done a side-by-side taste test of California versus Iranian pistachios while standing

A Middle Eastern welcome from Byblos Market.

in the parking lot of a Modesto farm stand, and the Iranian nuts were indeed plumper and just plain tastier.

Try for yourself at this large, bright market on the Eastside. The high turnover here guarantees freshness and variety. All kinds of pickles and olives, roasted seeds for snacking, spice mixes and flavorings, bread and rice—virtually everything you would need to put together a meal from *1,001 Arabian Nights* is for sale in the shop. They sell Iranian ice cream too, in fruit flavors scented with rose water or orange-flower water, pistachios, and cardamom.

Real Sweet-and-Sour Eggplant

Eggplant lovers will appreciate this Iraqi-Jewish dish of layered eggplant, onion, and tomato in a tamarind and curry sauce. Serve with lots of hot, white rice. Use any size baking dish and make any number of layers: it's pretty casual.

Serves 3 to 4

> 3 to 4 tablespoons olive oil
> 1 large eggplant, sliced into ½-inch-thick rounds
> 2 onions, sliced
> 1 large tomato, chopped
> 1 tablespoon curry powder
> Salt and pepper to taste
> ½ cup tomato sauce
> ½ cup water
> 2 tablespoons tamarind paste
> 1 to 2 tablespoons sugar or to taste

Preheat oven to 350 degrees F.

Use 1 tablespoon or less of the oil to lightly coat eggplant rounds. Broil 4 to 5 minutes on each side or till nicely browned. Set aside. You may also fry eggplant rounds on the stove, in which case they will absorb a lot more oil.

Fry onions in remaining oil over low heat till very soft and brown, or caramelized. Stir in chopped tomato, curry powder, and salt and pepper. Continue to cook for an additional 5 minutes.

In a baking dish, assemble alternating layers of eggplant and onion mixture, sprinkling with additional salt and pepper, and ending with a layer of eggplant.

For sauce, heat tomato sauce and water in small pan. Add tamarind paste and sugar; when paste has dissolved, pour liquid evenly over layers.

Bake for 25 to 30 minutes.

Variations: Stir-fry one pound of thinly sliced boneless, skinless chicken breast in 2 to 3 tablespoons of oil for 10 minutes, stirring often; then add to layers in baking dish. Or instead of tamarind paste, use the juice of 1 lemon.

Kitchree — Rice and Red Lentils

This hearty dish originated in India (it is related to kedgeree) and is served, with many variations, throughout the Middle East and India. This is my father's version, with one addition from me: garlic. My father abhorred the stuff, but I love it and it's a traditional ingredient of the dish. Many people like *kitchree* with a sunny-side-up egg fried in olive oil served on top. Others like a side of plain yogurt with it.

Serves 4 to 5

> *4 tablespoons olive oil*
>
> *1 onion, minced*
>
> *1 teaspoon cumin seed, crushed*
>
> *2 teaspoons paprika*
>
> *1 teaspoon turmeric*
>
> *2 tablespoons tomato paste*
>
> *4 cups water*
>
> *1 teaspoon salt*
>
> *1½ cups rice (preferably basmati), washed well and drained*
>
> *1 cup red lentils, washed and drained*

Topping

> *1 onion, sliced*
>
> *4 to 6 cloves garlic, sliced*
>
> *2 tablespoons olive oil*
>
> *1 teaspoon cumin seed*

In large pot with tight-fitting lid, heat the 4 tablespoons olive oil and fry onion till it just begins to turn yellow. Stir in crushed cumin, paprika, turmeric, and tomato paste.

Add water and salt. Bring to a boil. Slowly stir in rice and continue to boil, uncovered, for 5 minutes on medium-high heat.

Add lentils. Stir and check water level; it should be about ½ inch above the rice-lentil mixture. As soon as it returns to a boil, cover and simmer on very low heat for about 45 minutes, or until the rice is very hot. Be careful that it does not dry out or burn; add more water if necessary.

For topping, in large frying pan fry onion and garlic in the 2 tablespoons olive oil till golden. Stir in cumin seed and continue to fry for an additional minute till seeds start to brown and pop. Pour over rice and lentils.

scandinavian Jokes about lutefisk-starved

Scandinavians storming City Hall demanding to secede from Seattle and form the Independent Colony of Ballard have long since faded from fashion. And the waves of immigrants from the old countries crested generations ago. Still, there is no escaping the fact that Ballard, more than any other Seattle neighborhood, retains an indelible imprint of "Ya sure, you betcha" Nordic influence. Folks in this community band together and celebrate their heritage. In fact, there are some eighty clubs and organizations here that help give Ballard its strong cultural focus.

Of course, Scandinavians in Seattle are no longer exclusively located in Ballard, although it does remain the epicenter. Edmonds, Bellevue, and Redmond all contain scattered populations of people claiming Scandinavian heritage. Most Nordic folks, though, have been absorbed into the great digestive tract of America and have emerged scrubbed clean of obvious vestiges of ethnicity. But in stubborn dedication to their past, they return to the old ways on holidays. Christmas is closely associated with *pinnekjott*—cured and dried lamb ribs, patinated like ancient bronze and needing to be soaked overnight before being steamed over an interlaced "bridge" of small birch branches. Christmas breads and cakes redolent of cardamom and saffron and dried fruit fly out the door of bakeries. Families line up at Olsen's and Scandinavian Specialty Products to indulge in an orgy of nostalgia-infused eating. As I foraged and cadged samples while doing research for this chapter, I discovered a customer loyalty to the shops chronicled here that has made them some of the oldest food businesses in Seattle.

The real roots of Nordic food lie in the climate. People were forced to hunker down and stockpile supplies for the long winter, and in this way the process of preserving meat, fish, vegetables, and fruit was developed into a fine art. Cattle and goats gave little milk during the winter months, but the summer milk was made into cheese or churned into butter. Most meat was dried, salted, or smoked, so the abundance of sausages and delicate hams and bacons represented insurance against the uncertainties of the future. And of course, the sea was a source of life-giving food that was put up, salted, or pickled for generations of Scandinavians. Here in the Pacific Northwest, our mountains, rocky shores, fjords, and virgin forests must have reminded those first immigrants of home. And the fruits of our fields, our forests, and our sea must have seemed very familiar.

Long after the first generations of Danes, Finns, Icelanders, Norwegians, and Swedes landed, people still speak with fondness about the neighborhood food markets and bakeries that have served their community for so long. They enroll their children in cooking classes at the Nordic Heritage Museum and flock to pancake and lingonberry breakfasts and, yes, lutefisk feasts at church halls, community centers, and the Sons of Norway lodge. Nothing fancy, nothing gussied up by overly ambitious chefs—just real food for real people.

Glossary

aquavit: literally "water of life"; a liquor made from the distillation of potato or grain spirits, popular throughout most of Scandinavia.

cloudberry: a golden berry growing only within the Arctic Circle, usually found in preserves or jams.

fårerull: Norwegian larded and spiced lamb roll.

fenalår: salted, dried, and occasionally smoked leg of lamb.

fiskepudding: a Norwegian fish pudding, usually made with cod or haddock and potato starch.

frikadeller: Danish meat patties.

glögg: a hot punch served in Scandinavia during the winter, particularly for Christmas.

gravlax: raw salmon cured with pepper, dill, sugar, and salt; traditionally served with mustard-dill sauce.

Julekage: a Danish Christmas fruit loaf.

klippfisk: salted and dried cod, originally dried by laying it on cliffs in the open air.

knäckerbröd: a rye flat crispbread from Sweden.

kransekage: literally "wreath cake"; a Danish and Norwegian cake made largely of marzipan.

lefse: a Norwegian flat bread, thin and saucer-shaped, now mostly made with potatoes. Eaten buttered and sugared and folded like a handkerchief.

Norwegian trolls have been sighted in Ballard.

lutefisk: see page 289.

mämmi: a sweet dish from Finland, composed of baked rye flour and molasses, served cold with cream and sugar.

rakørret: trout that has been salted down and cured; a Christmas favorite in Norway.

rømmegrøt: a special Norwegian porridge made with sour cream, milk, and flour; served with cinnamon and crunchy sugar.

smørrebrød: literally "bread and butter"; typically an open-faced sandwich, usually made with rye bread and any number of special toppings.

tørrfisk: stockfish that is drier than salt cod, but isn't salted.

wienerbrød: literally "Vienna bread," which is what the Danes call Danish pastries.

CENTRAL SEATTLE

Nielsen's Authentic Danish Pastries

520 Second Ave. W, Seattle
Phone: 206/282-3004
Hours: 7:30AM–5:30PM Monday–Friday; 7:30AM–5PM Saturday; closed Sunday

Most Danish pastry in this country is a sad imitation, not comparable to the delectable *wienerbrød* (as Scandinavians know it) at this gem of a bakery. True Danish pastry is a sweet raised dough rolled "3 x 3"—that is, rolled in butter, folded in three, and rolled three times over. It is not as sweet as we are used to in this country and since it has no preservatives or chemical extenders, it's good for nothing after a day or two.

"Fresh yeast, milk from a bottle, and natural, unbleached flour—that's the way it's supposed to be, and that's the way we make it," says John Nielsen, former owner of this longtime bakery in lower Queen Anne. He recently sold the business to his assistant, Darcy Person, who has no intention of changing anything. Try the "potato," a sad-sack potato-shaped pastry with an almond base, custard topping, and cocoa powder coating. John says that by his reckoning he has made over 6 million of them, and they are his most popular item.

NORTH

Larsen's Original Danish Bakery . . . see Cakes, Pastries, Pies, and Other Baked Goods

Olsen's Scandinavian Foods

2248 NW Market St., Seattle
Phone: 206/783-8288
Hours: 9AM–5:30PM Monday–Saturday; closed Sunday

Petter Patterson, the chef at Hidden Harbor, one of Seattle's few remaining Scandinavian restaurants, told me that this bastion of old Ballard has the best pickled herring in town. Maybe that wouldn't appeal to everyone, but it did to me, so I quickly trotted down to Olsen's to check out their offerings. In a purely unscientific taste test, I can say that their firm, meaty, clove- and pepper-spiked fish definitely hit the mark. No fructose or corn syrup or chemical-laden mush here, I'm happy to report. I also found stockfish, looking like so many skeletal kites standing upright in a bucket for sale. Stockfish is an iconic food of the poverty-wracked Mediterranean regions as well as of Scandinavia. Fished in Norwegian waters and historically traded throughout the Mediterranean, it is a close relative of lutefisk and baccalà. Olsen's makes their own *lefse*, a crepe-shaped bread usually but not always made with potatoes, and very tasty too. They cure their own sausages, make their own breads, and sell cheeses and homemade *rømmegrøt*—a sour cream porridge (which sounds a lot worse than it tastes).

Lutefisk—The Simple Fish with the Unforgettable Scent

This most peculiar specialty of the Scandinavians has not made many converts in the rest of the world. What is lutefisk? The word *lut* literally means "lye," and *lute* means "to soak in lye water," a kind of water that traditionally was often derived from wood ashes. So you begin with stockfish (air-dried cod), which is soaked for a week, then submerged in a lye of birchwood ashes and slaked lime. After this, the fish is soaked for a further week with daily changes in water. During this time, it gives off an unforgettable odor, akin to dank wood shavings mixed with cod liver oil.

In years past, home cooks who wanted to serve lutefisk had no choice but to go through this complicated soaking procedure, but now frozen, presoaked lutefisk is readily available in most Scandinavian markets. To prepare the fish, wrap it in cheesecloth, cover it in salted water, and simmer it for about 10 minutes. The cooked fish will "shiver" if properly prepared, a sign of first-class lutefisk. Finish the dish with some melted butter or bacon fat, mustard sauce, or grated gjetost and a white sauce. It's a dish to either tug at the heartstrings or be considered a national disgrace.

Scandinavian Bakery

8537 15th Ave. NW, Seattle
Phone: 206/784-6616
Hours: 9AM–6PM Tuesday–Saturday; closed Sunday and Monday

Scandinavian Bakery has the feel of an old-fashioned bakery: no prominent espresso machine, no modern hip blond wood, no jazzy temple to haute patisserie—just a neighborhood bakery permeated with the sweet smells of sugar and wheat and toasted spices and a long glass case stuffed with delectable treats. Cardamom is a "must-use" spice in Scandinavian baking, and this bakery offers braided breads, little buns, and cookies all flavored with this highly aromatic spice. Based on my experience, I'd say that a raisin-cardamom roll—toasted, split, and buttered, with a dollop of lingonberry preserves—accompanied by a cup of tea will go a long way toward resuscitating you midway through the afternoon. Homemade rye and pumpernickel bread, fruit tarts, Danish pastries, and cookies round out the selection here.

Scandinavian Specialty Products

8539 15th Ave. NW, Seattle
Phone: 206/784-7020
Hours: 9AM–6PM Tuesday–Saturday; closed Sunday and Monday

This longtime fixture in north Ballard, also known as the Norwegian Sausage Co., has been curing and smoking various meats in-house for over thirty-five years. Surprisingly (to me at least), lamb figures in quite a few of them. This is the place to buy *pinnekjott* (dried lamb

ribs) as well as *fenalår*, a boneless cured "jerky" that is a must at
Christmas. The very tasty proscuitto-like ham called *spekeskine*,
sliced paper thin and perfumed with smoke, makes an admirable
companion to sliced honeyed melon, at considerably less cost than
Italian proscuitto. But what this shop is really known for is their fish
products. Fish cakes and fish puddings, fish balls and herrings—the
gamut of Scandinavian fish delicacies is made here. The fish cakes
are delicious, silky and nutmeg scented; bring them home to slice
and pan-fry with some wonderfully mealy buttered potatoes as an
accompaniment. The shop also has a large assortment of gift items
and books with a Nordic focus.

SOUTH

IKEA

600 SW 43rd St., Renton
Phone: 425/656-2980 or 800/570-IKEA
Hours: 10AM–9:30PM Monday–Friday; 10AM–8PM Saturday; 10AM–7PM
Sunday

This Swedish furniture and lifestyles giant has a small, well-stocked
grocery store and restaurant serving mostly authentic Scandinavian
food. Look for lovely lingonberry jams, enormous blue and red packages of Siljans crispbreads, and other *flatbrøds*. The freezer case holds
five-pound bags of Swedish meatballs, very handy for buffet tables
and actually quite tasty. Of course the Swedes are known to have
sweet tooths, and the store doesn't disappoint with its selection of
fine chocolates, lovely little tea biscuits, and toffees, jellies, gum-
drops, and the like.

Traditional Scandinavian Cheeses

Cheese lovers, be forewarned. Scandinavian cheeses run the
gamut from the commonest garden variety to some that are,
quite frankly, acquired tastes. There is no question, though, that
Scandinavians are a cheese- and dairy-loving people, and
cheeses figure in most meals. Nordic cheeses are usually mild in
flavor and semisoft in texture, and often feature some added
ingredient, such as caraway seed or dill.

Gammelost: the most traditional and least derivative Scandinavian cheese by far, according to Steve Jenkins, the premier authority on cheeses in this country. Unfortunately, it is very rare, so you're not likely to find it easily. Though its name means "old cheese," "old" refers not to the length of aging but to the use of soured rather than fresh, skimmed cow's milk. As the cheese ripens, it sprouts tufts of mold that are worked back into the surface of the cheese by hand. This results in a very rustic-looking cheese with a blue-green crust and a pronounced pungent taste and aroma. Be sure to try some if you see it in a market.

Gjetost: the staple breakfast in many a Norwegian home. Gjetost is a sweet, brown, firm cheese made from pure goat's milk or a cow-goat mix. It is cooked until caramelized (hence its color), then curded and pressed. The designation "ekte gjetost" on the label means that the cheese is made solely from goat's milk.

Jarlsberg: the industrial-grade, garden-variety Scandinavian cheese most familiar to non-Nordics. It is the largest-selling imported cheese in America. This cheese was created in the early 1960s at Norway's Agricultural School and was named after a similar one first produced in the early 1800s on the old Jarlsberg estate. Good, fresh Jarlsberg, with its soft, pliable texture and nutty taste, melts beautifully in cooking, but its flavor falls disappointingly short of a Swiss Emmental.

Tilsit: a Havarti-like cheese, with a kick and an aroma to match. Made in Denmark from partially skimmed cow's milk, it has tiny "eyes" throughout the loaves and is yellower than Havarti. It slices easily and melts beautifully.

indexes

specialty food index

bread

cakes, pastries, pies, and other baked goods

cheese

chocolates, candies, nuts, and ice cream

coffee, tea, and spices

fish

ethnic food index

index by location

CENTRAL

Columbia City / Seward Park

Mount Baker / Beacon Hill

Belltown

Capitol Hill / First Hill

Downtown

Pioneer Square

Fisherman's Terminal

International District

Eastlake

Madison Park

Madrona / Central District

Mercer Island

Pike Place Market

establishment index